India General Service Medal 1895

CASUALTY ROLL

Compiled by
Anthony Farrington

Published by

5 Buckingham Street, Strand, London WC2N 6BS
Telephone 01-839 4684
The Military Book & Medal Specialist

Copyright 1987 Anthony Farrington.

ISBN 0 948130 21 0

Printed & bound by Antony Rowe Ltd, Eastbourne

PREFACE

The present offering, my second reference aid for the medal collector, has been compiled from the official despatches (listed at pp.3-5) covering the campaigns and actions which earned the seven clasps to the India General Service Medal 1895.

Appearing first in Government of India General Orders and then (in most cases) in the London Gazette after an interval of a few weeks or months, the despatches at this period provide extremely detailed casualty returns and all the information they contain on the precise nature of wounds etc has been reproduced. Indian officers and men have been included and gallantry awards to casualties are also noted.

Arrangement is by clasp and regiment - slightly complicated perhaps and inevitably meaning that multi-clasp medals will need to be checked against each of the relevant sections - but my attempts at arrangement by regiment only proved even more complicated.

Under each clasp I have given edited facsimiles of the main despatch or despatches as a way of conveying the flavour and background, if not the full history, of these episodes in North-West Frontier warfare, varying from relatively small affairs to full scale campaigns involving a dozen or more British Army battalions.

Crown copyright material in the India Office Records has been arranged and edited by permission of the Controller of Her Majesty's Stationery Office.

A J F
April 1987

CONTENTS

	page
List of Despatches	3

Defence of Chitral 1895

Despatch from Cpt C V F Townsend, 26 April 1895	9
Casualties:	
15th Bengal Lancers	18
14th (Ferozepore Sikh) Bengal Inf	18
24th (Punjab) Bengal Inf	18
Central India Horse	19
Bengal Medical Service	19
Bengal Subordinate Medical Dept	19
Kashmir Imperial Service Troops	19
Gilgit Levy	21

Relief of Chitral 1895

Despatch from Lt-Gen Sir R C Low, 1 May 1895	25
Despatch from Lt-Gen Sir R C Low, 27 July 1895	31
Casualties:	
No 3 Mountain Battery RA	35
Royal Engineers	35
Devonshire Regt	35
Bedfordshire Regt	35
2nd Btn King's Own Scottish Borderers	35
1st Btn King's Royal Rifle Corps	36
Seaforth Highlanders	36
1st Btn Gordon Highlanders	37
Royal Irish Fusiliers	37
11th Bengal Lancers	37
Bengal Sappers & Miners	38
14th (Ferozepore Sikh) Bengal Inf	38
15th (Ludhiana Sikh) Bengal Inf	40
32nd (Punjab) Bengal Inf	40
37th (Dogra) Bengal Inf	41
2/4th Gurkhas	41
Punjab Frontier Force - Corps of Guides	42
4th Sikh Inf	43
Kashmir Imperial Service Troops - No 1 Kashmir Mtn Bty	43
Kashmir S & M	44
4th Kashmir Lt Inf	44

Punjab Frontier 1897-98

Despatch from Brig-Gen E R Elles, 10 August 1897	47
Despatch from Brig-Gen E R Elles, 13 October 1897	49
Despatch from Maj-Gen Sir B Blood, 27 October 1897	53
Casualties:	
Staff	58
51st Field Battery RA	58
No 1 Mountain Battery RA	58

	page
No 8 (Bengal) Mountain Battery	58
Royal Engineers	59
1st Btn Royal West Surrey Regt	59
1st Btn East Kent Regt	60
1st Btn Somerset Lt Inf	61
Lancashire Fusiliers	61
1st Btn Royal West Kent Regt	61
2nd Btn Highland Lt Inf	62
Argyll & Sutherland Hldrs	63
Army Veterinary Dept	63
11th Bengal Lancers	63
13th Bengal Lancers	63
Bengal Sappers & Miners	64
Bengal Subordinate Medical Dept	65
6th Bengal Lt Inf	65
20th (Punjab) Bengal Inf	65
22nd (Punjab) Bengal Inf	66
24th (Punjab) Bengal Inf	67
25th (Punjab) Bengal Inf	67
31st (Punjab) Bengal Inf	67
35th (Sikh) Bengal Inf	68
38th (Dogra) Bengal Inf	70
39th (Garhwal Rifle) Bengal Inf	71
45th (Rattray's Sikh) Bengal Inf	71
2/1st Gurkhas	71
Punjab Frontier Force - Corps of Guides	72
1st Punjab Cav	73
1st Sikh Inf	73
1st Punjab Inf	74
No 6 (Bombay) Mountain Battery	75
Bombay Sappers & Miners	76
28th Bombay Inf (Pioneers)	76

Malakand 1897

	page
Despatch from Brig-Gen W H Meiklejohn, 13 August 1897	79
Casualties:	
Staff	84
No 8 (Bengal) Mountain Battery	84
11th Bengal Lancers	84
Bengal Commissariat-Transport Dept	85
24th (Punjab) Bengal Inf	85
31st (Punjab) Bengal Inf	86
35th (Sikh) Bengal Inf	87
38th (Dogra) Bengal Inf	87
45th (Rattray's Sikh) Bengal Inf	87
Punjab Frontier Force - Corps of Guides	89
No 5 Co Madras Sappers & Miners	90

	page

Samana 1897
Despatch from Maj-Gen A G Yeatman-Biggs, 21 September 1897 — 95
Casualties:
    1st Btn Royal Scots Fusiliers — 97
    36th (Sikh) Bengal Inf — 97
    1/2nd Gurkhas — 99
    1/3rd Gurkhas — 100
    Punjab Frontier Force - 2nd Punjab Inf — 100

Tirah 1897-98
Despatch from Gen Sir W S A Lockhart, 26 January 1898 — 103
Casualties:
    Staff — 112
    Commissariat-Transport Dept — 112
    No 8 Mountain Battery RA — 112
    No 9 Mountain Battery RA — 113
    No 5 Co Bengal Sappers & Miners — 113
    1st Btn Royal West Surrey Regt — 113
    1st Btn Devonshire Regt — 114
    2nd Btn Yorkshire Regt — 115
    1st Btn Royal Scots Fusiliers — 116
    2nd Btn King's Own Scottish Borderers — 117
    2nd Btn Royal Inniskilling Fusiliers — 118
    1st Btn Duke of Cornwall's Lt Inf — 118
    2nd Btn Royal Sussex Regt — 119
    1st Btn Dorsetshire Regt — 119
    2nd Btn Oxfordshire Lt Inf — 122
    2nd Btn Derbyshire Regt — 122
    1st Btn Northamptonshire Regt — 124
    2nd Btn King's Own Yorkshire Lt Inf — 126
    1st Btn Gordon Hldrs — 127
    6th Bengal Cavalry — 130
    9th Bengal Lancers — 130
    17th Bengal Cavalry — 131
    18th Bengal Lancers — 131
    9th Gurkha (Rifle) Bengal Inf — 131
    12th (Kelat-i-Ghilzai) Bengal Inf — 132
    15th (Ludhiana Sikh) Bengal Inf — 132
    22nd (Punjab) Bengal Inf — 134
    30th (Punjab) Bengal Inf — 134
    34th (Punjab) Bengal Inf — 134
    36th (Sikh) Bengal Inf — 135
    45th (Rattray's Sikh) Bengal Inf — 137
    2/1st Gurkhas — 137
    1/2nd Gurkhas — 138
    1/3rd Gurkhas — 141
    2/4th Gurkhas — 143

	page
Punjab Frontier Force - No 1 (Kohat) Mtn Bty	143
No 2 (Derajat) Mtn Bty	144
3rd Sikh Inf	144
2nd Punjab Inf	145
1/5th Gurkhas	146
21st Madras Inf	147
No 5 (Bombay) Mountain Battery	147
No 3 Co Bombay Sappers & Miners	147
No 4 Co Bombay Sappers & Miners	148
28th Bombay Inf	148
Central India Horse	149
Imperial Service Troops - Jeypre Transport Train	149
Jhind Inf	149
Kapurthalla Inf	150
Maler-Kotla S & M	151
Nabha Inf	152

Waziristan 1901-02

	page
Despatch from Maj-Gen C C Egerton, 15 March 1902	155
Casualties:	
Gujarat Mountain Battery	159
Murree Mountain Battery	159
23rd (Punjab) Bengal Inf (Pnrs)	159
27th (Punjab) Bengal Inf	159
28th (Punjab) Bengal Inf	160
29th (Punjab) Bengal Inf	160
32nd (Punjab) Bengal Inf (Pnrs)	161
35th (Sikh) Bengal Inf	161
38th (Dogra) Bengal Inf	161
45th (Rattray's Sikh) Bengal Inf	161
1/2nd Gurkhas	162
1/3rd Gurkhas	163
Punjab Frontier Force - 1st Punjab Cav	163
5th Punjab Cav	163
3rd Sikh Inf	163
1st Punjab Inf	163
2nd Punjab Inf	164
5th Punjab Inf	165
9th Bombay Inf	165
Punjab Commission	165

List of abbreviations	166

DESPATCHES

IGS - B

Published in Government of India General Orders and the London Gazette

Defence of Chitral 1895

Cpt C V F Townsend, cmdg Chitral Fort, Chitral 26 Apr 1895
GGO 531/24 May 1895
LG 16 Jul 1895 pp.4006-16

Recognition of British and Indian officers
GGO 532/24 May 1895

Relief of Chitral 1895

Maj-Gen Sir R C Low, KCB, cmdg Chitral Relief Force, camp Khar 5 Apr 1895
GGO 380/19 Apr 1895

Maj-Gen Sir R C Low, camp Khar 7 Apr 1895
GGO 420/26 Apr 1895
LG 2 Jul 1895 p.3738

Maj-Gen Sir R C Low, camp Sado 13 Apr 1895
GGO 475/10 May 1895
LG 2 Jul 1895 p.3738

Maj-Gen Sir R C Low, camp Gjobani 18 Apr 1895
GGO 476/10 May 1895
LG 2 Jul 1895 p.3739

Maj-Gen Sir R C Low, camp Mundia Khan 19 Apr 1895
GGO 477/10 May 1895
LG 2 Jul 1895 pp.3739-40

Lt-Col J G Kelly, cmdg Gilgit Force, Chitral 6 May 1895; Cpt H B Borradaile, Laspur 7 Apr 1895
GGO 530/24 May 1895
LG 16 Jul 1895 pp.3999-4005

Lt-Gen Sir R C Low, camp Dir 1 May 1895
GGO 558/31 May 1895
LG 16 Jul 1895 pp.4017-20

Lt H J Jones, Fort Mastuj 2 Apr 1895
GGO 607/14 Jun 1895

Lts S M Edwardes & J S Fowler, camp Mandia 19 & 29 Apr 1895
GGO 608/14 Jun 1895

Lt F J Moberley DSO, Fort Mastuj 14 Apr 1895
GGO 609/14 Jun 1895

Lt-Gen Sir R C Low, Laram Pass 27 Jul 1895
GGO 998/27 Sep 1895
LG 15 Nov 1895 pp.6170-81

Punjab Frontier 1897-98

Lt-Col W duG Gray, Datta Khel 16 Jun 1897
GGO 773/9 Jul 1897
LG 7 Sep 1897 pp.4989-93

Maj-Gen Sir B Blood, 30 Aug 1897
GGO 1089/2 Oct 1897
LG 5 Nov 1897 pp.6068-76

Brig-Gen E R Elles, Peshawar 10 Aug 1897
GGO 1188/29 Oct 1897
LG 4 Jan 1898 pp.3-6

Maj-Gen Sir B Blood, 27 Oct 1897
GGO 1317/3 Dec 1897
LG 11 Jan 1898 pp.147-59

Maj-Gen E R Elles, Peshawar 13 Oct 1897
GGO 1318/3 Dec 1897
LG 11 Jan 1898 pp.159-64

Maj-Gen G C Bird, Datta Khel 25 Nov 1897
GGO 1432/31 Dec 1897

Maj-Gen Sir B Blood, camp Kunda 25 Dec 1897
Ggo 57/21 Jan 1898
LG 1 Mar 1898 pp.1270-72

Maj-Gen Sir B Blood - amendements to GGO 1317/1897
GGO 178/18 Feb 1898

Maj-Gen Sir B Blood, Ambela Pass 19 Jan 1898
GGO 217/25 Feb 1898

Malakand 1897

Brig-Gen W H Meiklejohn, Malakand 13 Aug 1897
GGO 1089/1 Oct 1897
LG 5 Nov 1897 pp.6060-67

Samana 1897

Maj-Gen A G Yeatman-Biggs, Kohat 28 Aug 1897
GGO 1141/15 Oct 1897
LG 21 Dec 1897 pp.7644-45

Maj-Gen A G Yeatman-Biggs, Fort Lockhart 21 Sep 1897
GGO 1417/24 Dec 1897

Tirah 1897-98

Gen Sir W S A Lockhart, camp Dwatoi 9 Dec 1897
GGO 58/21 Jan 1898
LG 1 Mar 1898 pp.1260-70

Gen Sir W S A Lockhart, Rawalpindi 26 Jan 1898
GGO 244/4 Mar 1898
LG 5 Apr 1898 pp.2171-95

Col G L R Richardson, camp Shinawari 28 Jan 1898
GGO 304/18 Mar 1898
LG 3 May 1898 pp.2738-40

Gen W S A Lockhart, Peshawar 4 Apr 1898
GGO 483/6 May 1898
LG 7 Jun 1898 pp.3506-10

Return of casulaties 12 Oct 1897-6 Apr 1898
GGO 620/3 Jun 1898

Waziristan 1901-02

Maj-Gen C C Egerton, Abbottabad 15 Mar 1902
GGO 611/1902
LG 8 Aug 1902 pp.5089-96

DEFENCE OF CHITRAL 1895

From Cpt C V F Townsend, Central India Horse, commanding the Escort to the British Agent, and Commandant of Chitral Fort during the siege, dated Chitral 26 April 1895

Reconnaissance, 3rd March 1895.—About 4-30. P.M. the news of the approach of Sher Afzal and a force was brought in, and I was ordered to take out 200 men of the 4th Kashmir Rifles by Captain Campbell, Central India Horse.

I threw out an advanced guard of one section under Subadar Badri Nar Singh and sent Captain Baird with them, and advanced in extended order. Captain Campbell ordered me to leave 50 men at the Serai, and so I left Subadar Harichand and 50 rifles at this place. Captain Campbell sent me orders to block the Ayun-Chitral road, and accordingly I occupied the eastern spur of the face on which the Political Officer's house stands, and which commands the road with a clear field of fire to the front up to over 1,000 yards; on reaching this spur I found that Captain Baird had been sent up on the high ground to the eastward among the trees, and had taken the section with him, and Captain Campbell soon ordered me to send another 25 men to Baird. This I did, sending Jemadar Shamu in command of it. After about half an hour Captain Campbell ordered me to advance on a house in which he said they had received news that Sher Afzal was to be found. He indicated the house on the plain, about a mile and a half to the south. I accordingly advanced in extended order, half company in firing line and half company in support. On reaching this house we found it empty, but I saw a hamlet about 500 yards further on, and I could see a lot of men moving about there among the trees and houses. I continued the advance. I could see our men (Baird's party) dotted up on the hill-side on the northern slopes of a nullah, and some men on the opposite (southern) side of the nullah, evidently Chitralis. Very soon I heard shots on these hill slopes, so concluded the men I could see in my front moving about in the village were the enemy, and I opened fire with a section volley. This fire was immediately returned by the enemy. I now advanced in the ordinary way, getting the men under cover as much as possible, and giving them steady volleys until I got to within 200 yards or so. The enemy now made most excellent shooting,—the Martini and Snider,—and men began to get hit, although I had got the men under a stone-reveted bank. I could see that the hamlet or village was full of men. I could see men in white clothes and standards, and they kept up a well-sustained fire from the walls and loop-holes and there was no more cover to my front.

I determined to hold on to this ground I had reached with my 100 men, until Baird should move along the hill slopes to the westward and so turn the village, and I could then rush it. However, time went on and I could see no signs of Baird, and small parties of the enemy of four and five began to overlap my left flank towards the river, and were enfilading us with their fire and in a similar way they began to move forward on my right. It was now 6-30 P.M., and it would soon be dark. Captain Campbell shortly after this arrived and said that the village must be rushed. I gave the order "to reinforce," but the support of men in rear did not come up. I kept on repeating the order, but no one came. Captain Campbell then went back to fetch the men himself, while I fixed bayonets preparatory to the charge, and kept up a heavy independent fire. The support was among some low walls 150 yards to the rear. Campbell managed to bring about a dozen men, and fell shot through the knee as he rejoined me. I then sent Colonel Jagat Singh, who only got one or two men. It was no good waiting any more, so I went round among the men, telling them that we must take the houses, rushing straight in, and I sounded the charge. We were met by a most close and destructive fire as we scrambled over the bank and rushed on. General Baj Singh was shot dead on one side of me and Major Bhikam Singh of the 4th Kashmir Rifles mortally wounded on the other side. After about 30 and 40 yards the men began to take cover, laying down behind stones, and the charge could not be carried home, though I tried all I could to get the men on.

Seeing that it was hopeless, that it was impossible to carry the village, I ordered the men to retire, and the men collected again under the bank whence we had charged from. It was getting rapidly dark and the enemy were overlapping us fast. I ordered a retirement, for I saw it would not do to be caught among the stone walls and hamlets between us and Chitral Fort in the dark. I told off some men to carry off Captain Campbell and Major Bhikam Singh, and sent them off. I then retired my party by alternate parties, keeping up a heavy fire whilst the men dribbled off to the rear in twos and threes by word of command, remaining with the last party myself. The enemy's fire being too close to carry out the retirement in any other manner, I carried out the retirement in alternate parties in this way, the enemy following us up very closely and getting round our flanks. I rallied the men for a stand at a small house with a half-walled enclosure, where I found the British Agent rallying the men. The British Agent then went to bring out the company of 14th Sikhs to support us. I begged him to get on his horse and told him that I would manage to get my party in all right; the enemy were now all round us and their swordsmen were getting bold. The British Agent was fired at on all sides as he rode across the polo-ground. I commenced the retirement again, the men now having very little ammunition left.

We were now fired into on all sides, front, flank and rear, from every hamlet and wall, and it was now quite dark and impossible at a short distance to distinguish friend from foe. Captain Campbell, who had been put on a pony, notwithstanding that he was severely wounded, helped me in keeping the men together. Crossing the polo-ground the enemy kept up a fire on us from the houses and the orchards. On reaching the serai I found 50 men of the 14th Sikhs under Lieutenant Harley, who had come out to cover our retreat. I directed him to cover our retirement into the fort, and, restoring order among the 4th Kashmir Rifles, retired into the fort; the Sikhs covered the retreat very steadily. I took command now at the fort, as Campbell was severely wounded. Every man was sent to his station. I heard that Captain Baird had been desperately wounded away on our right flank, and that he and Surgeon-Captain Whitchurch had not come into the fort. He had been wounded in the early part of the action. About 8 P.M. Surgeon-Captain Whitchurch came in, bringing Captain Baird, who was mortally wounded. Thirteen of the 4th Kashmir Rifles had stuck by them,—Gurkhas and one or two Dogras, under Subadar Badri Nar Singh. They had had a marvellous escape. They had to charge one or two walls or sangars where the enemy tried to stop them; several of the party were killed, Baird receiving another wound as he was being carried; they had to rush one sangar with the bayonets.

4th March 1895.—Engaged in demolitions in the garden, east front of fort stables and walls. The enemy's riflemen fired into the fort all day from sangars thrown upon the hill-sides.

Tuesday, 5th March 1895.—A flag of truce arrived from Sher Afzal, with a letter from Umra Khan to the British Agent. We expended 200 rounds to-day.

I had marksmen put in the towers to annoy the enemy, there being some very decent shots among the Sikhs.

6th March 1895.—Lieutenant Gurdon, Political Officer, was attached to the 4th Kashmir Rifles for duty.

Messengers were sent off with letters to try and get through the enemy to Mastuj on the nights of the 3rd, 4th, 5th and 6th.

Umra Khan's Diwan arrived with a flag of truce to see the British Agent.

Thursday, 7th May 1895.—Engaged in making volley loop-holes and log head-cover on parapets.

One sepoy of the 4th Kashmir Rifles wounded.

Friday, 8th March.—The enemy made a determined attempt on our waterway last night; they commenced a heavy and well-sustained fire from the trees on the north-west front of the fort, about one hour before dawn. As the men always slept on their alarm posts, every one was quickly in his place. Independent fire was not allowed at night: only section volleys. During the enemies' fire one of their men actually managed to get into the passage under the Water Tower and lit a huge fire; one or two men also with him had carried up bundles of faggots in the darkness. I opened the water-gate and sent out bhisties with mussacks to put the fire out, and this they did. Gave them Rs. 10 each afterwards.

Saturday, 9th March.—Nothing occurred in the night, our tower sentries firing a few shots at men seen lurking about among the trees on the north-west front. The enemy had improved their sangars in the night. A kahar was shot dead to-day in the fort by the riflemen in the sangars at Danin village, across the river; a Martini. This man caused us much annoyance throughout the siege.

Sunday, 10th March.—Nothing happened in the night; engaged in demolishing the old hospital and commissariat houses just outside the main gate at 9 P.M. I used the Punyalis and Guta syces to do this work; splendid fellows to work. They do everything in a quarter of the time that the sepoys do. The enemy fired a few shots at us at this work, but no damage done. One driver wounded in the fort to-day, and also a hospital dresser; both men were going down to get water.

We had now only 80 rifles of the 14th Sikhs fit for duty, and 240 rifles of the 4th Kashmir Rifles. The latter rather shaken by their losses on the 3rd of March. Taking into consideration the large number of guards, sentries and patrols we had to keep going in the fort, that the *morale* of the 4th Kashmir Rifles had suffered somewhat, that our siege was in all probability to be a very long one, I decided in my mind that the energy to be displayed in sorties must depend on circumstances; that the energies of the men must be husbanded as much as possible; that in always having to return after a sortie the men would soon be disheartened. Neither could we afford to lose a single man, and there were only three British officers, including myself, doing duty with the garrison. I therefore decided that we should begin sallying as soon as we heard of a force from Gilgit approaching, unless a sortie became absolutely necessary from the close approach of the enemy's sangars.

I laid down the following measures to be carried out as regards the defence of the fort :—

1. Fort police were established on account of the small number of Chitralis in the fort.
2. An organised system for putting out fires: bhistis slept with filled mussacks, and vessels were filled with water. Patrols went round at night, and also during the day, watching for accidents from fire. We feared fire greatly in the fort, as there is more wood almost than stones in it.
3. The sanitary arrangements were very bad, but the best that could be done under the circumstances. The latrines of necessity had to be in a little confined space of ground at the north flank wall.
4. As many walls and buildings as possible to be levelled outside the fort.
5. The sepoys to be spared as much fatigue and working parties as possible, getting the work done by the non-combatants.
6. Internal communications.
7. Hand-mills were made for grinding the grain, and all extra servants and odd hands were put on to this.
8. A careful watch was kept over the Chitralis in the fort, and a guard placed over them at night.
9. Every kind of cover that could be devised was thrown up ; traverses and parados were constructed out of beams taken from the buildings demolished ; wooden traverses erected on all the tower tops. Boxes filled with earth, commissariat bags filled with earth, carpets, doors taken off hinges ; all were utilised for cover. Finally I took care to instil into the minds of all the men that a relieving force would soon come, and then we should sally out and have our turn.

Monday, 11th March.—Messengers and letters from the enemy.

Tuesday, 12th March.—Managed to get all the outer wall knocked down on the west and south-west fronts last night, using the Punyalis to do the work ; and, as usual, the work was done excellently and marvellously quickly. The enemy fired pretty hotly from their sangar about 250 yards off on west front, and also they opened fire from the bazar on hearing the crash of the walls coming down. No one hit.

I ordered 30 rounds a day to be fired at Sher Afzal's house at 1,100 yards range, to cause him annoyance. Our average was 40 to 50 rounds of Martini daily expended, and 20 to 30 rounds of Snider, *i.e*, when we had a quiet night and there was no firing. We used the brass gun to-day in the fort, getting off two or three rounds at Sher Afzal's house from outside the garden gate (east face). One sepoy of the 4th Kashmir Rifles, one of the gun's crew, wounded in the arm by a Martini bullet.

Wednesday, 13th March.—I started watches for British officers, like on board ship, as regards night work ; this I found was the only way of ensuring a proper vigilance on the ramparts at night.

The rumour amongst the Chitralis in the fort is that Sher Afzal has sent a lot of men up the road towards Mastuj. We can get absolutely no information from outside. The enemy keep a close cordon round the fort at night to intercept messengers.

Thursday, 14th March.—The enemy made an attack last night on the east face in the garden ; much shouting and tom-toms and a straggling fire. They sounded the advance on a bugle.

We received them with a brisk fire, and they slunk off in the dark. During the time we were firing, a man was heard to shout to them repeatedly in Pashtu to come on and attack the water-way.

I loop-holed and occupied the stables outside the water-gate with one section to night. This picquet always to mount in the evening at 8 P.M.; in the day-time the east end of the stables was held by a Cossack post of six men, the wall being loop-holed.

15th March, Friday.—A few shots only were fired last night. The end of the covered way on the water's edge was enlarged a bit, loop-holes made, and occupied by a Cossack post of six Sikhs at night. A letter came from Sher Afzal to the British Agent to-day, saying that a party of our sepoys escorting an ammunition convoy had been surrounded and defeated at Reshun, and that a British officer who had come down from Mastuj had been taken prisoner also with this party. That he had written a letter to the British Agent which Sher Afzal would deliver if the British Agent would send some one to get it. We did not believe the story.

16th March, Saturday.—A quiet night last night. Sher Afzal forwarded a letter to-day from Lieutenant Edwardes dated Reshun, 13th March 1895. He said that he and Lieutenant Fowler, Royal Engineers, with a party of 20 sappers (Bengal Sappers and Miners) and 40 of the 4th Kashmir Rifles, on the march from Mastuj to Chitral, had been attacked just this (Chitral) side of Reshun on the road. They had lost 6 men killed and 13 wounded. They had concluded a truce with the enemy after three days' hard fighting. The Pathans with the Chitralis had proposed the truce to Edwardes, saying that the British Agent had made peace with Sher Afzal at Chitral. They had had to sally out of the house they had entrenched themselves in whenever they wanted water. The ammunition (60 boxes of Snider and engineer stores in this convoy) and stores, Edwardes said, were quite safe. Edwardes added a postscript to say that they could not hold out any longer if they were again attacked. A large force was all around them.

A truce of three days has been agreed to on both sides. Negotiations going on with reference to Lieutenants Edwardes and Fowler and party. We began digging out an old disused well in the fort, which had been filled in for many years.

17th March, Sunday.—I employed next two days in improving the traverses made of beams, boxes, etc., on the parapets, and the head-cover in the tower tops, making flanking loop-holes in lower story of flag tower (S. E.) and digging out the old well. Noticed that the enemy had shifted their quarters out of the bazar, which our marksmen had made fairly warm for them, and had moved south to Fateh Ali Shah's house and orchard walls.

18th March, Monday.—Nothing worthy of note.

19th March, Tuesday.—The look-out men on the towers reported that Chitralis had been seen arriving in batches from the direction of Mastuj at dusk yesterday evening.

Considerable numbers of the enemy arrived during the day from Mastuj-way. Should say quite 400 men during the day. Seven corpses were carried along past the fort into Chitral. These must have been men of note brought in, who had been killed at Reshun by our people.

Abdul Majid Khan, Umra Khan's lieutenant, who has been, with 300 Jandolis, with Sher Afzal all the time, sent a letter to the British Agent this evening. Says they are very sorry, but although they had sent off messengers to Reshun to say that peace was being made, a " row " had taken place in the meantime; that they had made prisoners of nine Mahommedan sepoys; and that the two British officers would be here to-morrow. This looked as if there had been treachery, and so it proved afterwards. I increased the picquet in the covered way to the water to-night to 20 rifles instead of 6, and arranged a picquet of 20 men to hold it by night and 20 by day. This made 70 men holding our water.

20th March, Thursday.—The enemy reinforced their sangars in the day with a lot of men, and sent 28 men across the bridge, and in a short time afterwards 80 men arrived across the bridge from Mastuj-way. The two British officers were being escorted in, but I could not make them out with the glass. However, Munshi Amir Ali was allowed to go and see them from the fort this evening, and our doubts were put an end to, as Amir Ali was allowed to see them and to converse with them, but in Hindustani only.

They were being well treated, but had been looted of all their kit.

21st March, Friday.—Constructed a semi-circular flèche, loop-holed, outside the water door.

Enemy trying to arrange that we should send a British officer up to Sher Afzal's house to see Fowler and Edwardes.

A note from Fowler, asking for medicine, said that the enemy had got all the stores, etc., so we suppose that they have got ammunition and all.

The British Agent told me that he has now heard the story of how Fowler and Edwardes were captured. During the truce they had with the enemy at Reshun, the Chitralis invited the British officers to look on at a game of polo on the Reshun polo ground. They went and were instantly thrown down and bound. What then happened to their men they do not know; they suppose that the 35 men remaining have been massacred with the wounded. We could hardly bring ourselves to believe the story, it was so astonishing.

22nd March, Sunday.—We had now to commence eating horse-flesh, and killed and salted ponies.

23rd March.—Poured with rain in the night.

Umra Khan's Diwan came to see the British Agent. The enemy announce that they will haul down the flag of truce this evening; this they did. We hauled down ours at the same time. Some desultory firing this night. It rained hard. We lit a fire outside the main gate to throw a light.

24th March.—The rain continues to pour in torrents. I hear that Lieutenants Edwardes and Fowler are to be taken down to Drosh to Umra Khan to-day. The enemy fired into the fort to-day from the hill sangars. A large piece of the parapet on the west front subsided, and we built it up with beams in the evening.

25th March.—Rained hard all night; evening quiet : 38 men in three parties observed to cross bridge from up road this evening. The surmise is that it is the captured 60 boxes of ammunition. I had a gun post made in the wall of the half demolished building outside the main gate during the night, also an embrasure close by in the wall for our brass gun to bear on the enemy's sangar in front of our west front. Took the gun out at 7 A.M. and opened fire on this sangar, but with no effect, as the gun has no sights, and we had to make a wooden one. The second shot hit the parapet of the sangar at the crest, but did it no damage. This sangar was made of fascines, and, as we found afterwards, excellently made, very strong, and rude earth casemates for their men to take cover in. All the sangars round opened fire on the fort. A Sikh was shot through the stomach and died in half an hour,—Martini bullet.

27th March.—Enemy fired from garden (east front) in the night, lighting a fire in the garden; supposed with object of drawing our fire, and thus wasting our ammunition.

During the night we put up a bullet-proof roof on the top of the water tower, and arranged screens of tents turned inside out to cover entrance into north tower, a favourite target for the riflemen in the Danin sangar; also screens rigged up over the gangway leading up on to the south parapet, a very exposed place. A bhisti shot dead this afternoon : this makes 10 casualties since the 3rd March.

28th March.—The Eed festival. Put up beams in stables to protect men going out of water gate to the latrines and down to the covered waterway. This is where the bhisti was shot yesterday. Also further strengthened top of water tower, and pierced its lower story for loopholes.

Ordered a board to assemble to-day, of which I was President, recommending Surgeon-Captain Whitchurch for the Victoria Cross for his conduct on the 3rd of March. Handed in the proceedings to the British Agent.

Constructed Machicoulis galleries to hold beacon fires, one on each parapet of fort. These a great success; the fires lit on them give a capital light in front of the parapet, lighting up the darkness, and at the same time do not light up our own loop-holes, as we were behind the fire. Two Chitralis told off to each fireplace to feed the fires under the watch of one sepoy. Before this we used fireballs to throw out when lighted over the parapets, and they acted very well indeed, only were expensive in oil. These balls consisted of resinous wood-shavings, tow, etc., compressed into a bag made of sacking tied up with stout string at the mouth, and kept handy on the parapets, with bottles of oil and matches close at hand. If the enemy attacked in the darkness, these were lit by a British officer, who soaked it with oil, applied the match, and hurled the ball out over the wall. They gave a clear light for about half an hour.

29th March.—Made and hoisted the Union Jack on the top of the highest tower (S. W.), called the Flag Tower. Improved head-cover on towers during night. The British Agent received a letter yesterday from Lieutenant Edwardes at Drosh, where he and Fowler were prisoners of Umra Khan. They were to start the next day for Jandol.

An attempt was made to send a messenger out to carry a letter to Mr. Udny, Asmar-way. The man returned saying he had nearly been captured by the enemy in the garden. Quiet night.

30th March.—Ammunition in hand this date :—

Martini 29,224 rounds, *i.e.*, 356 rounds per rifle, for 82 effective of 14th Sikhs.

Snider —68,587 rounds in hand for 261 rifles effective of the 4th Kashmir Rifles (5 men had recovered from wounds, but were not well enough to take their places at the alarm posts), *i.e.*, 262 rounds per rifle.

31st March.—The enemy made a new sangar last night on the opposite bank of the river, about 175 yards from our water place; this sangar about 30 yards in advance of their old sangar. At this point, screens of tents put up during the night to conceal bhistis and men going down to the covered way to the water, between the stables and the water tower. The enemy never fired if they could not actually see a man. Also had beams put up as screens outside the water gate, as the riflemen up at Danin made things warm for people at this doorway.

Enemy also last night commenced a covered way to the water from their lower sangar on our north-west front near the river ; they only managed to get up about eight yards of it, as our men fired at the noise of the stones. This waterway was running parallel to ours at a distance of about 80 yards. This lower sangar was only about 80 yards from our covered way to the water.

April 1st, 1895.—Desultory firing in the night ; loop-hole fire from the garden wall at our parapets. Sank a trench in the stables with a view to more protection for men going to the water-way. Made some volley loop-holes in the lower story of water tower.

We had now 37 men in hospital and 23 out-patients,—total 60 men.

April 3rd, 1895.—Nothing of importance since 1st April. Much rain on this date. The son of Mehtar Jan Bahadur Khan (who was in the fort along with us) was admitted to see his father. He had come from Mastuj, and said that 800 troops had arrived at Mastuj, and there were three British officers ; included 150 to 200 Hunza, Nagar, and Punyali levies. However, I believe, his statements were most contradictory, and he had evidently been told what to say.

4th April 1895.—Only a few stray shots last night fired by our people at men moving about by the enemy's sangar on north-west face in the chinar trees.

5th April 1895.—The enemy were at work in Nizam's summer-house in the garden at south-east angle of fort, about 50 yards from the gun tower. This place we had been unable to knock down owing to heavy fire on working parties. It was in reality a small servants' house, which had stood next door to the summer-house which had been levelled by us. The fire from the enemy got lively about 5 P.M. Bahadur Khan's son again came to see the British Agent, but late in the evening. He was not admitted into the fort, but told to come next morning.

6th April 1895.—Found in the morning that the enemy had been very active in the night. A large fascine sangar stood in front of the main gate at a distance of 40 yards only (west front).

A palisade-work sangar had also been made just under the chabootra (north-western face) ; also a sangar had been made in the middle of the garden (east face) about 40 yards from the garden gate. They fired with matchlocks in the night, mostly from the summer-house : this was no doubt to take off our attention.

I loop-holed the lower story of the east tower in the night to command the east end of the stables, which point in my opinion was a dangerous one. More loop-holes also made in stable buildings at west end.

I had occasion to find fault with the sentries of the 4th Kashmir Rifles in the gun tower this evening, and took steps to increase their vigilance.

They did not seem to like looking over the top of the tower owing to the enemy in the summer-house, who now made things warm for the sentries in the gun tower. Loop-holed the walls left outside the main gate ; enemy from near sangar firing.

7th April 1895—Last night I occupied the remaining walls standing outside the main gate, having loop-holed them, with 12 Sikhs and six Punyalis. About 5 A M, whilst I was having a look from the top of the north tower, a large number of the enemy opened a heavy matchlock fire from the chinar trees in front of the north tower. It seemed to me that this meant an attack on the covered way to the water at last, and having directed the Sikhs in the north tower to fire volleys, I went down and turned out the inlying picquet and sent round sending every one to their different alarm-posts. The enemy kept up a deal of shouting and yelling, our men in the water tower and the Sikhs on the west parapet giving them steady volleys, which the enemy could not face, but decamped towards the bazaar. Some of their men crept up to within twelve yards or so of our walls outside the main gate, firing at them, one Sikh being shot through the thigh by a Snider bullet.

During the firing, the enemy managed with great pluck to place huge faggots and logs of wood in a pile against the corner of the gun tower, and set light to it, and the tower was soon well on fire and blazing up. Things looked very bad; I sent up all the whole of the inlying picquet to run up with their greatcoats full of earth, sent up sacks of earth and as much water as we could get hold of.

A strong wind was blowing at the time. At one time the fire was got under; it then blazed up gain, the flames mounting up in the spaces between the beams in the tower. The Machicoulis galleries in the tower were the targets for a hail of Snider bullets from the summer-house at 50 yards, the bullets smashing through the planks. The British Agent, who was in the tower superintending the putting out of the fire, was wounded at a hole in the wall, and a Sikh shot there the next minute. A sentry of the 4th Kashmir Rifles also shot. I now went into the towers, as all seemed quiet around the fort, and it was getting quite light. Their riflemen from the sangars opened fire at the gun tower, from across the river and from high ground to the south-west, where they could hit our people going in and out of the tower with water and earth. My orderly was mortally wounded; altogether nine were wounded putting out the fire.

The fire was got under with great difficulty. We had to keep picking holes into the wall inside the tower as it mounted up, and pouring water down, and we got above the fire by means of ladders and by working *downwards* from the top story of the tower so as to meet the fire.

It was 10 A.M. before the fire was out, but water was kept pouring down inside the walls all day.

The enemy showed great courage and enterprise in firing our tower, and our sentries showed great slackness and want of vigilance.

I now changed the sentries of the 4th Kashmir Rifles, putting the men of the 14th Sikhs in their places. The Machicoulis were greatly improved and made very strong, and loop-holed with a large loop-hole to see a lot of ground at the foot of the tower. A sentry was always lying in each of these Machicoulis galleries.

Twelve corpses of the enemy were reported to have been seen by the look-out men in the towers.

During the afternoon I had heaps of earth collected and sent up on the parapets, vessels and ammunition boxes filled with water also and earth in plenty, and water in every story in all the towers. The mackintosh sheets of the 14th Sikhs were utilised to hold water. All the servants, syces, etc., were formed into a fire picquet under Surgeon-Captain Whitchurch. Also heaps of stones were placed in the tops of the towers for the sentries to throw down from time to time in the dark.

Rounds expended last night—
    Martini 127
    Snider of the 4th Kashmir Rifles 283

Subadar Badri Nar Singh, 4th Kashmir Rifles, has shown great bravery in the tower, going into the Machicoulis gallery when it was being ripped up with bullets; as did also Sepoy Awi Singh, of the 4th Kashmir Rifles, who was badly wounded—Snider bullet through the thigh. (Throughout the fighting, during the siege, and in the action of the 3rd March, I think not more than one man was wounded by matchlocks; all Martini and Snider.) The British Agent asked me to recommend these two men for the Order of Merit, and also Sepoy Bhola Singh, of the 14th Sikhs, also wounded in the tower. He displayed bravery in putting out the fire under the enemy's rifle fire. Subadar Badri Nar Singh had previously been recommended for the Order of Merit for his work on the 3rd March.

8th April 1895.—The enemy made no attack last night. There was an alarm of fire in the gun tower at 9 P.M. last night. I proceeded to the gun tower, and on looking out of the Machicoulis gallery on the south face, could see some red-hot embers placed quite close to the tower, and a bundle of faggots lay close by. We soon got this out by means of the bhistis in the tower. The enemy must have done this from the summer-house when the sentries were relieved in the evening; so I altered the time of reliefs from day to day.

Desultory firing in the night. Work done to-day as follows:—Decided to demolish the remaining walls and shell left of buildings in front of the main gate, doing it with the Punyalis at 12 noon; at the same time built a stone tambour loop-holed in front of the main gate before the walls outside were knocked down. This tambour held 10 men, and flanked capitally the whole of the west front with its two towers (north and flag towers).

The work was not finished till about 5 P.M. The outer walls were well prepared for knocking down, the uprights holding up the roof sawn through. Rajah Sipih Bahadur then suggested setting fire to them, and I allowed him to do so. The sangar 40 yards in front made it awkward for the working party; the fire burnt well, but only a part of the walls fell down; some remained the next morning, but the tambour made was a good piece of work. I left two perpendicular walls to the fort standing, knocking gaps through them.

During this work the Machicoulis in the gun tower were still more improved, and good loop-holes were made in the lower story, vertical to the ground at foot of tower; also a hole inside the tower dug in the floor to about four feet deep, and then a shutter-like loop-hole made which commanded the ground at the foot of the south face of the tower. Sentries placed in all these: 14 men now occupied this tower and I had an officer living in it.

9th April.—Quiet night; only a few shots from our men moving about.

We managed to knock the walls down clear outside the main gate to-day; no one hit doing it. I cannot speak too highly of the courage and skill of the Punyalis and Gilgit syces doing this work.

11th April 1895.—The enemy made an attack last night—supposed to be on our waterway. A tremendous din was suddenly raised. Yelling and tom-toms at 11-30 P.M. We went to our stations quietly. Section volleys from the east parapet, also from the west parapet, and a sharp fire at the gun tower corner. A large number of men came out of the sangars and were received by steady volleys from the water tower. We heard afterwards that this attack was really intended on the waterway, and that the Lutko men in these sangars had received orders from Sher Afzal to assault our waterway. The volleys, however, soon caused them to deploy off towards the bazaar, and they received some volleys from the Sikhs on the west parapet as they cleared off to the bazaar. The firing lasted half an hour. One man was wounded on our side in the gun tower, one of the levies. The Punyalis in the fort had been formed into a levy and armed with Sniders and placed in the tower-tops, where they were of great use. Some old Enfield rifles found in the fort were also put to use in the tower-tops, loaded with slugs. The riflemen in the sangars across the river kept up a fire on us and also from the direction of the bazaar. Rounds expended,—335 Snider, 341 Martini.

12th April 1895.—The enemy now began playing tom-toms and Pathan pipes in the summer-house at night, and shouting abuse at intervals; also men were set to work to sling stones into the fort, one man being wounded in the head by a stone. This, we found out at the end, was to drown the noise of their picks, as they had commenced a mine from the summer-house to undermine our gun-tower. The Pathans had guaranteed the taking of our gun-tower; they used to keep up a straggling matchlock fire from behind the trees in the garden. On the evening of the 11th, 40 to 50 men were seen going up the nullah to the south-west, where is a road leading up over the heights to the west of the fort going Drasan-way and to Mastuj. They never took the road leading to the bridge, as our Sikh marksmen in the north tower made this route too hot. At 11 A.M. on the morning of the 13th 100 men with flags and men on ponies seen going the same route up the nullah, and we began to speculate on the approach of a force from Gilgit. In the afternoon a lance-naick of the 14th Sikhs was shot through the head at a loop-hole. This made 23 men killed and wounded since the 3rd March. Parties of two and three were seen going Drasan-way all day on the 13th, and 25 cooly-loads.

On the nights of the 15th and 16th the usual din of tom-toms and pipes playing at the summer-house, and desultory firing.

17th April 1895, Wednesday.—Jemadar Rab Nawáz Khan, of the 15th Bengal Cavalry, warned us that he thought the tom-toms and band at the summer-house might possibly be to drown the noise of their making a mine. I warned the sentries in the gun-tower to be on the alert and to listen intently; also the sentries in the tambour at the main gate. At midnight on the 16th one of the sentries in the lower story of the gun-tower reported the noise of knocking. I went up and listened for some time but could hear nothing.

About 11 A.M. on the morning of the 17th the native officer in the gun-tower reported to me he could hear the noise of knocking. I went up into the tower in the lower story, and there was no doubt that a mine was being made, and it had reached within twelve feet of the foot of the tower. The British Agent came up, and we both agreed that there was only one thing to do, and that was the summer-house must be rushed, and that soon, and the mine destroyed.

There was no time to countermine. I told off Lieutenant Harley and 40 men of the 14th Sikhs and Major Bhagwán Singh, Subadar Gandib Singh and 60 men of the 4th Kashmir Rifles, and decided to let the party out of the garden-gate at 4 P.M. in the afternoon. They would only have to go fifty yards, and the enemy in all probability would be surprised, and 100 men would be ample to do the business. Men were told off to carry the powder-bags, powder-hose, matches and picks to destroy the mine. The shafts in all probability would be in the summer-house.

The gate was opened, and the party rushed out, a few hurried shots, and they were into the house, and had captured it, two men of the 4th Kashmir Rifles being shot dead as they got in. About 30 Pathans were in the house and they bolted down the garden wall, but stopped at the far end of the garden and kept up a heavy fire into the house and sustained it throughout, Harley's men keeping up a heavy fire in return. The mine shaft was found just outside the house behind the garden wall, and 35 Chitralis were bayoneted in the mouth of the mine as they came out, all being armed with swords. Two Pathans were shot in the house; two prisoners were taken. In the meanwhile we had gone to our stations on the parapet and kept up a lively fire from the parapet; several of the enemy were killed running away across the open towards the bazaar. It was several times reported to me from the towers that a considerable number of the enemy were making their way down to the river-bank from Fateh Ali Shah's house and coming round behind the garden wall, round towards our waterway; and they lined the garden wall at the east end of the garden, and opened fire on us with rifles. Two Gurkhas of the 4th Kashmir Regiment were shot dead in the garden, as they crept along the wall answering this fire. A considerable number of the enemy were seen gathering along the river-bank, and this made me anxious of a counter-attack on our waterway, so I occupied the stables with 20 men, withdrew the Sikhs from the west parapet, and put them in the north-east angle of the fort, to support and flank the waterway. I sent three different messages to Lieutenant Harley to hurry up in his work at destroying the mine, and warning him of the enemy gathering at the end of the garden. Soon after 5 P.M., I heard the explosion of powder and the party came rushing back into the garden-gate, the enemy from the end of the garden keeping up a furious fusillade on them. The party lost 8 killed and 13 wounded, *viz.*, 3 Sikhs killed and 5 wounded, and 5 of the 4th Kashmir Regiment killed and 8 wounded; total 21 killed and wounded out of 100 men.

18th April, Thursday.—Enemy very quiet to-day. Working hard at our countermines, gangs relieving all day and working in three hours' reliefs.

19th April.—About 3 A.M. this morning Lieutenant Gurdon, who was on middle watch, reported that a man was outside calling out under the fort-wall that he had important news to tell. All precautions were taken; he was admitted to the main gate, and he told us of the flight of Sher Afzal and the Jandol Chief about midnight, and of the near approach of Colonel Kelly's column from Mastuj. All the sangars were deserted. In the morning not a man was to be seen about Chitral. The siege, which had lasted 46 days, was at an end. A letter was received from Colonel Kelly this night, with news of his fighting on the road and of the Peshawar force advancing also. The Gilgit column accordingly arrived at 2 P.M. on the 20th, the 32nd Pioneers looking in very good trim and good condition.

Our losses ‡ throughout the siege including the 3rd of March amounted 104 killed and wounded of all ranks, out of 370 combatants forming the British Agent's escort.

‡ All the gunshot wounds caused by Martini and Snider bullets except two.

C. V. F. T.

15th (CURETON'S MULTANI) REGIMENT OF BENGAL LANCERS

Jemadar
Rab-Nawaz Khan   Khan Bahadur   very sev w 3 Mar 1895 Chitral Fort, tulwar

14th (FEROZEPORE SIKH) REGIMENT OF BENGAL INFANTRY

Havildar
 511 Mal Singh   sev w 17 Apr 1895 Chitral Fort, gs; awarded IOM 3rd Class

Naik
 829 Mota Singh   k 17 Apr 1895 Chitral Fort, gs

Lance-Naik
1442 Bakhtawar Singh   k 13 Apr 1895 Chitral Fort, gs

Sepoys
1932 Attar Singh   sev w 9 Apr 1895 Chitral Fort, gs
1501 Bhola Singh   very sev w 7 Apr 1895 Chitral Fort, gs; awarded IOM 3rd Class
 739 Fouja Singh   sl w 17 Apr 1895 Chitral Fort, gs
 772 Garja Singh   sev w 17 Apr 1895 Chitral Fort, tulwar
1510 Harnam Singh   very sev w 7 Apr 1895 Chitral Fort, gs
1540 Harnam Singh   sl w 17 Apr 1895 Chitral Fort, gs
1666 Jiwan Singh   k 17 Apr 1895 Chitral Fort, gs
1436 Keher Singh   sl w 17 Apr 1895 Chitral Fort, gs
1295 Narain Singh   k 17 Apr 1895 Chitral Fort, gs
1252 Partap Singh   sl w 24 Mar 1895 Chitral Fort, gs; awarded IOM 3rd Class
1804 Partap Singh   sl w 17 Apr 1895 Chitral Fort, tulwar
1950 Sawan Singh   k 16 Mar 1895 Chitral Fort, gs
1633 Thamman Singh   very sev w 7 Mar 1895 Chitral Fort, gs, dow 31 Mar

24th (PUNJAB) REGIMENT OF BENGAL INFANTRY

Captain
Baird, John McDonald   mort w 3 Mar 1895 Chitral Fort, gs, dow 4 Mar

CENTRAL INDIA HORSE

<u>Captain</u>
Campbell, Colin Powys   very sev w 3 Mar 1895 Chitral Fort, gs

<u>Sowar</u>
Mahmood   mort w 7 Apr 1895 Chitral Fort, gs, dow 16 Apr

BENGAL MEDICAL SERVICE

<u>Surgeon-Major</u>
Robertson, George Scott   CSI   British Agent in Chitral   sev w 8 Apr 1895 Chitral Fort, gs

BENGAL SUBORDINATE MEDICAL DEPARTMENT

<u>Hospital Assistant 3rd Grade</u>
Bhawani Dass   k 3 Mar 1895 Chitral Fort, gs

KASHMIR IMPERIAL SERVICE TROOPS

<u>General</u>
Baj Singh   k 3 Mar 1895 Chitral Fort, gs

4th (RAGHUNATH) REGIMENT OF KASHMIR LIGHT INFANTRY

<u>Major</u>
Bhikam Singh   k 3 Mar 1895 Chitral Fort, gs

<u>Havildar-Major</u>
 18 Durga Singh   sev w 3 Mar 1895 Chitral Fort, gs; awarded
                   IOM 3rd Class

<u>Kot-Havildar</u>
    Gulaboo   3rd Co   sl w 3 Mar 1895 Chitral Fort, gs

<u>Havildar</u>
 58 Dhani   very sev w 3 Mar 1895 Chitral Fort, gs; awarded
             IOM 3rd Class

Naiks
    Dhanbahadar 4th Co   k 3 Mar 1895 Chitral Fort, gs
408 Nain Singh 2nd Co   very sev w 3 Mar 1895 Chitral Fort, gs;
                             awarded IOM 3rd Class

Lance-Naiks
    Chanda Singh 2nd Co   sev w 3 Mar 1895 Chitral Fort, gs
    Jitman 5th Co   sev w 14 Mar 1895 Chitral Fort, gs
    Kishen Singh 5th Co   k 3 Mar 1895 Chitral Fort, gs
    Sri Man 5th Co   k 3 Mar 1895 Chitral Fort, gs
    Sundar 2nd Co   sl w 13 Apr 1895 Chitral Fort, gs

Sepoys
    Abhad Singh 3rd Co   sev w 7 Apr 1895 Chitral Fort, gs
    Amar Singh 3rd Co   w 3 Mar 1895 Chitral Fort, gs
    Arjan 1st Co   sev w 3 Mar 1895 Chitral Fort, gs
    Beli Ram 2nd Co   k 3 Mar 1895 Chitral Fort, gs
    Beli Ram 6th Co   sev w 18 Apr 1897 Chitral Fort, gs
    Bhogma 1st Co   sev w 12 Mar 1895 Chitral Fort, gs
    Chait Singh 2nd Co   sl w 8 Apr 1895 Chitral Fort, gs
    Chandarbir 5th Co   sev w 3 Mar 1895 Chitral Fort, gs
    Debi Singh 3rd Co   k 17 Apr 1895 Chitral Fort, gs
    Deedo 2nd Co   sev w 3 Mar 1895 Chitral Fort, gs
    Dewi 2nd Co   k 3 Mar 1895 Chitral Fort, gs
    Dhani Ram 6th Co   sev w 3 Mar 1895 Chitral Fort, tulwar
    Doolo 2nd Co   k 3 Mar 1895 Chitral Fort, gs
984 Gobind Ram 2nd Co   very sev w 18 Apr 1895 Chitral Fort, gs
    Gopal Singh 6th Co   k 3 Mar 1895 Chitral Fort, gs
    Gurkoo 2nd Co   k 3 Mar 1895 Chitral Fort, gs
    Hiroo 3rd Co   sev w 3 Mar 1895 Chitral Fort, gs
    Hushiara 2nd Co   k 3 Mar 1895 Chitral Fort, gs
    Hari Singh 3rd Co   sl w 18 Apr 1895 Chitral Fort, gs
    Ilahi Baksh 6th Co   sl w 15 Mar 1895 Chitral Fort, gs
    Jagat Deo 5th Co   very sev w 3 Mar 1895 Chitral Fort, gs
    Jagbir 4th Co   k 3 Mar 1895 Chitral Fort, gs
    Jamoher 2nd Co   sev w 3 Mar 1895 Chitral Fort, gs
748 Jebe 4th Co   k 17 Apr 1895 Chitral Fort, gs
    Jita 2nd Co   very sev w 3 Mar 1895 Chitral Fort, tulwar
    Jot Jaman   sl w 3 Mar 1895 Chitral Fort, tulwar
    Kakir 3rd Co   k 17 Apr 1895 Chitral Fort, gs
    Kakir 6th Co   sl w 3 Mar 1895 Chitral Fort, gs
    Kalbir 5th Co   k 3 Mar 1895 Chitral Fort, gs
    Kaloo 4th Co   k 3 Mar 1895 Chitral Fort, gs
    Kalu Raj 4th Co   sev w 3 Mar 1895 Chitral Fort, gs
    Karkbir 5th Co   sl w 3 Mar 1895 Chitral Fort, gs
    Kashi Nath 6th Co   mort w 3 Mar 1895 Chitral Fort, gs,
                            dow 27 Mar
    Kesar Singh 5th Co   k 3 Mar 1895 Chitral Fort, gs
    Kharak Singh 6th Co   mort w 18 Apr 1895 Chitral Fort, gs,
                            dow 19 Apr
    Khushia 2nd Co   sev w 3 Mar 1895 Chitral Fort, gs
    Khyali 3rd Co   sl w 3 Mar 1895 Chitral Fort, gs
    Kirpa 2nd Co   very sev w 3 Mar 1895 Chitral Fort, gs

```
    Lachhman    6th Co    k 3 Mar 1895 Chitral Fort, gs
    Lachman     3rd Co    k 3 Mar 1895 Chitral Fort, gs
    Madan Singh 5th Co    k 3 Mar 1895 Chitral Fort, gs
    Mian Singh  3rd Co    k 3 Mar 1895 Chitral Fort, gs
907 Mool Singh  4th Co    k 17 Apr 1895 Chitral Fort, gs
    Mukti Ram   5th Co    k 3 Mar 1895 Chitral Fort, gs
    Parti Man   6th Co    sl w 3 Mar 1895 Chitral Fort, tulwar
    Prem Singh  5th Co    sl w 7 Apr 1895 Chitral Fort, gs
    Pyar Singh    sev w 3 Mar 1895 Chitral Fort, tulwar
    Raghubir    6th Co    sl w 3 Mar 1895 Chitral Fort, gs
    Raghubir    6th Co    sev w 18 Apr 1895 Chitral Fort, gs
    Ram Ratan    k 3 Mar 1895 Chitral Fort, gs
    Rubela    k 3 Mar 1895 Chitral Fort, gs
    Santbir     5th Co    sev w 3 Mar 1895 Chitral Fort, gs
    Santoo    sl w 3 Mar 1895 Chitral Fort, gs
    Sant Ram    4th Co    sev w 3 Mar 1895 Chitral Fort, gs
    Singbir     4th Co    sev w 18 Apr 1897 Chitral Fort, gs
    Sono   4th Co    very sev w 3 Mar 1895 Chitral Fort, gs
    Sundar      3rd Co    k 17 Apr 1895 Chitral Fort, gs
    Surjan      4th Co    sev w 18 Apr 1895 Chitral Fort, gs
```

GILGIT LEVY

```
Rajab    sev w 7 Apr 1895 Chitral Fort, gs
Sultan Shah    very sev w 7 Apr 1895 Chitral Fort, gs
```

RELIEF OF CHITRAL 1895

From Lt-Gen Sir R C Low, KCB, commanding the Chitral Relief Force, dated camp Dir 1 May 1895

I have the honor to make the following report on the operations of the troops under my command since crossing the frontier on the 2nd April.

2. During this period of a month I have from time to time given brief accounts of each action as it took place, and of each further advance of this force; and now that the troops have arrived in Chitral territory, and the fort there is relieved, the British prisoners who were in Umra Khan's hands have been restored to freedom, and Umra Khan himself is a fugitive; now too that Sher Afzal, the Chitral usurper, is a prisoner in my hands, the time has arrived that I should make a more comprehensive report on the work done.

3. In my despatch dated the 5th April I gave a brief account of the assault and capture of the Malakand Pass. It must be remembered that this was written only two days after the action, and, being based on my own observation, was necessarily incomplete. Thus I have to make an important correction in this report regarding one battalion, namely, the 4th Sikh Infantry, who did not remain stationary guarding the left flank of the advance, as I wrote, but joined throughout in the advance up to the highest peaks of the enemy's position, parallel with the Guides Infantry, having an equally arduous climb with them, and meeting with and carrying many sangars full of the enemy. During this advance officers and men alike distinguished themselves. In my original report also the enemy at the Malakand Pass were estimated at 12,000 men, of whom 3,000 were said to be armed with fire-arms, but we afterwards ascertained that the number armed with fire-arms was much larger.

4. The following day, 4th April, the 1st Brigade was ordered to descend the Malakand Pass into the Swat Valley, its place on the pass being taken by the 2nd Brigade, while the 3rd Brigade remained on the south side of the pass, pending the passage of the baggage and supplies of the rest of the force.

6. On the 4th April the advance of the 1st Brigade down the pass towards the Swat Valley was opposed by the enemy. In this action the Guides Cavalry, under Captain Adams, made two brilliant charges, before which the enemy in largely superior numbers, scattered and fled up the hills.

7. During the 5th and 6th April the 2nd Brigade marched down the pass and encamped opposite the crossing over the Swat river, north of the village of Aladand. Reconnaissances were made which shewed that the gatherings we had fought on the 3rd and 4th had retired up the Swat Valley without entirely dispersing.

8. On the 7th April the 2nd Brigade was opposed by the enemy at the passage of the Swat river. The action commenced by several bodies of the enemy being seen advancing down the Adinazai Valley from the direction of Uch, and the Sappers, then collected on the river, making a bridge, were fired at from the hills on the opposite side. I should mention that the previous evening the 11th Bengal Lancers, which had crossed the pass and joined the head-quarters camp with the 1st Brigade at Khar, had been ordered to march early on the morning of the 7th to the 2nd Brigade camp opposite the

crossing over the Swat river, and from thence to ford the river and make a reconnaissance up the Adinazai Valley towards Uch, being supported by other arms from the 2nd Brigade, the Brigadier-General Commanding the 2nd Brigade being also directed to cross the river and destroy the fort of Ramora.

The 11th Bengal Lancers, conveying these orders, joined Brigadier-General Waterfield and his brigade at 9 A.M., before which time the enemy had commenced the attack, and the 4th Sikhs had been ordered down to the river bank to support the Sappers, as also the Maxim guns under Captain Peebles, Devonshire Regiment. On the arrival of the 11th Bengal Lancers, that regiment, with a squadron of the Guides Cavalry, the whole under Lieutenant-Colonel Scott, 11th Bengal Lancers, was directed to cross the river, under cover of the fire of No. 8 Mountain Battery, Royal Artillery, and part of the King's Own Scottish Borderers, and attack the enemy, while the remainder of the King's Own Scottish Borderers, supported by No. 2 (Derajat) Mountain Battery, crossed later opposite Ramora fort and took possession of it. As soon as the 11th Bengal Lancers began to cross the river the enemy were seen to begin retiring, but were too late, for the Lancers, led with great dash, pursued and overtook them, and are reported to have killed at least 100. The pursuit was continued after Umra Khan's horsemen up to the top of the Katgola Pass.

Our loss was trivial, while that of the enemy was considerable; and this was mainly due to the able manner in which Brigadier-General Waterfield handled his troops. In the original report on this action the enemy were estimated at 1,500, but I have since ascertained that there were quite three times that number opposed to us.

Two battalions occupied Chakdara and the adjoining villages on the right bank of the Swat river on the night of the 7th April.

9. The 3rd Brigade crossed the Malakand Pass and joined me at Khar on the 8th. To feed the troops on the north side of the pass, I had been obliged to utilize during the 4th, 5th and 6th all the mules of the force, as these were the only animals that could cross the pass by the zig-zag road already described, and consequently it was not till the 8th, when camels had been streaming across with supplies for two days, that it was possible to equip the 2nd and 3rd Brigades with transport for their baggage and for twenty days' supplies.

The 2nd Brigade were entirely across the river by the evening of the 8th.

10. On the 9th April head-quarters crossed the Swat river and joined the 2nd Brigade at Chakdara, the 3rd Brigade encamping on the opposite bank at Aladand.

11. Before I moved on from the Swat river an advanced guard had been sent on ahead, consisting of the 11th Bengal Lancers, two squadrons of the Guides Cavalry, the Guides Infantry and the 4th Sikhs, which had arrived at Sado on the 10th. The cavalry forded the river and reconnoitred up the Bajaur Valley on the 10th, finding Umra Khan's forts held, and on that evening, owing to the river rising, they experienced considerable difficulty in recrossing to the left bank. On my arrival it was clear that nothing but a bridge could get the troops across, and this was at once commenced by Major Aylmer, V.C., Royal Engineers, with the 4th Company, Bengal Sappers and Min-

ers, under the direction of Colonel Leach, D.S.O., Commanding Royal Engineer with the force. The bridge was built on raft-piers constructed from the logs lying on the banks of the river. On the evening of the 12th, men on foot could cross, and there being every hope of my being able to cross the troops and their baggage the following day, the Guides Infantry were passed over to cover the bridge, and formed an entrenched post at the apex of a re-entering angle of the right bank, on which the end of the bridge rested. This post had a level space of some hundreds of yards in front, and being with its surroundings thoroughly commanded at short range by the high ground on the left bank, was extremely strong.

12. On the morning of the 13th, between 3 and 5 A. M., an unexpected misfortune happened. The river rose suddenly and brought down large logs of timber which broke the bridge, and as the current increased at the same time to such an extent as to make a raft-bridge useless, it was seen at once that the only resource was to make a suspension bridge. A suitable place, about two miles down stream from the site of the raft-bridge, was accordingly selected, and a design was adopted by which the cables of the bridge were to be made of many strands of telegraph wire. Work was commenced immediately, but the bridge could not be expected to be ready for three or four days. The site selected being, as I have said, about two miles down stream, a new road was required along the hillside on the right bank back to the mouth of the Bajaur Valley, which road could only be commenced when men could be passed over the river.

Meanwhile, on the morning of the 13th, the Guides Infantry had received orders to march down the right bank of the Panjkora river, and punish certain villages on that side from which men had been persistently firing on the transport, which, till the completion of the Kamrani route, was forced to use the Shago Kas defile road. The whole of the route which should have been followed by the Guides Infantry was in full view of the left bank, and could easily be protected by infantry posted thereon. By some mistake, which can never now be accounted for, Lieutenant-Colonel Battye, Commanding the Guides Infantry, led his battalion up the Ushiri river into Bajaur. At noon he sent a message by heliograph that two large bodies of the enemy were advancing against him. His battalion could not be supported, as troops could not cross the river to do so. It was therefore ordered to retire to its entrenched post, and the 2nd Brigade at once lined the high banks overlooking the Panjkora river to cover its retirement. The battalion retired most deliberately, and this retirement was covered first by artillery fire from the left bank, and afterwards, as the enemy approached nearer, by fire of the infantry and Maxim guns. The enemy were in considerable strength, probably about 4,000 all told, and I do not doubt had heard of the broken bridge, and thought that our troops on their side of the river might be cut off. With the knowledge that troops could not be sent to his assistance, the visible strength of the advancing enemy, and the distance of his battalion from the covering fire of the troops on the left bank, it would undoubtedly have been wiser if the officer commanding had retired at once without waiting for orders. However, the disinclination to retire is a fault on the right side, and the retirement as it was carried out was a splendid performance. It is deeply to be deplored that when the battalion had reached the level ground, and was about to cross the Ushiri river to its entrenched post, Lieutenant-Colonel Battye was killed. In his death the Corps of Guides has lost an able commander, and the State a gallant and valuable officer. After the Guides reached their post, they were reinforced by a company of the 4th Sikhs, which crossed on rafts, and the enemy did not attack with any boldness, but contented themselves with long range firing, which they continued up to about 11 P.M. The loss on the enemy's side was reported by their own people afterwards to be over 500.

On this day, 13th April, Lieutenant Edwardes, 2nd Bombay Grenadiers, who had been a prisoner, was sent in by Umra Khan to my camp.

13. On the 14th the gathering of the previous day gradually disappeared, but not before we had to lament the loss of another valuable officer, *viz.*, Captain Peebles, Devonshire Regiment, in charge of the Maxim guns, who was mortally wounded in the entrenchment whither he had crossed the previous evening with one of his guns, on a mussuck-raft.

14. During the 14th the remainder of the 4th Sikhs was crossed on mussuck-rafts, and joined the Guides Infantry, and a strong position on spurs on the other side of the river and to the north of the Ushiri stream was occupied by these two battalions. The crossing on the few small rafts at my disposal became every moment more difficult and slower, owing to the river continuing to rise. On the night of the 14th very bad weather set in, and rain continued all that night, and through the day and night of the 15th, much delaying work on the suspension bridge, and the rising water approached nearer and nearer to its piers.

The Guides Infantry and the 4th Sikhs with them had the previous evening been ordered, as the only means of feeding them, to be ready to park their ammunition and baggage in the entrenched post of the Guides Infantry, and make their way to the suspension bridge, so that they might re-cross before the bridge was swept away, and things looked so serious on the morning of the 16th that they were ordered to commence this movement. When, however I visited the bridge, early on the morning of the 16th, I was informed that no further rise had taken place in the last three or four hours; and, during the time that I was there, the water, if any thing, fell, and the rain ceased. I therefore sent orders to the Guides Infantry and 4th Sikhs to stand fast. At noon it was clear that the water was falling, and that the danger was over for the time. But the necessity for a bridge above high flood-level was evidently urgent and the Commandant, Royal Engineers, put it in hand at once; and I trust it may be ready before the river rises again.

Lieutenant Fowler, Royal Engineers, was on this day sent in by Umra Khan.

15. On the morning of the 17th the two brigades were ordered to advance. One squadron of the Guides Cavalry marched at an early hour to reconnoitre up the valley towards Miankila, under the orders of Brigadier-General Blood, C.B., and the 11th Bengal Lancers and the two infantry brigades followed across the river.

At 10 A.M., after the troops of the 3rd Brigade (which was leading) had crossed, I received a message from Brigadier-General Blood that the enemy were in sight near the village of Miankila, and were advancing from thence. The road on the right bank of the Panjkora river from the bridge up to the open valley was only a footpath fit for mules, over which every man and animal had to go in single file, horses having to be led, and it was clear that both brigades could not hope to get across and move up to the scene of action during the day.

I therefore directed Brigadier-General Waterfield to pass over the baggage of the 3rd Brigade which could reach that brigade before night, and then only to cross the bridge with his own brigade and its transport, and to join me the first thing next morning.

Then pushing on myself, I reached Ghobani just as the 3rd Brigade were going into action. The enemy occupied the hills on the left or southern side of the valley, and held the villages of Gulderi and Andak to the west on some bluffs above the river and the hills to the south of the Ushiri. The 4th Gurkhas were directed up the southern hills and then to move along them to the west; the Seaforth Highlanders being on the slopes below them, and the 25th Punjab Infantry in support. Two companies of the Buffs occupied the hills to the north, with No. 2 (Derajat) Mountain Battery in action on a knoll in the centre, and the remainder of the Buffs in reserve. While the infantry cleared the southern hills, the 11th Bengal Lancers advanced up the centre of the valley to a small village, Gosam, where their horses got protection from the enemy's fire, but the cavalry got no opportunity of charging, the ground in their front being too broken. The enemy on this occasion did not show the bold front of previous days, but retired as the infantry advanced, and though the guns were sent forward about 1,000 yards to hasten their retreat, the loss of the enemy was not great. Throughout the action the troops were well handled by Brigadier-General Gatacre, D.S.O.

16. On the morning of the 18th Brigadier-General Waterfield with the 2nd Brigade joined me, and the 2nd and 3rd Brigades advanced against Miankila and Mundar. The latter, a fort on the left bank of the Jandol river, is the home of Umra Khan, and it was expected that he would make a final stand at one of these places. Both were, however, deserted, and it was reported that Umra Khan had fled towards Asmar, and had asked for an asylum from the Amir of Kabul. I may add that he has been a fugitive ever since.

17. The same afternoon Brigadier-General Gatacre, with the Buffs, the 4th Gurkhas, half of No. 4 Company, Bengal Sappers and Miners, No. 2 (Derajat) Mountain Battery, and the two Maxim guns of the Devonshire Regiment, pushed on to Barwa, *en route* for Dir and Chitral, with twenty days' supplies; and the remainder of the brigade, *viz.*, the Seaforth Highlanders and the 25th Punjab Infantry, were taken on by me on the morning of the 20th to Kambat (called Chashma at first) at the foot of the Janbatai Pass.

18. On the afternoon of the 20th April, Brigadier-General Gatacre sent a message back to me that Major Deane, Chief Political Officer (who accompanied him), had received news that the garrison of Chitral was reduced to great straits, and that the mines of the enemy had reached to within ten yards of the walls of the fort, and he suggested that he should advance rapidly with a small body of 500 men. To this I consented, as being the only way of passing quickly through the intricate country we were now traversing, and the only chance of rescuing the garrison. To support him while out of communication, I sent forward on the 21st the Seaforth Highlanders with all the supplies I could collect, and arranged to move on myself with the 25th Punjab Infantry when more supplies arrived. On the following day, 21st, reassuring news came regarding the garrison of Chitral Fort, *viz.*, that it was holding out on the 17th, and later that Sher Afzal had abandoned the siege and had absconded; this was confirmed on the following day, the 22nd.

At that time it was not known whether the relief of Chitral Fort had been effected by Colonel Kelly, or by the occupation of Kila Drosh by the Khan of Dir acting under my orders, or by the advance of my force and the defeat of Umra Khan. Probably it was the result of all three, but it is now known that Colonel Kelly was the first to arrive at Chitral, on the 20th April.

19. When this news was received, Brigadier-General Gatacre was directed not to advance hurriedly, but with due consideration for his troops. The Janbatai Pass (7,400 feet) was found to be a very difficult one, and the hills beyond it were very much more difficult to traverse than any that had yet been passed over, and it was only possible to move over this pass by single battalions at a time.

20. On my arrival at Dir on the 25th April, Brigadier General Gatacre was crossing the Lowarai Pass, which was accomplished by the Buffs and half a battalion of the 4th Gurkhas on the 26th and 27th without any loss, though it was only done by all the troops following the example of Brigadier-General Gatacre himself, and exhibiting the most determined perseverance and energy. The troops above named, *viz.*, the Buffs and half a battalion of the 4th Gurkhas, are now at Ashreth in Chitral, where they have been ordered to halt pending further orders, as with the capture of Sher Afzal, who was brought into my camp a prisoner on the 27th, peace in the Chitral Valley is re-established.

When not fighting or marching, every man has laboured with the greatest cheerfulness all day on road-making, and altogether the month has been one of continued exertion, and cheerful self-denial and devotion, under circumstances of unusual difficulty and hardship.

I cannot speak too highly in this respect of the conduct of all ranks, both British and Native.

From Lt-Gen Sir R C Low, KCB, commanding the Chitral Relief Force, dated Laram Pass 27 July 1895

I have the honor to submit the following report in continuation of my No. 296-A of the 1st May last.

1. After the capture of Sher Afzal the troops were halted, and it was a question as to whether it was desirable to move up to the Chitral Fort. The British Agent there advised that the troops should not advance, on the ground that the valley, already devastated by Umra Khan, could not give supplies.

2. The Government of India, however, decided that British troops should be shown at Chitral.

Brigadier-General Gatacre, D.S.O., Commanding the 3rd Brigade, was ordered to move on the three marches from Ashreth to Chitral.

He found the track up the Kunar River quite as bad as, if not worse than, the defiles on each side of the Lowarai Pass, and, as before, the track had to be made passable by the skill of engineer officers and sappers and by the willing labor of the troops.

3. During the first week of May I was detained at Dir. The Khan of Dir at this time wanted our constant support. He had, by capturing Sher Afzal and handing him over to me, done good service and simplified the political situation at Chitral, but the duty was a very unpleasant one for him, and he incurred a great deal of unpopularity amongst the people of his own country, in which he was not yet firmly established as ruler.

4. It is only right that I should here record the military services of the Khan of Dir during the advance of the Force, as it bears considerably on the main object of the expedition,—namely, the relief of Chitral Fort.

Mahomed Sharif Khan, the Khan of Dir, some years ago was dispossessed of the whole of his territory by Umra Khan, and at the time of the mobilization of the Chitral Relief Force he was a refugee in Upper Swat. On hearing that the Government of India intended to send a force against Umra Khan, he joined me at the front, avowedly with the object of regaining his lost territory and position, but offering his services at the same time,—services which, as will be seen, were afterwards of great importance.

After the action of the 4th April, on the descent from the Malakand Pass to the Swat Valley, the Khan of Dir was sent on in advance across the Laram Pass into Dir territory, with orders to raise his tribes and recapture, if possible, all the forts in Dir territory then held by detachments of Umra Khan's men, and then to push men across the Lowarai Pass to the assistance of the besieged garrison of Chitral.

The delay to the advance of the Force caused by the floods in the Panjkora River, the washing away of the first bridge, and the necessity of building a suspension bridge, have been duly reported in my despatch of which this is a continuation. At that time it was believed that the garrison of Chitral had food only till the 20th April, and after the defeat of Umra Khan on the 17th, and his flight, it was clear that, using the utmost exertions, the leading troops could hardly reach Chitral before the 25th, and that the action of the Khan of Dir might have an important effect on the fate of the besieged garrison.

The Khan carried out his instructions most loyally, not only in capturing the different forts in Dir territory, in doing which, it may be said, he acted as much for himself as for us, but also in pushing forward men into the Chitral Valley, which is outside his territory, and which was done entirely in our interests.

He captured the Fort of Dir from Umra Khan's troops on the 12th April, with the loss of sixty of his own men, and he pushed forward men under his brother, who took and occupied the fort of Kila Drosh, the most important fort in the Chitral Valley, on the 18th April. Kila Drosh is two marches south of Chitral Fort, and on the same date Colonel Kelly's troops were two marches north of Chitral Fort, while Brigadier-General Gatacre's brigade had reached Barwa, five marches south of Kila Drosh. The siege of Chitral was raised that night, the garrison finding themselves free on the morning of the 19th April.

It is due to the Khan of Dir that the active part he took should be recognized, since, if he did nothing more, he heralded our arrival in the Chitral Valley.

5. Leaving Dir on the 9th of May, I marched to Chitral and reached it on the 16th. The troops were drawn up to receive me, and in front of them I met the British Agent, Surgeon-Major G. S. Robertson, C.S.I., and the provisional Mehtar, the boy Shujah-ul-Mulk.

The parade was made as impressive as possible, for the Chitralis had never seen British soldiers, and as a matter of fact did not believe that we had any. A portion of the garrison that had defended the fort during the siege, *viz.*, one company of the 14th Sikhs, was in the centre, supported on the right by the Gilgit Field Force, consisting of the 32nd Pioneers and two guns of the Kashmir Mountain Battery, the whole under Lieutenant-Colonel J. G. Kelly, 32nd Pioneers; on the left were the troops of the 3rd Brigade, *viz.*, the 1st Battalion of "The Buffs," No. 2 (Derajat) Mountain Battery, No. 4 Company, Bengal Sappers and Miners, a detachment of the 2nd Battalion, 4th Gurkha Rifles, and my escort of one company of the Seaforth Highlanders: the whole parade being under the command of Brigadier-General Gatacre, D.S.O. After inspecting the troops, I formed them into three sides of a square and, addressing them, pointed out that the parade was a very remarkable one, in that every man present had received the congratulations of Her Majesty the Queen-Empress; that the gallantry of the besieged garrison of Chitral was the pride and admiration of all their comrades in the army; as was also the determined march of Lieutenant-Colonel Kelly and his troops, who were the first to reach Chitral.

6. Prior to my departure from Chitral, the British Agent heard rumours of disturbances in Kohistan, and asked that the troops of this Force should hold the valley and relieve Lieutenant-Colonel Kelly's troops. This was sanctioned by Government, and Chitral was occupied by the 2nd Battalion, 4th Gurkha Rifles, and the whole line from Chitral to our frontier in India has since been held by the troops of this Force.

7. During the operations of the month of April the troops of the Force under my command advanced from our Indian frontier into Chitral territory, crossing five mountain passes, three of which—the Malakand (2,900 ft.), the Janbatai (7,400 ft.), and the Lowarai (10,200 ft.)—were of the most difficult character; and having also to throw bridges over two large rivers, the Swat and the Panjkora, besides innumerable smaller streams. The tracks across the mountains were so narrow and difficult that it is no exaggeration to say that the troops had to make them passable for baggage animals every yard of the way.

8. During the first advance of the Force the object was speed, and the labour of the troops was spent in making the mountain tracks passable. Since the 1st May the troops have been employed in improving these tracks into roads, over which the transport can work without exhaustion.

9. The heat in the valleys has been intense during May and June, but posts have been found on or close to the line of communications for the British soldiers of the Force, namely, on the Laram, the Janbatai and Lowarai passes, where they have had a comparatively cool climate.

10. The operations of the Force being throughout in a country which has hitherto been closed to us, has afforded special opportunities for certain branches of the service to earn distinction. This is notably the case as regards the Sappers and Miners and Pioneers. The rapid way in which almost impassable footpaths over mountain passes were converted into excellent mule and camel roads, testifies to the energy and zeal of the officers and the endurance and physique of the men of these branches of the service; while the hastily-constructed bridges over unfordable rivers and mountain torrents, with many of the gallery passages along bare cliffs built out from sheer precipices with cantilevers of beams, doors, etc., from the nearest villages, were marvels of ingenuity and resource.

11. The survey party with the Force has done most valuable work, which has principally consisted in triangulation, traversing, and large-scale surveys of country, and plans of various places. The extent of this work may be judged when I say that the area embraced by the triangulation has been upwards of 1,500 square miles; 60 miles have been traversed, while the country mapped at two inches, one inch, half an inch, and quarter inch to a mile scale has been respectively 40 square miles, 450 square miles, 100 square miles, and 1,200 square miles.

12. The Intelligence Branch also has lost no opportunity of adding to our knowledge of the country. Stage by stage as the Force advanced the officers of the Intelligence Department reconnoitred, sketched, and reported on the route to be followed by the troops in rear, the mileage of this alone being about 186 miles. In addition 600 miles of branch roads were sketched and reconnoitred as well as between 30 and 40 passes, and the whole country embraced by these reconnaissances was gazetteered and much new information collected.

13. The different actions in which the troops of the Force have been engaged have already been reported, but I may now briefly refer to them with the view of bringing to His Excellency's notice the names of officers who have earned distinction.

At the storming of the Malakand Pass, the attack, as already reported, was made by seven battalions of the 1st and 2nd Brigades, two battalions, the 4th Sikhs and Guides Infantry, being sent up the highest peaks with orders to make a turning movement on reaching the crest, while the direct frontal attack on the enemy's main position was made by the King's Own Scottish Borderers and the Gordon Highlanders, supported on the left by the King's Royal Rifle Corps, and on the right by the Bedfordshire Regiment and the 37th Dogras. The action commenced at 8-45 A.M., and the pass was captured at 2 P.M. I attach a casualty return, Appendix A, which shows the losses on our side. The enemy numbered about 12,000, and afterwards admitted a loss of over 300 killed.

14. On the descent into the Swat Valley on the 4th April, the troops of the 1st Brigade were met by the advancing enemy. The troops held the eastern hills of the descent, while the baggage passed through the defile to the open in the Swat Valley. The brunt of the fighting fell on the 37th Dogras, supported by No. 4 Company of the Bengal Sappers and Miners, and by one company of the 15th Sikhs, who were ordered to hold a low hill which commanded the passage, and who repulsed repeated attacks of large bodies of the enemy; the final and most determined attempt being frustrated and enemy routed by a brilliant charge of the Guides Cavalry. I attach a statement (Appendix B) of our casualties on this occasion.

15. On the 7th April the enemy disputed the passage of the Swat River, which was effected by the advance of the 11th Bengal Lancers and Guides Cavalry to the river bank under cover of artillery and infantry fire, the crossing of the river by those regiments, and their brilliant charge and pursuit of the enemy for many miles, while the infantry forded the river and seized the positions of the enemy and Umra Khan's fort of Ramora. I attach a statement of our losses on that occasion (Appendix C)

16. The next action was that of the Guides Infantry at the Sado ferry on the Panjkora River on the 13th April, which has already been described in detail, at the conclusion of which the regiment lost their commanding officer, Lieutenant-Colonel F. D. Battye. The attack of the enemy continued during the night of the 13th and till the morning of the 14th. I attach a casualty return (Appendix D) of our losses on the occasion

17. The three days following the above action, while full of anxiety regarding the rising of the Panjkora River in front and the Swat River in rear, were notable for the arrival in camp of Lieutenants Edwardes and Fowler, who had been prisoners in Umra Khan's hands; their safe arrival in camp being a great relief, as I had constant fears as to what their fate would be on my advancing into Umra Khan's territory.

18. I may record here an instance of the promptitude of Brigadier-General Gatacre, D.S.O., and the gallantry of Major Aylmer, V.C., Royal Engineers, which occurred on the 15th April. On that day I had only three rafts left, and in the last attempt to cross the Panjkora River one of these three rafts was overturned, having on it at the time two British soldiers, Private Hall and Private Ellwood of the Maxim gun detachment of the Devonshire Regiment, one sepoy and one boatman. When the raft was overturned Brigadier-General Gatacre was standing on the bank, and seeing that one of the British soldiers (Private Hall) and the sepoy and boatman had regained the raft, which was being carried down the stream bottom upwards, and knowing that the stream took a considerable bend before it came to the point where the suspension bridge was being built, he galloped down to that point and informed Major Aylmer, who was superintending the construction of the bridge, of the accident. At that time there was no superstructure to the bridge—merely the standards and wire suspension ropes. Major Aylmer ordered a rope to be passed across to the right bank, but the slack was caught by the current, and the rope was carried away. At this moment the raft appeared in sight about 200 yards off, and Major Aylmer, seeing the urgency of the case, got into a sling cradle and was pulled to the centre of the stream. The raft immediately after passed under him, and he grasped Private Hall who left his hold on the raft, whereupon his extra weight immersed the cradle in the water, so that officer and man were in great danger of being swept away. However, Major Aylmer held on manfully, and with the assistance of No. 3189, Lance-Naick Sham Singh of No. 4 Company, Bengal Sappers and Miners, who got down into the cradle to help Major Aylmer, the whole party were landed, though with much difficulty and danger.

19. The last action in which the force has been engaged was that of the 17th of April. In this fight the enemy did not make any stand, possibly owing to the able manner in which the attack was directed by Brigadier-General Gatacre; for the positions of the enemy were taken in flank from east to west, and they were abandoned one after the other as the troops advanced. I append (Appendix E) a casualty return of our losses on this occasion.

20. I cannot conclude this portion of my report without bringing to His Excellency's notice the passage of the Lowarai Pass by the troops of the 3rd Brigade under the direction of Brigadier-General W. F. Gatacre, D.S.O., at the time there was about three miles of ascent to be made over snow, and the same extent of snow on the descent. The pass was crossed in very bad weather, which added to the difficulties and to the time taken in crossing the mules and supplies. The time of year (early spring) necessitated the passage being, if possible, done in the very early morning while it was yet freezing and the snow was as sound as possible. The start, therefore, was made from Gujar at the foot of the snow at 1-30 A.M. by torch-light. A strong working party led the advance armed with improvised snow-ploughs to cut through drifts when necessary, but their main duty was to steadily tramp down a track all the way, which in this manner hardened sufficiently to bear the weight of the mules, while men with torches were left at turns and dangerous places; for if once a mule left the track, it at once sank into the adjoining snow and had to be unladen and lifted again on to the beaten path. In this way the top of the pass was reached in the middle of heavy rain and sleet at 7 A.M. The descent on the north side is very steep, never less than 1:4 and often 1:3, and the track had to be tramped down in zigzags. The laden mules found it almost impossible to control their movements, especially as the rain, freezing on the snow, had made the top layer into a sheet of ice, and large numbers of them were constantly slipping off and, so to speak, "tobagganing" straight down the mountain. General Gatacre in his report says he saw as many as twenty at a time solemnly sliding down on their haunches for distances varying from 100 to 200 feet or more, when they turned complete somersaults into the snow, whence they could not move till dug out; and as it was impossible to load them again there, the bags or boxes carried by them were sent sliding down the mountain, guided by ropes from party to party of men stationed on the descent, while the animals, replaced without loads on the path, found their way down the beaten track.

The column reached Ziarat, on the north side of the pass, below the snow line by nightfall. I may add that the pass became more and more dangerous from this time till the snow melted sufficiently to admit of a summer road being made above the snow-covered torrent by the Pioneers. The only passage, until the snow melted sufficiently to admit of this being done, was up and down the centre of the snow-covered torrent, and for about ten days in the spring this becomes very dangerous, owing to the liability to sink through into the water beneath and from the avalanches of snow from the adjoining cliffs. Probably the best time to cross this and other passes of this nature is on a fine day at the latter end of winter when the snow is hard.

No 3 MOUNTAIN BATTERY, ROYAL ARTILLERY

<u>Naik</u>
134 Dabiya   sl w 3 Apr 1895 Malakand Pass, gs left arm

ROYAL ENGINEERS

<u>Lieutenant</u>
Fowler, John Sharman   w 15 Mar 1895 Reshan, taken prisoner, released 16 Apr; awarded DSO

DEVONSHIRE REGIMENT

<u>Captain</u>
Peebles, Allan Laing   mort w 14 Apr 1895 Panjkora River, gs, dow 15 Apr

<u>Private</u>
3194 Northway, R.   sev w 13/14 Apr 1895 Panjkora River, gs leg

BEDFORDSHIRE REGIMENT

<u>Corporal</u>
1786 Killington, J.   sl w 4 Apr 1895 nr Khar, spent bullet foot

<u>Privates</u>
2981 Cox, T.   sl w 3 Apr 1895 Malakand Pass, gs ear
4364 Stevens, G.   k 3 Apr 1895 Malakand Pass, bullet head

2nd Btn KING'S OWN SCOTTISH BORDERERS

<u>Captain</u>
MacFarlane, Duncan Alwyn   dang w 3 Apr 1895 Malakand Pass, gs arm

<u>Second-Lieutenant</u>
Coke, Edward Sacheverell D'Ewes   sev w 3 Apr 1895 Malakand Pass, gs thigh

Corporals
1343 Larkins, P.   sl w 3 Apr 1895 Malakand Pass, gs knee
2677 Melville, W.   sl w 3 Apr 1895 Malakand Pass, gs chest
2964 Smith, James   k 3 Apr 1895 Malakand Pass, gs chest

Lance-Corporal
3856 McKinnon, J.   sev w 3 Apr 1895 Malakand Pass, gs chest

Privates
2107 Blades, W.   sl w 3 Apr 1895 Malakand Pass, gs face
4089 Blakey, J.   sev w 7 Apr 1895 Swat River, gs shoulder
4499 Brown, J.   sev w 3 Apr 1895 Malakand Pass, gs shoulder
2969 Bunney, J.   sev w 3 Apr 1895 Malakand Pass, gs knee
4450 Chalmers, W.   sev w 3 Apr 1895 Malakand Pass, gs neck
3902 Dundas, H.   sev w 3 Apr 1895 Malakand Pass, gs face
4343 Finlay, R.   sev w 3 Apr 1895 Malakand Pass, gs chest
4829 Gordon, J.   sl w 13/14 Apr 1895 Panjkora River, gs hand
4930 Graham, G.   sev w 3 Apr 1895 Malakand Pass, gs neck
3995 Henry, James   dang w 3 Apr 1895 Malakand Pass, gs head
2546 O'Neil, J.   sev w 3 Apr 1895 Malakand Pass, gs arm
2414 Simpson, T.   sev w 3 Apr 1895 Malakand Pass, gs hip
3836 Smith, John   k 3 Apr 1895 Malakand Pass, gs chest

1st Btn KING'S ROYAL RIFLE CORPS

Captain
Nugent, Oliver Steward Wood   sl w 3 Apr 1895 Malakand Pass; awarded DSO

Privates
7406 Bradbury, T.   sev w 3 Apr 1895 Malakand Pass, gs left arm
5915 Carter, W.   k 3 Apr 1895 Malakand Pass, bullet head
5827 Gardiner, H.   k 3 Apr 1895 Malakand Pass, bullet head
4640 Gillard, A.E.   k 3 Apr 1895 Malakand Pass, bullet neck
3667 Palmer, A.   sev w 3 Apr 1895 Malakand Pass, gs right leg
5344 Richards, W.   sev w 3 Apr 1895 Malakand Pass, gs left buttock
6116 Rudd, E.   sl w 3 Apr 1895 Malakand Pass, gs left hand
7179 Walker, J.   k 3 Apr 1895 Malakand Pass, bullet head

SEAFORTH HIGHLANDERS

Private
1830 Taylor, J.   sl w 17 Apr 1895 Mamagai, bullet left shoulder

1st Btn GORDON HIGHLANDERS

Captain
Burney, Herbert Henry   sl w 3 Apr 1895 Malakand Pass, gs hand

Lieutenant
Watt, Donald Munro   sl w 3 Apr 1895 Malakand Pass, gs shoulder

Second-Lieutenant
Hesketh, Walter   attchd   sev w 3 Apr 1895 Malakand Pass, gs chest

Lance-Corporals
3191 Edmonstone, R.   sl w 3 Apr 1895 Malakand Pass, gs
4847 Mann, W.   dang w 3 Apr 1895 Malakand Pass, gs abdomen

Drummer
2240 Brown, J.   sev w 3 Apr 1895 Malakand Pass, gs forearm

Privates
3915 Bree, J.   sl w 3 Apr 1895 Malakand Pass, gs chest
4315 Capewell, A.   sl w 13/14 Apr 1895 Panjkora River, graze
4090 Collie, A.   sl w 13/14 Apr 1895 Panjkora River, gs arm
1638 Cowborough, J.   k 3 Apr 1895 Malakand Pass, gs chest
3975 Davidson, D.   sev w 3 Apr 1895 Malakand Pass, gs leg
4541 Francis, Thomas   k 3 Apr 1895 Malakand Pass, gs head
4689 Pardoe, F.   k 3 Apr 1895 Malakand Pass, gs chest
4311 Purkiss, G.   sev w 3 Apr 1895 Malakand Pass, gs shoulder
3238 Smith, A.   sev w 3 Apr 1895 Malakand Pass, gs arm
3932 Smith, A.   sev w 3 Apr 1895 Malakand Pass, gs leg
3783 Wheatley, F.   sev w 3 Apr 1895 Malakand Pass, gs leg

ROYAL IRISH FUSILIERS

Captain
O'Leary, Tom Evelyn   sl w 13/14 Apr 1895 Panjkora River, gs chest

Private
3188 Mullins, M.   sev w 13/14 Apr 1895 Panjkora River, gs forearm

11th REGIMENT OF BENGAL LANCERS

Daffadar
1847 Issar Singh   very sl w 7 Apr 1895 Swat River

Lance-Daffadar
1529 Jowda Singh   very sl w 7 Apr 1895 Swat River

Sowars
2174 Bal Singh   sev w 7 Apr 1895 Swat River, sword cuts left leg
2306 Ganda Singh   very sl w 7 Apr 1895 Swat River
2015 Hainan Singh sev w 17 Apr 1895 Mamagai, gs right leg
1889 Hussein Khan sl w 17 Apr 1895 Mamagai, graze
2271 Kapur Singh   very sl w 7 Apr 1895 Swat River
1941 Sad-ud-Din   sev w 17 Apr 1895 Mamagai, gs right thigh
2407 Sant Singh   very sl w 7 Apr 1895 Swat River
2345 Surain Singh k 7 Apr 1895 Swat River

BENGAL SAPPERS & MINERS

Jemadar
Lal Khan   w 9 Mar 1895 Reshan, spent bullet right arm

Havildar
3568 Ram Jas Upadhya   k 15 Mar 1895 Reshan

Naiks
3050 Jai Singh   k 15 Mar 1895 Reshan
2888 Kala Singh   k 15 Mar 1895 Reshun; awarded IOM 3rd Class
                  pension

Sappers
     Amir Shah   w 12 Mar 1895 Reshan, bullet splinter centre
                  forehead
4188 Anokh Singh   k 15 Mar 1895 Reshan
4791 Bhau Singh   sl w 7 Apr 1895 Swat River, gs knee
3754 Bhola Singh   k 15 Mar 1895 Reshan
4108 Bir Singh   mort w 7 Mar 1895 Reshan, dow 8 Mar
4148 Chanda Singh w 15 Mar 1895 Reshan, sword cuts head & back;
                   awarded IOM 3rd Class
3376 Dal Singh   w 7 Mar 1895 Reshan, gs through calf; k 15 Mar
4028 Man Singh   w 7 Mar 1895 Reshan, spent bullet; k 15 Mar
4022 Nadhan Singh w 11 Mar 1895 Reshan, gs fracture skull;
                   k 15 Mar
4280 Nadir Khan   k 15 Mar 1895 Reshan; awarded IOM 3rd Class
                   pension
3941 Natha Singh   k 15 Mar 1895 Reshan
3759 Rulya Singh   k 15 Mar 1895 Reshan

14th (FEROZEPORE SIKH) REGIMENT OF BENGAL INFANTRY

Captain
Ross, Claye Ross   k 10 Mar 1895 Koragh

Lieutenant
Jones, Herbert John   w 10 Mar 1895 Koragh, gs right arm & large contusion right forearm; awarded DSO

Naiks
1149 Hardit Singh   k 10 Mar 1895 Koragh
1009 Sahib Singh   k 10 Mar 1895 Koragh; awarded IOM 3rd Class pension

Lance-Naiks
1469 Bhanga Singh   k 10 Mar 1895 Koragh
1402 Burh Singh   w 10 Mar 1895 Koragh, gs above left nipple; awarded IOM 3rd Class
1587 Indar Singh   k 10 Mar 1895 Koragh
1257 Talok Singh   k 10 Mar 1895 Koragh

Drummer
1054 Kishan Singh   k 10 Mar 1895 Koragh

Sepoys
1664 Bhagat Singh   k 10 Mar 1895 Koragh
 866 Bhan Singh   k 10 Mar 1895 Koragh
1367 Bishan Singh   k 10 Mar 1895 Koragh
1986 Bishan Singh   k 10 Mar 1895 Koragh
1916 Bukan Singh   k 10 Mar 1895 Koragh; awarded IOM 3rd Class pension
1651 Dasondhu Singh   k 10 Mar 1895 Koragh; awarded IOM 3rd Class pension
1674 Dayal Singh   w 10 Mar 1895 Koragh, contusion; awarded IOM 3rd Class
1981 Dewa Singh   k 10 Mar 1895 Koragh
1859 Ganda Singh   k 10 Mar 1895 Koragh
1922 Ganga Singh   w 10 Mar 1895 Koragh, bullet graze left forearm; awarded IOM 3rd Class
1610 Gayan Singh   sl w 4 Apr 1895 Mastuj
 547 Ghanda Singh   k 10 Mar 1895 Koragh
1390 Gopal Singh   k 10 Mar 1895 Koragh
1842 Gujjan Singh   k 10 Mar 1895 Koragh
1649 Gurmukh Singh   k 10 Mar 1895 Koragh
1676 Hardit Singh   k 10 Mar 1895 Koragh
1888 Jiwan Singh   k 10 Mar 1895 Koragh
 778 Jodh Singh   w 10 Mar 1895 Koragh, contusion right hand; awarded IOM 3rd Class
1550 Kehar Singh   k 10 Mar 1895 Koragh
1891 Kesar Singh   k 10 Mar 1895 Koragh
1082 Khem Singh   k 10 Mar 1895 Koragh
1746 Kheta Singh   k 10 Mar 1895 Koragh
1618 Khizan Singh   k 10 Mar 1895 Koragh
1643 Kirpal Singh   k 10 Mar 1895 Koragh
1826 Kishan Singh   k 10 Mar 1895 Koragh
1834 Kishan Singh   k 10 Mar 1895 Koragh
1928 Kishan Singh   k 10 Mar 1895 Koragh
1725 Mal Singh   w 10 Mar 1895 Koragh, bullet graze back & hand; awarded IOM 3rd Class

1516 Nand Singh   k 10 Mar 1895 Koragh
1909 Nand Singh   k 10 Mar 1895 Koragh
1740 Narain Singh   k 10 Mar 1895 Koragh
1895 Natha Singh   k 10 Mar 1895 Koragh
1699 Nidhan Singh   k 10 Mar 1895 Koragh
1670 Nikka Singh   k 10 Mar 1895 Koragh
2017 Phuman Singh   k 10 Mar 1895 Koragh
1490 Pirthi Singh   k 10 Mar 1895 Koragh
1712 Prem Singh   w 10 Mar 1895 Koragh, contusion left foot;
                    awarded IOM 3rd Class
1656 Ram Singh   k 10 Mar 1895 Koragh
1163 Rattan Singh   k 10 Mar 1895 Koragh
1782 Roor Singh   k 10 Mar 1895 Koragh
1629 Saddah Singh   w 10 Mar 1895 Koragh, gs abdomen; awarded IOM
                    3rd Class
1228 Sant Singh   k 10 Mar 1895 Koragh; awarded IOM 3rd Class
                    pension
1856 Sarmukh Singh k 10 Mar 1895 Koragh
1577 Sham Singh   w 10 Mar 1895 Koragh, contusion left foot;
                    awarded IOM 3rd Class
1884 Sobha Singh   k 10 Mar 1895 Koragh
1530 Sundar Singh   k 10 Mar 1895 Koragh
1634 Thamman Singh w 10 Mar 1895 Koragh, contusion right foot;
                    awarded IOM 3rd Class
1874 Wariyam Singh k 10 Mar 1895 Koragh
1836 Wazir Singh   k 10 Mar 1895 Koragh

15th (LUDHIANA SIKH) REGIMENT OF BENGAL INFANTRY

Sepoy
2452 Jita Singh   sl w 7 Apr 1895 Swat River, gs forearm

32nd (PUNJAB) REGIMENT OF BENGAL INFANTRY (PIONEERS)

Jemadar
Sher Singh   sev w 13 Apr 1895 Nisa Gol, gs right side chest;
              awarded IOM 3rd Class

Havildar
1699 Wadhawa Singh   dang w 13 Apr 1895 Nisa Gol, gs chest;
                      awarded IOM 3rd Class

Naik
1867 Harnam Singh   sev w 13 Apr 1895 Nisa Gol, gs left thigh

Lance-Naik
2167 Jawahir Singh   sev w 13 Apr 1895 Nisa Gol, gs neck

Sepoys
3006 Bhagat Singh   k 13 Apr 1895 Nisa Gol, gs chest
2633 Budha Singh   sev w 9 Apr 1895 Chakalwat, gs neck & right shoulder
2448 Duma Singh   sl w 13 Apr 1895 Nisa Gol, gs graze forehead
2835 Ishar Singh   sev w 13 Apr 1895 Nisa Gol, gs right ankle
1893 Jiwan Singh   k 13 Apr 1895 Nisa Gol, gs chest
2991 Mal Singh   sev w 13 Apr 1895 Nisa Gol, gs left foot
2978 Wazir Singh   sev w 13 Apr 1895 Nisa Gol, gs right leg

37th (DOGRA) REGIMENT OF BENGAL INFANTRY

Lieutenant
Wynch, Frederick John Henry   sl w 4 Apr 1895 nr Khar, gs right arm

Naiks
119 Jai Singh   sev w 3 Apr 1895 Malakand Pass, bullet right leg
308 Sundar   sl w 3 Apr 1895 Malakand Pass

Sepoys
1156 Bishen Singh   sev w 4 Apr 1895 nr Khar, bullet left shoulder
 845 Ganesha   dang w 3 Apr 1895 Malakand Pass, bullet shoulder
 613 Ghepi   dang w 4 Apr 1895 nr Khar, bullet head
1138 Gurditta   sl w 4 Apr 1895 nr Khar, bullet thigh
 534 Lalu   sl w 3 Apr 1895 Malakand Pass
1268 Nathu   sev w 4 Apr 1895 nr Khar, bullet left hand
 869 Nauranga   sl w 4 Apr 1895 nr Khar, sword cut hand
 293 Nihala   sl w 4 Apr 1895 nr Khar, bullet hand
 833 Nihala   sl w 4 Apr 1895 nr Khar, bullet wrist
1084 Nihala   k 4 Apr 1895 nr Khar, bullet neck
 880 Prema Singh   k 4 Apr 1895 nr Khar, bullet head
 643 Ram Ditta   dang w 4 Apr 1895 nr Khar, bullet head
 969 Ram Singh   sev w 4 Apr 1895 nr Khar, bullet right foot
 282 Roda   dang w 4 Apr 1895 nr Khar, bullet forearm & right thigh
 611 Sohanu   sl w 4 Apr 1895 nr Khar, bullet hand

2nd Btn 4th GURKHA (RIFLE) REGIMENT

Sepoys
 568 Bhawan Singh   sev w 17 Apr 1895 Mamagai, gs right arm
 355 Goria Gurung   sev w 17 Apr 1895 Mamagai, gs right thigh
1470 Man Sing Garti   sev w 17 Apr 1895 Mamagai, gs left forearm
1402 Sarbar Garti   sl w 17 Apr 1895 Mamagai

CORPS OF GUIDES CAVALRY, PUNJAB FRONTIER FORCE

Lieutenant
Baldwin, Guy Melfort   sl w 4 Apr 1895 nr Khar, sword cut back of hand; awarded DSO

Lance-Daffadar
1070 Suba Singh   sl w 4 Apr 1895 nr Khar, sword cut head

Sowars
1425 Bhan Singh   sl w 4 Apr 1895 nr Khar, sword cut head
1126½ Budh Rai   sl w 4 Apr 1895 nr Khar, sword cut back of hand
 975 Mul Rai   sl w 4 Apr 1895 nr Khar, sword cut head

CORPS OF GUIDES INFANTRY, PUNJAB FRONTIER FORCE

Lieutenant-Colonel
Battye, Frederick Drummond   k 13 Apr 1895 Panjkora River, gs abdomen

Lieutenant
Ommanney, Arthur Hammond   sev w 3 Apr 1895 Malakand Pass, gs leg

Havildar
2365 Bhola Singh   sl w 13/14 Apr 1895 Panjkora River, gs left ankle

Lance-Havildar
2798 Hushyar Singh   sl w 13/14 Apr 1895 Panjkora River, gs right leg

Sepoys
3832 Baggat Singh   k 13/14 Apr 1895 Panjkora River, gs head
1998 Dur Jan   sl w 13/14 Apr 1895 Panjkora River, gs face
4052 Fateh Khan   sev w 13/14 Apr 1897 Panjkora River, gs face
3611 Ghani Shah   sev w 3 Apr 1895 Malakand Pass, gs shoulder
3920 Kalu   k 13/14 Apr 1895 Panjkora River, gs chest
3380 Kharku   k 13/14 Apr 1895 Panjkora River, gs chest
3607 Khazana   sl w 13/14 Apr 1895 Panjkora River, gs left ear
2997 Maitaba   sev w 13/14 Apr 1895 Panjkora River, gs wrist
3850 Partab Singh   sev w 3 Apr 1895 Malakand Pass, gs chest
3773 Ram Singh   sl w 13/14 Apr 1895 Panjkora River, gs ankle
3671 Siyah   dang w 13/14 Apr 1895 Panjkora River, gs fracture thigh
3074 Sonu   sl w 13/14 Apr 1897 Panjkora River, gs arm

4th REGIMENT OF SIKH INFANTRY, PUNJAB FRONTIER FORCE

Major
Tonnochy, Valens Congreve   sev w 3 Apr 1895 Malakand Pass, gs thigh

Lieutenant
Harman, Richard DSO   sev w 3 Apr 1895 Malakand Pass, gs thigh

Subadars
Rae Singh   sev w 3 Apr 1895 Malakand Pass
Sawan Singh   sev w 3 Apr 1895 Malakand Pass

Havildar
715 Tulsi   sev w 3 Apr 1895 Malakand Pass, gs leg

Naik
71 Umar Shah   sev w 3 Apr 1895 Malakand Pass, gs head

Sepoys
163 Bir Singh   sl w 3 Apr 1895 Malakand Pass
449 Bir Singh   k 3 Apr 1895 Malakand Pass
835 Chain Singh   k 7 Apr 1895, shot through head while crossing Swat River
444 Dewan Singh   sev w 13/14 Apr 1895 Panjkora River, gs ankle
1068 Gannu   sev w 3 Apr 1895 Malakand Pass, gs thigh
741 Gurdit Singh   drowned 7 Apr 1895 crossing Swat River
978 Jagat Singh   dang w 3 Apr 1895 Malakand Pass
911 Sohel Singh   sev w 3 Apr 1895 Malakand Pass, contusion face

KASHMIR IMPERIAL SERVICE TROOPS

No 1 KASHMIR MOUNTAIN BATTERY

Havildar-Major
38 Piranditta   sl w 13 Apr 1895 Nisa Gol, gs right arm & shoulder

Havildar
63 Bulwan Singh   sl w 13 Apr 1895 Nisa Gol, gs right buttock

Naik
14 Kojoo   k 13 Apr 1895 Nisa Gol, gs chest

Gunner
182 Sonoo   dang w 13 Apr 1895 Nisa Gol, gs right side, left groin & left thigh

Drivers
Alewah   k 13 Apr 1895 Nisa Gol, gs head
Suja Shah   k 13 Apr 1895 Nisa Gol, gs head

KASHMIR SAPPERS & MINERS

Subadar
Manktu   sl w 9 Apr 1895 Chakalwat, gs neck

Havildar
 71 Kiwan Singh   dang w 13 Apr 1895 Nisa Gol, gs thigh

Sepoys
395 Guta   sl w 9 Apr 1895 Chakalwat, gs crown of head
407 Kaku   sl w 9 Apr 1895 Chakalwat, gs finger
 51 Rupa   sev w 13 Apr 1895 Nisa Gol, gs shoulder

4th (RAGHUNATH) REGIMENT OF KASHMIR LIGHT INFANTRY

Subadar
Dharm Singh   k Mar 1895 Reshan; awarded IOM 3rd Class pension.

Havildar
    Ranjit Singh   k Mar 1895 Reshan; awarded IOM 3rd Class pension

Lance-Naik
    Budhia   k Mar 1895 Reshan; awarded IOM 3rd Class pension

Sepoys
342 Maniram Rana   k 13 Apr 1895 Nisa Gol, gs chest
421 Parbir Gharti   k 13 Apr 1895 Nisa Gol, gs chest

PUNJAB FRONTIER 1897-98

From Brig-Gen E R Elles, CB, commanding Peshawar District, dated Peshawar 10 August 1897

I have the honour to make the following report on operations carried out against a rising of Mohmands and other tribes led by the Adda Mullah.

2. Two or three days before the 7th August rumours had reached the Commissioner that the Adda Mullah with his gathering was somewhere in the hills near by, and intended attacking the Hindu village of Shunkargarh under the walls of Fort Shabkadr. I offered to reinforce the Border Police in the Fort with a squadron and two companies, but the Commissioner declined.

3. At about 8-30 P.M. on the evening of the 7th, Saturday, the Commissioner came to me and informed me that Shunkargarh would be attacked and that he wanted troops sent out.

I at once issued orders for the following troops to move without delay:

51st Field Battery	4 Guns.
13th Bengal Lancers	2 Squadrons.
Somersetshire Light Infantry	2 Companies.
20th Punjab Infantry	The Battalion.

The troops marched between 12 and 1 A.M. on the 8th. The distance to Shabkadr is fully 19 miles, and there was a ferry at 13 miles, the *Adizai*. It was an intensely hot night and the troops reached the ferry by daylight. Owing to paucity of boats a large number of the cavalry horses were swum across the stream over 200 yards wide and running very strong.

Adizai.—At Adizai, which I visited at daybreak, I heard and saw that Shunkargarh had been burnt, and from a report by the Border Police "Subadar" at Shabkadr it appeared that the enemy had come down at 4 P.M. on the 7th, and after burning the village and attacking the Fort had retired in the morning to the low hills. Cavalry were pushed on to reconnoitre, and at 8·30 Lieutenant-Colonel Woon moved on Shabkadr with the remainder of the Cavalry, 2 guns 51st Field Battery, 2 companies Somersetshire Light Infantry and $2\frac{1}{2}$ companies 20th Punjab Infantry. He reconnoitred the enemy and found them occupying the low hills west of Shabkadr covering the Gandab Pass. The heat was intense the troops done up, and the column was not yet concentrated, so Lieutenant-Colonel Woon withdrew to the Fort.

4. I returned myself to Peshawar by noon on the 8th as it was absolutely necessary for me to do so.

5. On the morning of the 9th, in accordance with my orders, which were to attack the enemy as soon as possible, Lieutenant-Colonel Woon moved out with the force given in margin and found the enemy occupying the position on the undulating plateau at the foot of the hills. He determined to make a frontal attack with his Infantry whilst moving his Cavalry and Artillery to turn the enemy's left flank. He came into contact with the enemy at 7-40 A.M., but his guns, owing to getting into bad ground, only came into action at 8-30.

51st Field Battery	4 guns.
13th Bengal Lancers	151 Lances.
Somersetshire Light Infantry	186 Rifles.
20th Punjab Infantry	400 ,,

The engagement soon became very hot and the enemy made a determined attempt to turn Colonel Woon's left flank and he was forced to commence a retirement to prevent the enemy getting between his force and the Fort. At this period of the engagement I arrived on the scene having left Peshawar early, as I thought it necessary to proceed personally to Shabkadr and inform myself of the situation. I had started four companies of the 30th Punjab Infantry during the night as a re-inforcement, but there was a very heavy storm in the night with torrents of rain which delayed them.

On nearing Shabkadr I heard the guns and pushed on, reaching the scene of action a little before 9. I found that the enemy's line extended for about two miles, the left being on the lower spurs of the main hills. Our small force was outflanked and was too cramped up, being subject to cross-fire. The Artillery were close to the Infantry, and Cavalry with the guns. I brought the guns into action again to support the Infantry and sent the Cavalry well to the right flank, telling Major Atkinson to be prepared to charge. I also saw the necessity of extending the Infantry more to the left.

About this time there were many casualties, including Captain Blacker, the only officer with the guns, so I sent Captain Graham, Deputy Assistant Adjutant-General, to take charge of them.

When Major Atkinson, 13th Bengal Lancers, had got into position, I ordered him to charge from under the hills right along the enemy's front and to double up his line. He carried out the order in the most brilliant manner covered by Artillery fire, charging for $1\frac{1}{2}$ miles over nasty stony ground and completely cleared the enemy from the front. The effect of bolder tactics was such that the enemy at once retired into the hills. With the small force at my disposal suffering from the heat and hard work of the last 36 hours I did not think it desirable to follow the enemy into the hills. I formed up the force on the edge of the plateau in an extended line and waited for an hour. It was then reported by the Cavalry that the enemy had completely cleared off to the hills and I ordered the troops to withdraw to the Fort. The Cavalry and part of the Infantry advanced some distance to the front before retiring. Two companies of the 30th Punjab Infantry came up as a reserve under Captain Dobbie just after the Cavalry charge.

7. The steadiness of the Infantry under trying circumstances was very noticeable, more especially considering the small number of British officers present.

8. I attach casualty reports on Army Form B. 103. The enemy's numbers have been estimated at 5,000 to 6,000 men, and they appear to have lost heavily,[*] and some 30 or 40 headmen of note were killed, whose names are known. Our losses were, I regret, heavy for the small force engaged, amounting to 4 officers wounded, 9 non-commissioned officers and men killed and 61 wounded.

[*] Has been since confirmed from other sources.

From Maj-Gen E R Elles, commanding the Mohmand Field Force, dated Peshawar 13 October 1897

I have the honour to submit the following report on the operations of the Mohmand Field Force.

2. The object for which these operations were ordered was to punish the Mohmands for an unprovoked attack on British territory, to destroy the Hadda Mullah's power, disperse his hostile gathering, and clear any hostile forces from the Mohmand country.

3. The force, the composition of which is given in the margin, was at first ordered to concentrate at Shabkadar on the 11th September, in view to advancing on the 13th, but under orders from Army Head-Quarters the advance was postponed for two days, and I consequently ordered the concentration for the 13th, with the intention of advancing on the 15th September.

1st Brigade.
1st Battalion, Somersetshire Light Infantry.
Maxim Gun Detachment, 1st Battalion, Devonshire Regiment.
20th Punjab Infantry.
2nd Battalion 1st Gurkhas.
Sections A and B, No. 5 British Field Hospital.
Three Sections No. 31 Native " "
Section A, No. 45 " " " "

2nd Brigade.
2nd Battalion, Oxfordshire Light Infantry.
9th Gurkha Rifles.
37th Dogras.
Sections C and D, No. 5 British Field Hospital.
No. 44 Native Field Hospital.

Divisional Troops.
13th Bengal Lancers.
No. 3 Mountain Battery, Royal Artillery.
No. 5 (Bombay) Mountain Battery.
No. 5 Company, Bengal Sappers and Miners.
28th Bombay Pioneers.
1st Patiala Infantry.
Sections C and D, No. 63 Native Field Hospital.

4. On the 15th September the advance across the border commenced. Opposition was expected, as the Hadda Mullah was reported to have arrived in Gandab.

The 1st Brigade, with No. 3 Mountain Battery, Royal Artillery, the 28th Bombay Pioneers and No. 5 Company, Bengal Sappers and Miners, advanced prepared for action followed by part of the 2nd Brigade with baggage and supplies.

The leading brigade met with no resistance and succeeded in reaching Gandab that day notwithstanding the difficulty of the road, but the Pioneers and Sappers and the 2nd Brigade, with all camel transport, were halted some miles short at Dund and Melmiana. The road for the last seven miles into Gandab was in parts very difficult for mules, and quite impossible for plain camels. As all my supplies were on camels, I had to wait at Galanai until the road was made practicable. On the 16th the force halted, and every effort was made to improve the road.

On the 17th, the 13th Bengal Lancers were brought through to Galanai from Shabkadar, and Brigadier-General Westmacott, with the 20th Punjab Infantry, No. 3 Mountain Battery, Royal Artillery, and two Maxims, was pushed on to the foot of the Nahakki Pass, seven or eight miles further on. On this date a letter was received from Major-General Sir Bindon Blood, stating that the Hadda Mullah was at Bedmanai with a large gathering.

On the 18th, thanks to the excellent work done by the 28th Bombay Pioneers and No. 5 Company, Bengal Sappers and Miners, under the superintendence of Captain Kelly, R.E., Field Engineer, the road to Galanai had been made practicable for camels, and I was relieved of all anxiety about supplies.

On the 19th, the Pioneers and Sappers were pushed on at daybreak and worked all day at the Nahakki Pass, and, thanks to their unremitting labour, I concentrated the 1st Brigade, No. 3 Mountain Battery, Royal Artillery, two Maxims, the 13th Bengal Lancers, the 28th Pioneers, and No. 5 Company, Bengal Sappers and Miners, at Nahakki on the 20th.

5. Helio communication had been established with Major-General Blood from the 19th, and daily letters were also received from him. General Blood had ordered me to join him at Nawagai as soon as possible, in view to attacking the Mullah, for, owing to Brigadier-General Jeffreys' brigade having been detached to punish the Mamunds, Brigadier-General Wodehouse's brigade was not strong enough alone to force the very strong position of the Bedmanai Pass. A telegram from the Adjutant-General in India absolved me from acting under Major-General Blood's orders, but further events in the Mohmand country convinced me that it was desirable to act up to his wishes, and I consequently informed him that I would move on Nawagai as he desired, and place myself under his orders.

6. On the 21st September, I moved the 1st Brigade, with No. 3 Mountain Battery, Royal Artillery, four guns of No. 5 (Bombay) Mountain Battery, two Maxims, three squadrons of the 13th Bengal Lancers and half No. 5 Company, Bengal Sappers and Miners, to Lakarai in the Nawagai

Valley, about six miles from Brigadier-General Wodehouse's camp, and I met Major-General Blood. He informed me of the attack on the 3rd Brigade camp on the previous night, and that he proposed to place the 3rd Brigade, Malakand Field Force, at my disposal, in view to forcing the Bedmanai Pass and punishing the Mittai and Suran Valleys.

I must acknowledge my great obligations to Sir Bindon Blood for placing the combined force under my command.

On the 22nd, the whole force moved into a combined camp at Kuz Chinari, facing the Bedmanai Pass, where a few shots were fired into the 3rd Brigade camp at night.

On the morning of the 23rd, at 7-15 A. M., I moved to the attack of the pass with the force as per margin, leaving the baggage loaded and massed at Kuz Chinari, with one company per corps, three squadrons of the 13th Bengal Lancers and one squadron of the 11th Bengal Lancers, the whole under Lieutenant-Colonel G. W. Deane, 13th Bengal Lancers. My plan of attack was to advance up the long spur on the left (east) of the pass with the 1st Brigade, supported by one battery, whilst the 3rd Brigade moved up the centre of the pass and covered the right flank, supported by ten guns between the brigades with an escort of the Somersetshire Light Infantry. The Garhwalis moved to occupy the detached hill covering both entrances to the Pass, viz., that from Nawagai and that from the Mittai Valley. Their advance was covered by the cavalry, and they were fired on by a party of 200 of the enemy.

1st Brigade, Mohmand Field Force.
Brigadier-General R. Westmacott, C.B., D.S.O.

1st Somersetshire Light Infantry.
2nd Battalion, 1st Gurkha Rifles.
20th Punjab Infantry.
28th Bombay Pioneers.
† No. 5 Company, Bengal Sappers and Miners.

3rd Brigade, Malakand Field Force.
Lieutenant-Colonel B. C. Graves, 39th Garhwalis.

The Queen's.
22nd Punjab Infantry.
39th Garhwalis.
No. 3 Company, Bombay Sappers and Miners.

Royal Artillery.
Lieutenant-Colonel A. E. Duthy, Royal Artillery.

No. 1 Mountain Battery, Royal Artillery.
No. 3 Mountain Battery, Royal Artillery.
No. 5 (Bombay) Mountain Battery (4 guns).

At 8·15 the 20th Punjab Infantry advanced up the wooded spur south of Khalil Kor village, driving in the enemy's picquets concealed amongst trees and rocks. The 20th was accompanied by two Maxims under Lieutenant B. Logan, Devonshire Regiment, and followed by the 2-1st Gurkhas and 28th Bombay Pioneers. The enemy were never in very great strength, and information goes to show that there were not more than 700 or 800 men, with whom both the Hadda Mullah and the Sufi Mullah were present, but the former left at the beginning of the action. There was, however, considerable opposition to the advance of the 20th Punjab Infantry and 2-1st Gurkhas, but the enemy were driven from ridge to ridge by the 20th, the firing line being led most energetically by Captain P. G. Walker. The leading regiment was well supported by the Maxims, which kept up with the firing line. No. 3 Mountain Battery, Royal Artillery, had very bad ground to contend with, but gave great assistance to the infantry.

By 10-30 the 20th Punjab Infantry had, without a check, pushed on to a hill with a *sungar* on it (5,500 feet) and 2,700 feet above the Bedmanai Pass, which it completely commanded, and the enemy had retired in different directions, mainly to a higher peak with a strong *sungar*. In the mean time the batteries in the gorge had been shelling and clearing the heights on the right of the pass and its summit. The enemy had been seen coming up to the top of the pass in some strength, but did not stand before artillery fire. By 11 A.M. the 20th Punjab Infantry and 2-1st Gurkhas had seized the key of the position, a peak on the east of the pass (6,760 feet) nearly 4,000 feet above Kuz Chinari, the Maxims were firing on the retreating enemy, and the Pioneers and No. 3 Mountain Battery, Royal Artillery, were on the 5,500 feet peak.

The pass was now occupied by the Queen's and 22nd Punjab Infantry, and I ordered up all mule baggage; but, as the road was bad, decided not to bring up camels that day. Camp was placed in the village of Karmanzai, about one mile beyond the pass, and was not disturbed at night.

The position was a very strong one, and necessitated the crowning of the 6,960 peak, nearly 3,000 feet above the pass itself; had a determined defence been made by a strong body of the enemy, the losses of the attacking force must have been very great. That the resistance was so slight was due to the heavy losses incurred by the enemy in their attack on the 3rd Brigade camp on the night of the 20th, which caused a large part of the Mullah's gathering to disperse, and also to the fact that the enemy were uncertain up to the last movement whether we meant to attack the Bedmanai Pass or the Mittai Valley on the 23rd. The effect of the advance of the Mohmand Field Force appears to have been first felt on the 20th, when I occupied Nahakki in force. No doubt the fear of being cut off and the approach of a strong force influenced the Mullah's gathering to make a supreme effort, and led them to attack the 3rd Brigade camp on the night of the 20th.

On the 24th the 1st Brigade moved on to Sarfaraz Kili in the Bohai Dag, and the whole of the baggage and supplies were brought through from Kuz Chinari.

The 3rd Brigade, Malakand Field Force, had returned to Kuz Chinari on the 23rd, and aided by the 1st Patiala Regiment, were engaged in punishing the Mittai and Suran Valleys on the 24th and 25th.

On the 25th the force marched to Jarobi. The route led for six or seven miles up a stony valley running under the Ilazai mountain. The Jarobi glen, called the Shindara in its lower part, runs down from the back of Ilazai and is 400 to 500 yards at the mouth, gradually narrowing as you get into the hills, with steep rocky mountain ridges and cliffs on each side. The cavalry were fired at near the entrance by parties of the enemy. Seeing that it would be impossible to take the force up to Jarobi and camp there, I ordered camp to be formed near the entrance, as much in the open as possible, and decided to move up and punish the glen during the afternoon, returning before dark. The distance to the Mullah's mosque was about four miles, and the gorge took a sharp turn at 2½ miles.

The Somersetshire Light Infantry, 28th Pioneers and No. 5 (Bombay) Mountain Battery were left in position at the mouth of the gorge to cover the retirement; the 2-1st Gurkhas (four companies) crowned the rocky hill on the left (west), commanding the turn in the glen. Four companies of the 20th Punjab Infantry and No. 3 Mountain Battery, Royal Artillery, pushed up the gorge with half No. 5 Company, Bengal Sappers and Miners, to the turn. Here the main village of Tola Kili was seen filling up the gorge on a small hill three-quarters of a mile in front.

No. 3 Mountain Battery was here brought into action and four companies of Gurkhas brought up, whilst the 20th Punjab Infantry pushed on up the gorge to the Mullah's mosque about half a mile beyond the village. Four companies of Gurkhas were pushed on to Tola Kili in support, and the 28th Pioneers ordered up on firing taking place. The advance of the 20th was unopposed until they reached the Mullah's mosque, which Lieutenant-Colonel Woon describes as being little more than a cowshed, when fire was opened from both sides and from the front, and about a dozen *ghazis* charged from the mosque on to the leading party of the 20th. Six of these men were shot down and the rest bolted. This was about 3 P.M. No. 3 Mountain Battery was in action covering the 20th by fire on to the hills to the left. As the whole gorge from its winding character, narrowness and the precipitous hills on each side formed a regular trap, I sent an order by Lieutenant Elles, Aide-de-Camp, at 3 P.M., to retire without fail at 3-30, as I was determined to get all troops clear of the gorge by dark. There is no Jarobi village, but the village of Tola Kili, the chief one, and three fort villages in the gorge had been destroyed, and there was nothing to gain by remaining. Orders had been given before the expedition that all mosques were to be respected.

Lieutenant-Colonel Woon carried out the retirement very steadily, and suffered no more casualties, and was supported by the Gurkhas; the Pioneers in turn covered them when they had passed through and had a few casualties, but any following up ceased two and-a-quarter miles before the entrance was reached, being checked by the 2-1st Gurkhas on the hill to the left.

The whole retirement was most steadily carried out by the troops under Brigadier-General Westmacott's orders in one of the nastiest gorges I ever saw. The steepness of the hills may be judged by the fact that the top of the Ilazai Mount is only two miles distant horizontally from the Mullah's mosque, the drop being 4,400 feet in that distance. The enemy were chiefly Musa Khel from Mittai, for the Jarobi glen is only separated by a low pass from the Mittai Valley. Ten of the enemy are known to have been killed; it is not known whether they had further loss.

On the 26th I moved in two columns down the two valleys forming the head of the Bohai Dag, and thoroughly punished the Baizai; the columns joined hands and camped at Khawarina.

On the 27th Brigadier-General Westmacott, with the force in the margin, punished the Kuda Khel, whose fortified villages are situated close to the Durand boundary, and a small column visited Torakhwa, a reserve remaining in a central position. Brigadier-General Westmacott's column found the Kuda Khel forts occupied by the enemy, as well as the heights above the village. The forts were cleared by the fire of No. 5 (Bombay) Mountain Battery, Captain Knapp's horse being shot whilst coming into action.

4 guns, No. 5 (Bombay) Mountain Battery.
Oxfordshire Light Infantry.
1 Squadron, 13th Bengal Lancers.
2-1st Gurkhas.
4 Companies, 28th Bombay Pioneers.
½ No. 5 Company, Bengal Sappers and Miners.

The 2-1st Gurkhas were sent to clear the heights, from which a galling fire was kept up, and the heights were shelled by the battery in various directions. The Gurkhas crowned the ridge forming the Durand line and looked down into the Dakha plain. The work of destroying the forts and towers was completed, and the force was carefully withdrawn by Brigadier-General Westmacott, covered by the Oxfordshire Light Infantry.

On the 29th the force returned to Nahakki, two battalions and a battery being detached to the Sam Ghakke Pass in consequence of a cavalry reconnaissance being opposed.

On the 30th September I moved with the 2nd Brigade under Brigadier-General C. R. Macgregor to Yakhdand, Pipal and Danish Kul, the districts inhabited by the Dawezai, Utmanzai and Isa Khel, returning to Nahakki on the 3rd October, after detaching a small column* under Lieutenant-Colonel H. O. Woodhouse to move into the Peshawar Valley by the Alikandi route, through the Burhan Khel country, the district of Pindiali.

* 9th Gurkha Rifles.
2 guns, No. 5 Mountain Battery.
‡ Company, Bengal Sappers and Miners.

The evacuation of the country was now carried out without incident, and the last of my troops reached Peshawar on the 7th October.

7. The expedition proved productive of little fighting, but the splendid force under my command would, I believe, have made little of any possible opposition. I cannot speak too highly of the 20th Punjab Infantry and 2-1st Gurkhas, on whom the brunt of the work fell. I would wish for no better regiments for hill fighting under their respective commanders.

The work done during the expedition by the 28th Bombay Pioneers and No. 5 Company, Bengal Sappers and Miners, is worthy of the highest commendation. The 28th Pioneers also did excellent work in reserve to the 1st Brigade in the attack at Bedmanai, and at Jarobi covered the retirement, showing high soldierly qualities in both instances.

The main difficulties to contend with were the passes, over which roads had always to be made, and anxiety regarding water, as in the western Mohmand country; the supply is almost entirely from tanks, the dams of which had been cut by the Mohmands, and they often only contained a little dirty water.

8. The Imperial Service Troops under my command proved their fitnes to fight in the first line, and were utilised exactly the same as the regular Native troops. The cavalry escorts of the Patiala and Jodhpore Cavalry did good reconnaissance work on more than one occasion and came under fire. The 1st Patiala Regiment was employed under Lieutenant-Colonel Graves in the operations in the Mittai and Suran Valleys, and covered the retirement of the brigade under fire; their good service was brought to my notice by the General Officer Commanding the 3rd Brigade. The Nabha Regiment, owing to its having been added to my force late in September, had to be kept on the Line of Communications.

9. I trust the objects of the expedition were fully carried out, thanks to the fine body of troops I had the honour of commanding and to the hearty co-operation of my staff and of all ranks in the force, in attaining the objects in view.

From Maj-Gen Sir B Blood, commanding the Malakand Field Force, dated 27 October 1897

3. The period from the 27th August to the 6th September was taken up with routine work, and latterly with movements preparatory to the expedition into the Mohmand country, an account of which I will now proceed to give.

4. On the 6th September, in pursuance of orders which I had received, to march two brigades vid the Panjkora Bridge and Nawagai to Shabkadr in the Peshawar Valley, the disposition of the Malakand Field Force was generally as follows:—

    3rd Brigade, equipped with camels and a few mules, at the Panjkora Bridge and Uch.
    2nd Brigade, equipped entirely with mules, at Chakdara.
    1st Brigade, equipped with camels, carts, and a few mules, at Khar, the Malakand and the Line.
    Divisional head-quarters, with camp offices, at Chakdara.

7. On the 13th the 3rd Brigade halted, the 2nd Brigade moved to a point close to and south-west of Khar, and I personally examined the Rambat Pass, finding that the country to the south of it was very deficient in water and forage. This being so, I directed Brigadier-General P. D. Jeffreys, C.B., Commanding the 2nd Brigade, to encamp on the 14th, north of Markhanai, to improve the Rambat Pass, to cross it into Butkor on the 15th with two battalions, a company of sappers and miners, a squadron, and five days' supplies, and to send the remainder of his brigade on the same day, under Colonel T. H. Goldney, 35th Sikhs, to join me at Nawagai, to which place I intended to march on the 14th with the 3rd Brigade. I further directed Brigadier-General Jeffreys to move his special force through Butkor as quickly as possible to Danish Kol, where I promised to join him, or send him further instructions. Both brigades carried with them rations for men up to the 23rd September; and I had arranged to drop my communications with the Malakand and draw my next supplies from Shabkadr, where the Mohmand Field Force, under Major-General E. R. Elles, C.B., was waiting to march on the 15th to join me in the Mohmand country south of Nawagai.

8. The movements detailed in the foregoing paragraph were duly carried out by the 2nd and 3rd Brigades, so far as the 14th was concerned; the 3rd Brigade, with divisional head-quarters, being encamped on the evening of that day about a mile south of the village of Nawagai while Brigadier-General Jeffreys, with three battalions, a mountain battery and a squadron, was on the right bank of the Chaharmung stream, north of Markhanai, having detached the Buffs and the 4th Company, Bengal Sappers and Miners, to the crest of the Rambat Pass, to prepare it for the passage of his special force next morning.

9. At about 8 P.M. on the 14th, while it was still quite dark before the moon rose, Brigadier-General Jeffreys' camp was suddenly assailed by a heavy musketry fire from the ravines close by. The attack was continued with little intermission for six hours, being directed at first chiefly against the faces of the camp held by the Guides under Major F. Campbell and the 35th Sikhs under Colonel T. H. Goldney, and afterwards against that defended by the 38th Dogras under Lieutenant-Colonel F. G. Vivian. The enemy showed no inclination to come to close quarters, and ultimately drew off about 2 A.M., doubtless having in view the desirableness of getting beyond reach of cavalry before day-light. This, however, they did not succeed in doing, as they were overtaken in the Mamund Valley about 8 A.M. on the 15th by Captain E. H. Cole and his squadron of the 11th Bengal Lancers, who killed 21 of them and dispersed the rest.

12. Early in the morning of the 15th I received a brief report by heliograph of the attack on Brigadier-General Jeffreys' camp the night before, and at once sent him orders to concentrate his force and proceed to the punishment of the tribes concerned. Later in the day I received a fuller report of what had happened, together with information from Brigadier-General Jeffreys that he had received my orders and was concentrating his brigade at Inayat Kili in the Mamund Valley, with a view to carrying them out. He had ascertained that the attack on his camp had been made by a small gathering of Mamunds, who had been reinforced by some of Umra Khan's followers from Zagai, a village in the Mamund Valley, and by a few men from the neighbouring tribes.

13. Naturally the night attack of the 14th-15th, with the consequent turning aside into the Mamund Valley of Brigadier-General Jeffreys' brigade, made a considerable change in the aspect of affairs in South Bajaur and the Mohmand country; and the strategical

situation which had now developed itself was interesting. I found myself at Nawagai with a brigade of all arms ‡ in a strongly entrenched position, faced by the Hadda Mullah's gathering in the Bedmanai Pass,—a not very difficult defile some six or eight miles in length, the mouth of which is about seven miles south-west in a straight line from the site of my camp,—itself about one mile south of Nawagai village. The intervening ground is a plain of which the western half is cut up by ravines, while the rest is favourable for cavalry. East of and behind me lay the road to the camp of the 2nd Brigade at Inayat Kili running for about six miles through a net work of deep ravines, and then for the remaining six or seven over a plain. I was not strong enough to attack the Mullah's gathering in their position with a sufficient amount of odds in my favour, while I did not think it advisable to rejoin Brigadier-General Jeffreys,—first, because he was strong § enough already for immediate requirements; secondly, because it would have been most unwise to have retired through the ravines above mentioned in face of the Mullah's gathering; thirdly, because I expected that one of Major-General Elles' brigades would join me in the Nawagai Valley on the 17th or the 18th at latest, and, finally, because my support was necessary to keep the Khan of Nawagai with us,—as, if I had deserted him, he would have been compelled by the Mullah's men to throw in his lot with them, which would have been a serious matter on account of his influence in Bajaur. Accordingly, I determined to stay where I was until Major-General Elles' advance should make it possible to dispose effectually of the Mullah's gathering, and to clear out the Bedmanai Pass and the Mittai and neighbouring valleys with completeness.

‡ 3 Battalions.
1 Mountain Battery.
3 Squadrons.
1 Company of Sappers.

§ 4 Battalions.
1 Mountain Battery.
1 Squadron
1 Company of Sappers.

14. At about 6-30 on the morning of the 16th September, Brigadier-General Jeffreys moved out from his camp at Inayat Kili, with the greater portion of his force in three columns, to deal with the villages of the Mamunds.

15. The right column under Lieutenant-Colonel Vivian, 38th Dogras, consisting of six companies and a detachment of sappers, was directed along the eastern side of the Mamund Valley on the villages of Shinkot, Chingai 1st, Damadolah and Badam Kili; the central column under Colonel Goldney 35th Sikhs, consisting of six companies, four guns, one squadron and a detachment of sappers, was directed against the villages of Munar, Hazarnao and Badalai; while the left column, under Major Campbell of the Guides, was composed of five companies and a detachment of sappers, and was directed along the right bank of the Watelai ravine parallel to the centre column.

16. The right column, under Lieutenant-Colonel Vivian, having advanced by the route ordered as far as Damadolah, found that place too strong and too strongly held to be reasonably attempted without artillery, and returned thence to camp, arriving at 4 P.M., with two men slightly wounded.

17. The centre column, under Colonel Goldney, 35th Sikhs, advanced some six miles up the valley without seeing anything of the enemy, who were first reported at Badam Kili, to which place a detachment under Lieutenant-Colonel A. E. Ommanney was sent to dislodge them. The remainder of the column pushed on, and at about 10-30 A.M. two companies of the 35th Sikhs, which led the advance, occupied a knoll near Shahi Tangi, upwards of nine miles from camp. In this movement, however, the two companies advanced too far from their supports, and as the enemy promptly attacked them in force, they were compelled to retire about a mile, with the loss of one British officer and one sepoy killed and sixteen non-commissioned officers and sepoys wounded. Soon afterwards the Buffs, under Lieutenant-Colonel Ommanney, coming up, the knoll was again occupied without much opposition, being the furthest point reached by the column.

18. During this advance the guns came into action,—first on the spur north of Badalai, and afterwards on that north of Chingai 2nd. They were covered in the first position by two companies of the 35th Sikhs, posted to their right; and on their moving towards the second position, one-and-a-half of these companies, under Captain W. I. Ryder, were ordered to cover the movement by climbing to the top of the high ridge to their right, and then advancing along it towards the north. Owing to subsequent orders not reaching him, Captain Ryder went further than was intended.

19. In the earlier part of the day the left column had remained far behind, being fully occupied for some considerable time in dealing with the numerous villages met with along the road shortly after leaving camp. Towards 9 A.M. it was called up by Brigadier-General

Jeffreys, as the enemy began to appear in force on his left near Agrah, and it joined the centre column about noon.

20. At about 2-30 P.M., as soon as the fortified villages of Chingai 2nd and Shahi Tangi had been dismantled, Brigadier-General Jeffreys ordered the troops to return to camp. Captain Ryder was still on the high ridge above Chingai 2nd, along which he attempted to retire in a direction which diverged from the line of retreat of the main body of the force. Soon after the retirement commenced, a message was received from him stating that he was hard pressed and could not rejoin the main body, whereupon Brigadier-General Jeffreys ordered Major Campbell, with six companies of the Guides Infantry, to go to his assistance, which they did about 4 P.M., a short time being taken up in assembling the companies, which were in extended order.

21. The fact of this movement having to be undertaken so late in the afternoon was a most unfortunate occurrence, since Brigadier-General Jeffreys had to wait until the safety of the Guides and Captain Ryder's detachment was assured, and the consequent delay at that time of day made it impossible for him to reach camp before dark.

22. The Guides, under Major Campbell, most successfully and gallantly relieved and brought off Captain Ryder's detachment, which had suffered heavy losses. The combined detachments did not, however, succeed in rejoining Brigadier-General Jeffreys, being prevented by nightfall and a thunderstorm which came on about the same time. Ultimately they made their way to camp without further loss, arriving about 9 P.M.

23. Meanwhile, as soon as the safety of Captain Ryder's detachment was certain, Brigadier-General Jeffreys continued his retirement towards camp. So long as daylight lasted the enemy kept at a respectful distance from him, but as it got dark they got bold, and the ground being broken and difficult, they were able to bring a hot fire to bear on the troops, while a heavy thunderstorm, which came on at dusk, greatly increased the difficulties of the situation. Ultimately, however, by about 8-30 P.M., all the troops had arrived in camp, except Brigadier-General Jeffreys, four guns of No. 8 (Bengal) Mountain Battery, a small party of sappers and a few men of the Buffs and 35th Sikhs, who got separated from the rest in the darkness.

24. About dusk Brigadier-General Jeffreys, then about three miles and half from camp, decided to occupy a neighbouring village, called Bilot, for the night, chiefly with a view to sheltering the battery mules with him from the enemy's sharp-shooters; and while he was engaged in arranging this, the thunderstorm before referred to came on, causing sudden and complete darkness. In the consequent confusion the troops got separated, and only the detachments above detailed remained with Brigadier-General Jeffreys. He proceeded to occupy and entrench a re-entering angle of the village, part of which was burning, while the rest was soon occupied by the enemy, who fired on the General and his detachment from behind walls at a few yards' range, inflicting serious losses in men and animals. This state of things continued, in spite of several gallant attempts to clear the village, which were led by Lieutenants T. C. Watson and J. M. C. Colvin, R.E., until the arrival about midnight of Major J. F. Worlledge, 35th Sikhs with two companies of the Guides and two of his own regiment. After this the enemy were easily driven off and gave no further annoyance during the night.

25. Major Worlledge had left camp about 5-30 P.M. in obedience to an order from Brigadier-General Jeffreys, and on joining the General about dark had been sent to find and support the Guides under Major Campbell. Failing to find the Guides in the dark, Major Worlledge tried to retrace his steps to the General, but only succeeded in finding him after the moon rose about midnight, although he had been close to him for some time previously without knowing it. Brigadier-General Jeffreys ultimately reached camp at 8 A.M. on the 17th, some of the troops there having been sent out to his assistance, and returning with him.

30. On the 17th September, the troops of the 2nd Brigade rested, and timely arrangements were made for bringing up supplies of ammunition and food and for sending the wounded down the line. On the 18th, Brigadier-General Jeffreys resumed the punishment of the Mamunds, attacking and destroying the strongly fortified village of Damadolah, with a loss of two sepoys killed and six wounded. On this occasion the enemy lost many killed and wounded, and some 300 loads of their grain and other supplies were carried off for the use of our troops. On the 19th, Brigadier-General Jeffreys seized and destroyed the group of villages called Hazarnao without opposition. On the 20th, he captured and burned Umra Khan's strong village of Zagai, some seven miles from camp, with the loss of two British

officers, nine other British ranks, and two sepoys wounded. On the 22nd, he took and destroyed the fortified village of Dag, with the loss of one sepoy killed and two wounded. On this day I arrived at Inayat Kila from Nawagai.

31. While the events above described were occurring in South Bajaur, nothing of special interest happened at Nawagai until the 19th September. The Hadda Mullah's gathering was reported to be increasing, and some men belonging to it fired ineffectually at our evening patrols on the 15th and 16th from the ravines near the mouth of the Bedmanai Pass. The country was regularly reconnoitered in various directions, and the cavalry under Major S. B. Beatson, 11th Bengal Lancers, accompanied by Captain Stanton, D.S.O., R.A., Deputy Assistant Quartermaster-General for Intelligence, penetrated on the 15th as far as Ato Khel, five or six miles north of the Nahakki (or Nakki) Pass, over which the Mohmand Field Force under Major-General Elles, C.B., was daily expected to appear. On the afternoon of the 17th, some 1.500 men of the Hadda Mullah's gathering appeared close under the hills at the mouth of the Bedmanai Pass, about seven miles from camp, and I turned out part of the brigade to meet them if they should advance. Nothing happened, however, as the enemy remained where they were, too far off for me to reach them without being benighted in the ravines afterwards. On the 18th, Captain Norie, Superintendent of Signalling with my force, opened heliographic communication with a detachment of Major-General Elles' force, which had arrived at the top of the Nahakki Pass.

32. At 5-30 P.M., on the 19th, about 2,000 of the Hadda Mullah's men appeared at the mouth of the Bedmanai Pass, and seemed to be engaged for an hour or so in some kind of dance. Ultimately, about dusk, they commenced to move towards our camp, and soon afterwards I was informed by the son of the Khan of Nawagai that they meant to attack us before morning. Accordingly at about 11 P.M. some 150 men, chiefly swordsmen, made a rush at the portion of the camp defended by the 1st Battalion, Queen's West Surrey Regiment, under Lieutenant-Colonel J. S. Collins, who easily repulsed them, when, after trying other parts of the camp in a half-hearted way for a few minutes, they drew off and commenced skirmishing with the Khan of Nawagai's men, who were on outpost duty about a mile off, finally disappearing about 12·30 A.M. Our losses in the affair were, one British soldier killed and one severely wounded, besides several horses and transport animals killed or wounded. We were afterwards informed that about 1,200 men advanced against our camp on this occasion, but that the warm manner in which their first line was received stopped the rest.

33. On the 20th, I received a message from Major-General Elles, C.B., saying that he would meet me at 10 A.M. next day at Lakarai with his 1st Brigade under Brigadier-General Westmacott, C.B., D.S.O, to concert arrangements for further joint action. To this I replied that I would place my 3rd Brigade at his disposal with a view to his attacking the Hadda Mullah's gathering as soon as possible, and that I intended to join my 2nd Brigade at Inayat Kili in the Mamund Valley on the 22nd. In the afternoon I made a reconnaissance in force towards Kuz Chinarai, at the mouth of the Bedmanai Pass, whereupon the enemy appeared at the adjoining mouth of the Mittai Valley in considerable force; but as they remained at such a distance that I could not deal with them without being benighted during my return to camp, I did not attack them. Ultimately when I retired they advanced at a very respectful distance, and when last seen before dark they were about two miles from camp. On this occasion also I was warned by the Khan of Nawagai that the enemy meant to attack before morning, and I was informed, besides, that some fresh contingents had joined them.

34. Accordingly, at about 9 P.M., we were vigorously attacked by a force probably not less than 3,000 strong, with about 100 Martini-Henry and several Lee-Metford rifles, besides many other fire-arms.

The attack was well carried out by rushes of swordsmen covered by a smart fire of small arms; and the firing, with rushes at intervals, sometimes against three sides of the camp at the same time, went on till about 2 A.M., when the enemy drew off. They were nowhere to be seen at daylight when I sent the cavalry out in pursuit.

36. On the 21st, I met Major-General Elles at Lakarai and made the arrangements with him which I have already detailed. Next morning, the 22nd September, my 3rd Brigade, the command of which had devolved on Lieutenant-Colonel B. C. Graves, 39th Garhwalis, after Brigadier-General Wodehouse was wounded, marched to Kuz Chinarai to join Major-General Elles, while I proceeded to Inayat Kili, in the Mamund Valley, and joined my 2nd Brigade under Brigadier-General Jeffreys.

37. Next day, the 23rd September, my 3rd Brigade took part in the seizure of the Bedmanai Pass, one British soldier being wounded in the operations. On the 24th the brigade attacked and destroyed the fortified villages in the Mittai Valley, two men of the 1st Battalion of the Queen's being wounded in the skirmishing which took place; and on the 25th a similar operation was carried out in the Suran Valley, without loss, by a column detached from the brigade, under Lieutenant-Colonel Collins, of the Queen's. On the 26th, the brigade marched to Lakarai, and thence viâ the Gandab Valley to Peshawar, where it was broken up and its troops merged into the Tirah Expeditionary Force.

38. On my arrival at Inayat Kili, on the 22nd, I found that about 170 sick and wounded were with the 2nd Brigade, and that arrangements were in progress to send all the serious cases down the line, starting on the 26th. On the 22nd, Brigadier-General Jeffreys destroyed the fortified village of Dag, as already related in paragraph 30, ante.

39. On the 23rd September, Brigadier-General Jeffreys proceeded to deal with the village of Tangai, near Dag. The opposition on this day was slight, and the casualties were one officer, Major R. S. H. Moody, of the Buffs, and one sepoy wounded.

45. On the 30th September, Brigadier-General Jeffreys attacked and took the villages of Agrah and Gat, about seven miles north of Inayat Kili. These villages are strongly placed for mutual support on the southern face of a spur which runs eastwards from the high range of mountains whose crest forms the Afghan boundary. There are minor spurs on the east and west of the two villages, that to the eastward being rather far off; a third spur, crowned by huge boulders, runs up between the others to a small peak below Gat, and adds greatly to the strength of the position. On the 30th September, the enemy held Agrah and Gat in considerable force, and departing from their usual tactics vigorously opposed the advance of our troops; but after some fighting at close quarters the villages were carried by the 1st Battalion, Royal West Kent Regiment, under Major C. W. H. Evans,—the Guides Infantry, under Major F. Campbell, seizing and occupying the spurs on the left, and the 31st Punjab Infantry the rugged central spurs; while No. 7 Mountain Battery, Royal Artillery, under Major M. F. Fegan, covered the advance with their fire; and the Guides Cavalry, under Lieutenant-Colonel R. B. Adams, held in check in the most bold and brilliant manner a considerable force of the enemy who advanced from the westward towards our left flank. Lieutenant-Colonel J. L. O'Bryen, 31st Punjab Infantry, was mortally wounded while gallantly leading his battalion, and our other casualties were—killed, Second-Lieutenant W. C. Browne-Clayton, 1st Battalion, Royal West Kent Regiment, three British and seven native soldiers; wounded, six British officers, twenty-one British and twenty-two native soldiers,— total 61 casualties. The enemy suffered severely in this action, and did not display their usual enterprise in following our infantry to the level ground, on their withdrawal and return to camp.

46. The next operation of interest was on the 3rd October, when Brigadier-General Jeffreys, whose force had now been increased by half a battalion and four mountain guns, seized and destroyed the village of Badelai without opposition During his return to camp, however, the enemy showed in great force at the upper end of the valley, and advanced among the ravines to within 1,000 to 1,200 yards of the troops covering his withdrawal. They were kept in check without any difficulty, but as they had many Martini-Henry rifles and expended a great quantity of ammunition, they caused a loss on our side of two killed and sixteen wounded, in spite of the long ranges at which they fired.

47. On the 4th October, the arrival of four guns of the 10th Field Battery, under Major Anderson, R.A., and of the 2nd Battalion, Highland Light Infantry, under Lieutenant-Colonel R. D. B. Rutherford, brought the force at my disposal at Inayat Kili up to the strength detailed in paragraph 43. Major H. A. Deane, C.S.I., the Political Agent of Dir, Swat and Chitral, arrived the same day, and as he recommended a cessation of hostilities for a few days to enable the Khan of Nawagai, and his brothers, the Khans of Khar and Jhar, to recommence negotiations with the tribes, who were reported to be again anxious to make terms, I discontinued operations with the exception of the daily foraging.

48. Ultimately the Mamund *jirga* came in and made submission on the 11th October, and on the following day the force marched to Jhar, advancing on the 13th to a position about three miles up the Salarzai Valley. Here the force halted until the 19th October while negotiations were carried on by the political officers with the Salarzai tribe, who were required to surrender some rifles and other fire-arms as a punishment for joining in the attack on Chakdara Fort in July and August last. These negotiations having been successfully concluded, the force moved back to Jhar on the 20th October, where the Shamozai section of the Utman Khels, who had also taken part in the attack on Chakdara Fort, were in like manner called upon to surrender arms; and after they had done so the force started on the 22nd for the Swat Valley, where they were all assembled on the 27th October.

STAFF

Brigadier-General
Wodehouse, Josceline Heneage   sev w 20/21 Sep 1897 Bedmanai Pass, gs

51st FIELD BATTERY, ROYAL ARTILLERY

Captain
Blacker, Stewart Ward William   sev w 9 Aug 1897 Shabkadr, bullet perforating thigh

Sergeant-Major
10529 Wallman   sl w 9 Aug 1897 Shabkadr, bullet graze hand

Sergeant
15882 Chase   sl w 9 Aug 1897 Shabkadr, bullet graze hand

No 1 MOUNTAIN BATTERY, ROYAL ARTILLERY

Gunner
6971 Francy, James   sl w 20/21 Sep 1897 Bedmanai Pass, gs head

Drivers
   2 Jaggana   sl w 20/21 Sep 1897 Bedmanai Pass, contusion shoulder
 131 Sham Singh   sl w 20/21 Sep 1897 Bedmanai Pass, gs leg

No 8 (BENGAL) MOUNTAIN BATTERY

Lieutenants
Crawford, Alfred Temple   k 16 Sep 1897 Dabar, gs
Wynter, Francis Arthur   sev w 16 Sep 1897 Dabar, gs

Jemadar
Ishar Singh   sev w 16 Sep 1897 Dabar, gs

Havildar
 66 Sirandad   k 14 Sep 1897 Markhanai, gs skull

Lance-Naiks
 22 Gul Ahmed   sev w 16 Sep 1897 Dabar, gs
 10 Rahman Khan   sl w 16 Sep 1897 Dabar, gs

Trumpeter
253 Jawan   sl w 16 Sep 1897 Dabar, gs finger

Gunners
401 Bahadur   k 16 Sep 1897 Dabar, gs
 92 Bhagga   dang w 16 Sep 1897 Dabar, gs left knee
340 Fateh Ali   sev w 16 Sep 1897 Dabar, gs buttock
353 Hayat Muhammad   sl w 16 Sep 1897 Dabar, gs chest
  9 Karim Chand   sev w 16 Sep 1897 Dabar, gs chest & back
260 Kashim Khan   sev w 14 Sep 1897 Markhanai, gs loins
314 Magh Singh   sev w 16 Sep 1897 Dabar, gs knee; awarded IOM
            3rd Class
322 Makhan   k 16 Sep 1897 Dabar, gs
261 Mehtab Shah   sl w 16 Sep 1897 Dabar, gs right shoulder
 17 Natha Singh   sev w 16 Sep 1897 Dabar, gs arm & chest

Drivers
436 Bonoo   sl w 16 Sep 1897 Dabar, gs upper lip
120 Gamah (Lce-Naik)   k 16 Sep 1897 Dabar, gs
278 Ghulam Hussain   sev w 16 Sep 1897 Dabar, gs hand
399 Ibrahim   dang w 16 Sep 1897 Dabar, gs left arm
396 Imam Din   sev w 16 Sep 1897, gs abdomen
122 Kamina   dang w 16 Sep 1897 Dabar, gs right shoulder
224 Karam Elahi   k 16 Sep 1897 Dabar, gs
393 Karam Khan   sl w 16 Sep 1897 Dabar, stone on eyebrow
149 Lal Din   sl w 16 Sep 1897 Dabar, gs elbow
152 Mal Singh (Naik)   sev w 16 Sep 1897 Dabar, gs knee, leg
            & forearm
283 Mangi Khan   sev w 16 Sep 1897 Dabar, gs foot
228 Maula Buksh   k 16 Sep 1897 Dabar, gs
327 Mota Singh   k 16 Sep 1897 Dabar, gs
460 Muhammad   dang w 16 Sep 1897 Dabar, gs chest
306 Sultan Mahomed   sev w 16 Sep 1897 Dabar, gs finger

ROYAL ENGINEERS

Lieutenants
Hingston, George Bennett   sl w 12 Oct 1897 nr Charmina, gs hip
Watson, Thomas Colclough   sev w 16 Sep 1897 Dabar, gs left hand;
            awarded VC

1st Btn ROYAL WEST SURREY REGIMENT

Corporal
1816 Fletcher, John   sl w 20/21 Sep 1897 Bedmanai Pass,
            gs shoulder

Lance-Corporal
3886 Ware, Frederick   sl w 20/21 Sep 1897 Bedmanai Pass, gs arm

Privates
 408 Bradford, Maurice   sev w 19 Sep 1897 Bedmanai Pass, gs upper arm
3142 Hughes, John   dang w 24 Sep 1897 Mittai Valley, gs
4781 O'Brien, Patrick   k 19 Sep 1897 Bedmanai Pass, gs neck
3146 Stevens, William   k 20/21 Sep 1897 Bedmanai Pass, gs head
2588 Watson, William   sev w 24 Sep 1897 Mittai Valley, gs
2164 Wentham, James   sl w 20 Sep 1897 Bedmanai Pass, gs back
3374 Willett, Albert   k 19 Sep 1897 Bedmanai Pass, stab in lung & abdomen

1st Btn EAST KENT REGIMENT

Major
Moody, Richard Stanley Hawks   sl w 23 Sep 1897 Bedmanai Pass, gs

Captain
Hulke, Lewis Iggulden Backhouse   sl w 20 Sep 1897 Zagai, gs

Lieutenant
Power, Rowland Edward   sl w 20 Sep 1897 Zagai, gs

Second-Lieutenant
Keene, Geoffrey Norman Stewart   dang w 20 Sep 1897 Zagai, gs

Corporal
3152 Strutt, John   sl w 20 Sep 1897 Bedmanai Pass, gs

Lance-Corporals
3980 Boorman, C.   sl w 16 Sep 1897 Dabar, gs back
4584 Clarke, Charles   sev w 20 Sep 1897 Bedmanai Pass, gs, dow
3165 Judges, F.   sl w 16 Sep 1897 Dabar, gs right forearm
2872 North, Arthur   sev w 20 Sep 1897 Bedmanai Pass, gs
4288 Smith, James   sev w 16 Sep 1897 Dabar, gs left thigh; awarded VC

Privates
4219 Austin, A.   k 16 Sep 1897 Dabar, gs brain
3174 Belcher, Charles   sev w 20/21 Sep 1897 Bedmanai Pass, gs
4572 Clements, Robert   sev w 20 Sep 1897 Bedmanai Pass, gs
3824 Clow, George   sev w 20/21 Sep 1897 Bedmanai Pass, gs
4734 Davis, Edward   sev w 20 Sep 1897 Bedmanai Pass, gs
4779 Dodd, W.   k 16 Sep 1897 Dabar, gs abdomen
4549 Fox, Robert   sev w 20 Sep 1897 Bedmanai Pass, gs
4840 Heffernan, M.   sev w 16 Sep 1897 Dabar, gs left arm
3186 Lever, James   sev w 16 Sep 1897 Dabar, gs right thigh; awarded DCM
3088 May, H.   dang w 16 Sep 1897 Dabar, gs right forearm

3182 Nelthorpe, H.   sl w 16 Sep 1897 Dabar, gs left thumb; awarded DCM
4825 Ovenden, Arthur   sev w 20 Sep 1897 Bedmanai Pass, gs
3997 Poile, C.   sl w 16 Sep 1897 Dabar, gs forehead; awarded DCM
4384 Weller, W.   sl w 16 Sep 1897 Dabar, gs back of head
3387 Williams, William   sl w 20 Sep 1897 Bedmanai Pass, gs

1st Btn SOMERSET LIGHT INFANTRY

Major
Lumb, Anthony   sev w 9 Aug 1897 Shabkadr, gs neck & shoulder

Second-Lieutenant
Drummond, Eric   sev w 9 Aug 1897 Shabkadr, gs upper arm

Sergeants
1202 Miles, Jesse   sev w 9 Aug 1897 Shabkadr, gs back
2173 White, William   k 9 Aug 1897 Shabkadr, gs chest

Privates
3199 Atkins, Thomas   k 9 Aug 1897 Shabkadr, body cut up
3520 Barker, William   sev w 9 Aug 1897 Shabkadr, gs head
3539 Eyles, Henry   sev w 9 Aug 1897 Shabkadr, gs head
3734 Fisher, Ernest   k 9 Aug 1897 Shabkadr, body cut up
1776 Gatehouse, John   sev w 9 Aug 1897 Shabkadr, gs abdomen
3369 Gleed, Charles   sev w 9 Aug 1897 Shabkadr, gs head
3205 Langford, George   sev w 9 Aug 1897 Shabkadr, gs shoulder
2872 Miles, Albert   sl w 9 Aug 1897 Shabkadr, gs shoulder
3327 Troake, Thomas   sev w 9 Aug 1897 Shabkadr, gs head
1310 Walker, Thomas   sev w 9 Aug 1897 Shabkadr, contusion chest

LANCASHIRE FUSILIERS

Lieutenant
Greaves, Robert Thurston   k 17 Aug 1897 Landakai, gs & sword cuts (with the force as Correspondent of the 'Times of India')

1st Btn ROYAL WEST KENT REGIMENT

Major
Western, William George Balfour   sl w 30 Sep 1897 nr Inayat Kili, gs

Captains
Lowe, Noel Herbert Strode   sl w 30 Sep 1897 nr Inayat Kili, gs
Style, Rodney Charles   sl w 30 Sep 1897 nr Inayat Kili, gs

Lieutenant
Isacke, Hubert   sev w 30 Sep 1897 nr Inayat Kili, gs

Second Lieutenants
Browne-Clayton, William Clayton   k 30 Sep 1897 nr Inayat Kili, gs
Jackson, Freeman Astley   sl w 30 Sep 1897 nr Inayat Kili, gs

Sergeants
1804 Ashby, George   sl w 3 Oct 1897 Badalai, gs
2350 Regan, John   sl w 3 Oct 1897 Badalai, gs
1341 Warner, J.   sev w 30 Sep 1897 nr Inayat Kili, gs

Drummer
3357 Berry, F.   k 30 Sep 1897 nr Inayat Kili, gs

Privates
2625 Bright, R.   sev w 30 Sep 1897 nr Inayat Kili, gs
4179 Brooker, H.   sl w 30 Sep 1897 nr Inayat Kili, gs
3350 Buckland, H.   dang w 30 Sep 1897 nr Inayat Kili, gs
3712 Clipham, Percy   dang w 3 Oct 1897 Badalai, gs
3114 Crampton, C.   sl w 30 Sep 1897 nr Inayat Kili, gs
3354 Edwards, W.   dang w 30 Sep 1897 nr Inayat Kili, gs
3346 Evans, F.   sl w 30 Sep 1897 nr Inayat Kili, gs
4004 Eversett, G.   sl w 30 Sep 1897 nr Inayat Kili, gs
3471 Gadd, C.   sl w 30 Sep 1897 nr Inayat Kili, gs
2738 Gibson, P.   sl w 30 Sep 1897 nr Inayat Kili, gs
2613 Gregory, A.   sl w 30 Sep 1897 nr Inayat Kili, gs
3454 Herrin, G.   sl w 30 Sep 1897 nr Inayat Kili, gs
1320 Hills, J.   sl w 30 Sep 1897 nr Inayat Kili, gs
3393 Hutson, T.   k 30 Sep 1897 nr Inayat Kili, gs
4303 Jarvis, E.   sl w 30 Sep 1897 nr Inayat Kili, gs
4092 Jipps, J.   sev w 30 Sep 1897 nr Inayat Kili, gs
3998 Jones, G.   k 30 Sep 1897 nr Inayat Kili, gs
4720 King, C.   sl w 30 Sep 1897 nr Inayat Kili, gs
4140 Latter, H.   sl w 30 Sep 1897 nr Inayat Kili, gs
2952 Meagher, A.   sev w 30 Sep 1897 nr Inayat Kili, gs
3545 Morgan, D.   k 30 Sep 1897 nr Inayat Kili, gs
2777 Scudder, W.   sl w 30 Sep 1897 nr Inayat Kili, gs
4202 Sullivan, D.   dang w 30 Sep 1897 nr Inayat Kili, gs

2nd Btn HIGHLAND LIGHT INFANTRY

Private
4409 McMasters, John   dang w 7 Jan 1898 Tanga Pass, bullet chest, dow

ARGYLL & SUTHERLAND HIGHLANDERS

Lance-Corporal
3276 Ward, J.   sl w Jul 1897 Sheranni, gs left leg

ARMY VETERINARY DEPARTMENT

Veterinary-Captain
Mann, Henry Thomas William   sl w 20/21 Sep 1897 Bedmanai Pass, contusion

11th REGIMENT OF BENGAL LANCERS

Daffadar
1686 Bijai Singh   sl w 17 Sep 1897 Damadolah, gs left eye & finger

Trumpeter
1995 Bishan Singh   sl w 20/21 Sep 1897 Bedmanai Pass, gs finger

Sowars
1962 Abdul Kadir   sl w 20/21 Sep 1897 Bedmanai Pass, gs left arm
2449 Arjan Singh   sl w 20/21 Sep 1897 Bedmanai Pass, gs thigh
1542 Buta Singh   sl w 20/21 Sep 1897 Bedmanai Pass, gs thigh
     Makhan Singh   sl w 20/21 Sep 1897 Bedmanai Pass, gs back
1984 Sher Singh   sl w 20/21 Sep 1897 Bedmanai Pass, gs neck
2136 Taja Singh   sev w 16 Sep 1897 Dabar, gs left shoulder

Recruit
     Dal Singh   sev w 16 Sep 1897 Dabar, gs neck

13th REGIMENT OF BENGAL LANCERS

Lieutenant
Cheyne, Archibald Ythen   sl w 9 Aug 1897 Shabkadr, sword cut & bullet

Ressaidar
Khuda Buksh   sl w 9 Aug 1897 Shabkadr, sword cut right hand

Jemadar
Mohamed Azim Khan   sl w 9 Aug 1897 Shabkadr, sword cut right thigh

Daffadars
- 198 Ghazan Khan   sl w 9 Aug 1897 Shabkadr, bullet left thigh
- 202 Jagat Singh   sl w 9 Aug 1897 Shabkadr, bullet chest
- 135 Uttam Singh   sev w 8 Aug 1897 Shabkadr, bullet right thigh

Lance-Daffadar
- 787 Atma Singh   sev w 8 Aug 1897 Shabkadr, bullet right forearm

Sowars
- 1310 Bostan Khan   sev w 9 Aug 1897 Shabkadr, bullet left thigh
- 1137 Chanda Singh   k 9 Aug 1897 Shabkadr, bullet
- 1228 Gholam Hussain   sl w 9 Aug 1897 Shabkadr, sword cut right hand
- 811 Gopal Singh   sl w 8 Aug 1897 Shabkadr, bullet right forearm
- 1151 Hurnam Singh   sl w 8 Aug 1897 Shabkadr, bullet right hand
- 324 Kahn Chand   sev w 9 Aug 1897 Shabkadr, sword cut left hand
- 1319 Khudadad Khan   sl w 8 Aug 1897 Shabkadr, bullet left thigh
- 771 Mihr Singh   sev w 9 Aug 1897 Shabkadr, sword cut left hand
- 1073 Shamas Khan   sev w 9 Aug 1897 Shabkadr, bullet right shoulder
- 1218 Sheibaz Khan   sl w 9 Aug 1897 Shabkadr, two bullets, chest & back
- 918 Sultan Khan   sl w 9 Aug 1897 Shabkadr, sword cut right shoulder
- 867 Zaman Ali Khan   sl w 9 Aug 1897 Shabkadr, sword cuts right hand & toe

BENGAL SAPPERS & MINERS

Subadar
Fateh Ali   sl w 25 Sep 1897 Jarobi, gs

Havildar
2936 Baryam Singh   4th Co   sl w 16 Sep 1897 Dabar, gs head

Naik
3382 Khan Singh   5th Co   sev w 25 Sep 1897 Jarobi, gs

Sappers
- 4951 Azad Khan   4th Co   dang w 16 Sep 1897 Dabar, gs right thigh
- 4831 Chet Singh   4th Co   dang w 16 Sep 1897 Dabar, gs back
- 4781 Gharib Singh   4th Co   sev w 16 Sep 1897 Dabar, gs chest & foot
- 4826 Hardett Singh   4th Co   sl w 16 Sep 1897 Dabar, gs face
- 4172 Harnam Singh   4th Co   sev w 16 Sep 1897 Dabar, gs left arm
- 4166 Ibrahim Khan   4th Co   sev w 16 Sep 1897 Dabar, gs leg & hand
- 3580 Jey Singh   5th Co   sev w 25 Sep 1897 Jarobi, gs
- 4163 Kan Singh   4th Co   sl w 16 Sep 1897 Dabar, gs chin
- 4779 Kehar Singh   dang w 16 Sep 1897 Dabar, gs arm & thigh
- 4659 Mahbut Khan   4th Co   sev w 16 Sep 1897 Dabar, gs right shoulder
- 4846 Natha Singh   4th Co   sev w 16 Sep 1897 Dabar, gs thigh

```
4398 Ram Singh       4th Co   sl w   16 Sep 1897 Dabar, gs head
4200 Ramzan Khan     4th Co   sev w  16 Sep 1897 Dabar, gs thigh
4766 Safadar Ali     4th Co   sev w  16 Sep 1897 Dabar, gs thigh
3566 Sahib Din       4th Co   dang w 16 Sep 1897 Dabar, gs knee & hand
2455 Sayyid Khan     4th Co   k      16 Sep 1897 Dabar, gs
4784 Sayyid Muhammad 4th Co   k      16 Sep 1897 Dabar, gs
4765 Sherdil Khan    4th Co   k      16 Sep 1897 Dabar, gs
4674 Unais Khan      4th Co   k      16 Sep 1897 Dabar, gs
```

BENGAL SUBORDINATE MEDICAL DEPARTMENT

Hospital Assistant 2nd Grade
144 Saadut Husain   sev w 20/21 Sep 1897 Bedmanai Pass, gs thigh

6th REGIMENT OF BENGAL LIGHT INFANTRY

Sepoys
943 Punna   k 2 Sep 1897 nr Miram Shah, gs abdomen & thigh
995 Ranji Nal dang w 16 Jul 1897 nr Idak, gs right knee, leg amputated

20th (PUNJAB) REGIMENT OF BENGAL INFANTRY

Jemadar
Arjan Singh   sev w 9 Aug 1897 Shabkadr, gs right buttock

Havildars
4335 Nur Jung   sev w 9 Aug 1897 Shabkadr, gs right forearm
3942 Pian Khan   sev w 9 Aug 1897 Shabkadr, gs chest
4351 Sharifulla sev w 25 Sep 1897 Jarobi, gs left thigh

Naik
4674 Ajmeer   sev w 9 Aug 1897 Shabkadr, gs left thigh

Lance-Naik
4588 Lalla   sev w 23 Sep 1897 Bedmanai Pass, gs leg

Sepoys
3780 Alam Khan   sev w 9 Aug 1897 Shabkadr, contusion lower jaw
2716 Atar Singh   sev w 9 Aug 1897 Shabkadr, gs right foot

```
4881 Azad Khan     sev w 9 Aug 1897 Shabkadr, gs head
4343 Bachan Singh  sev w 9 Aug 1897 Shabkadr, gs left buttock
 128 Bahadar Singh sev w 9 Aug 1897 Shabkadr, gs groin
4771 Baloock Khan  sev w 9 Aug 1897 Shabkadr, contusion left foot
4289 Bazai    sev w 9 Aug 1897 Shabkadr, gs right foot
4897 Bazira   sev w 9 Aug 1897 Shabkadr, gs left forearm
4781 Chet Singh   sl w 9 Aug 1897 Shabkadr, gs left arm
3741 Devi Ditta   sl w 25 Sep 1897 Jarobi, gs left arm
4819 Diyan Singh   k 9 Aug 1897 Shabkadr, bullet
4698 Eshan Singh  sev w 9 Aug 1897 Shabkadr, contusion left knee
4178 Fakir    sev w 9 Aug 1897 Shabkadr, gs buttock
4044 Fazal Shah   sev w 9 Aug 1897 Shabkadr, gs right buttock
4381 Feoo     k 9 Aug 1897 Shabkadr, bullet
 424 Ghazau Khan  sev w 9 Aug 1897 Shabkadr, gs left leg
4696 Hanina   sl w 9 Aug 1897 Shabkadr, contusion head
     Isa Khan  k 9 Aug 1897 Shabkadr, bullet
 130 Jehan Gul    sev w 9 Aug 1897 Shabkadr, gs buttock
2935 Kabir    sl w 9 Aug 1897 Shabkadr, gs left thigh
4632 Khairai  sev w 9 Aug 1897 Shabkadr, gs left hand
4504 Khushal Singh  k 9 Aug 1897 Shabkadr, bullet
4932 Kishna    k 9 Aug 1897 Shabkadr, bullet
3051 Laloo    sl w 9 Aug 1897 Shabkadr, contusion chest
3908 Makhan   sl w 9 Aug 1897 Shabkadr, contusion buttock
4682 Mir Baz  sev w 9 Aug 1897 Shabkadr, contusion left thigh
4375 Mohammad Ali   sev w 9 Aug 1897 Shabkadr, gs chest,abdomen
                        & arm
4510 Nikoo    sev w 9 Aug 1897 Shabkadr, contusion left arm
4588 Nur Gul  sev w 9 Aug 1897 Shabkadr, gs right foot
  63 Nur Khalim  sl w 23 Sep 1897 Bedmanai Pass, gs face
4559 Nur Khan sev w 9 Aug 1897 Shabkadr, contusion foot
4786 Saidai   sl w 25 Sep 1897 Jarobi, bullet scalp
3748 Said Akhmad   sev w 25 Sep 1897 Jarobi, gs right hip
4871 Sandoo Khan   sev w 9 Aug 1897 Shabkadr, gs chest
4685 Sodama   sevw 9 Aug 1897 Shabkadr, contusion right arm
3890 Tajah    sev w 9 Aug 1897 Shabkadr, contusion buttock &
                    ankle
 138 Umra Khan    k 25 Sep 1897 Jarobi, gs abdomen
4464 Zar Gul Khan  sl w 9 Aug 1897 Shabkadr, contusion back
  18 Zar Khan    sev w 9 Aug 1897 Shabkadr, contusion left arm
```

Recruits
```
     Naham Singh  sl w 9 Aug 1897 Shabkadr, gs left foot
     Sohbat Khan  sev w 9 Aug 1897 Shabkadr, contusion right leg
```

22nd (PUNJAB) REGIMENT OF BENGAL INFANTRY

Sepoys
```
3547 Dewah Singh   sev w 20/21 Sep 1897 Bedmanai Pass, gs thigh
```

4350 Khan Muhammad   sev w 20/21 Sep 1897 Bedmanai Pass, gs left arm
3858 Nauroz Khan   sl w 20/21 Sep 1897 Bedmanai Pass, gs foot
4054 Rajab Ali   sl w 20/21 Sep 1897 Bedmanai Pass, gs leg
3613 Sham Singh   sev w 20/21 Sep 1897 Bedmanai Pass, gs abdomen

24th (PUNJAB) REGIMENT OF BENGAL INFANTRY

Lance-Naik
3017 Tya Singh   sl w 17 Aug 1897 Landakai, contusion

Sepoys
3576 Aslam   sl w 17 Aug 1897 Landakai, gs right thigh
3751 Hans   sl w 17 Aug 1897 Landakai, contusion

25th (PUNJAB) REGIMENT OF BENGAL INFANTRY

Sepoys
1019 Bala Singh   k 19 Aug 1897 nr Idak, gs chest & head
1045 Sawan Singh   k 19 Aug 1897 nr Idak, gs abdomen

31st (PUNJAB) REGIMENT OF BENGAL INFANTRY

Lieutenant-Colonel
O'Bryen, James Loughnan   k 30 Sep 1897 nr Inayat Kili, gs abdomen

Lieutenant
Peacock, Edward Barnes   sev w 30 Sep 1897 nr Inayat Kili, gs thigh

Jemadar
Dip Singh   sev w 30 Sep 1897 nr Inayat Kili, gs

Lance-Naik
2016 Rija   dang w 30 Sep 1897 nr Inayat Kili, gs

Bugler
2595 Sahib Ram   sl w 3 Oct 1897 Badalai, gs

Sepoys
1922 Bachittar Singh   sl w 30 Sep 1897 nr Inayat Kili, gs
2528 Belam Khan   sl w 3 Oct 1897 Badalai, gs

```
2287 Beli        dang w 30 Sep 1897 nr Inayat Kili, gs
2803 Bhola Singh    k 30 Sep 1897 nr Inayat Kili, gs
2859 Dhowkal Singh  k 3 Oct 1897 Badalai, gs
2831 Gurdit Singh   sl w 30 Sep 1897 nr Inayat Kili, gs
2710 Harnam Singh   sl w 30 Sep 1897 nr Inayat Kili, gs
1693A Jagat Singh   sev w 30 Sep 1897 nr Inayat Kili, gs
1961 Jewan Singh    sev w 3 Oct 1897 Badalai, gs
2573 Khewa Singh    sev w 3 Oct 1897 Badalai, gs
2577 Kirpal Singh   sev w 30 Sep 1897 nr Inayat Kili, gs
2426 Lal Singh   sl w 30 Sep 1897 nr Inayat Kili, gs
2628 Madat Khan   k 30 Sep 1897 nr Inayat Kili, gs
2827 Magar     sev w 17 Aug 1897 Landakai, gs
2237 Mika Singh   k 30 Sep 1897 nr Inayat Kili, gs
2609 Muhammad Hossain   sev w 30 Sep 1897 nr Inayat Kili, gs
2660 Pakhar Singh   k 30 Sep 1897 nr Inayat Kili, gs
2340 Paras Ram   sev w 30 Sep 1897 nr Inayat Kili, gs
2804 Raja Singh    dang w 30 Sep 1897 nr Inayat Kili, gs
1814 Ralla Singh   sl w 30 Sep 1897 nr Inayat Kili, gs
2551 Sawan Singh    dang w 30 Sep 1897 nr Inayat Kili, gs
2306 Sher Khan   k 30 Sep 1897 nr Inayat Kili, gs
2720 Sucha Singh   sl w 30 Sep 1897 nr Inayat Kili, gs
2813 Sundar Singh   k 30 Sep 1897 nr Inayat Kili, gs
2603 Udey Singh    k 30 Sep 1897 nr Inayat Kili, gs
1823 Uttam Singh   sl w 3 Oct 1897 Badalai, gs foot
```

35th (SIKH) REGIMENT OF BENGAL INFANTRY

Captain
Ryder, William Ironside   (attchd from 2/1st Gurkhas)   sl w 16 Sep 1897 Dabar, gs ankle

Lieutenants
Cassels, Gilbert Robert   dang w 16 Sep 1897 Dabar, gs head
Gunning, Orlando George   sev w 16 Sep 1897 Dabar, gs head, swordcuts back
Hughes, Victor   k 16 Sep 1897 Dabar, gs chest

Subadar
Thakur Singh   sl w 16 Sep 1897 Dabar, gs shoulder

Jemadars
Basawa Singh   sl w 14 Sep 1897 Markhanai, gs chest
Hazara Singh   sev w 16 Sep 1897 Dabar, gs forearm

Havildars
    Badhawa Singh   missing 16 Sep 1897 Dabar
 119 Ram Singh   sl w 16 Sep 1897 Dabar, gs shoulder, thigh & loin
 311 Kishan Singh   sl w 16 Sep 1897 Dabar, gs toe

Naiks
  217 Buddon Singh   sev w 16 Sep 1897 Dabar, gs arm
  356 Isar Singh   k 16 Sep 1897 Dabar, gs
  297 Ram Singh   sl w 16 Sep 1897 Dabar, gs hand
  239 Sundar Singh   sl w 16 Sep 1897 Dabar, gs forehead

Lance-Naiks
  205 Narain Singh   sev w 16 Sep 1897 Dabar, gs forearm
  234 Surmukh Singh   sev w 16 Sep 1897 Dabar, gs scrotum

Buglers
  903 Kartara Singh   k 16 Sep 1897 Dabar, gs
  906 Sohan Singh   dang w 16 Sep 1897 Dabar, gs compound fracture

Sepoys
  478 Atar Singh   sl w 16 Sep 1897 Dabar, gs shoulder
 1330 Basant Singh   sl w 14 Sep 1897 Markhanai, gs chest
 1327 Bela Singh   sl w 16 Sep 1897 Dabar, gs thigh
 1340 Bir Singh   k 16 Sep 1897 Dabar, gs
  749 Buddon Singh   k 16 Sep 1897 Dabar, gs
  867 Budh Singh   sl w 16 Sep 1897 Dabar, gs skull
 1051 Dhyam Singh   sev w 16 Sep 1897 Dabar, gs
  862 Didar Singh   sev w 16 Sep 1897 Dabar, gs leg
 1258 Dyal Singh   k 16 Sep 1897 Dabar, gs
 1552 Fatteh Singh   sl w 16 Sep 1897 Dabar, gs leg
 1184 Gahna Singh   sl w 14 Sep 1897 Markhanai, gs head
 1286 Ganda Singh   k 16 Sep 1897 Dabar, gs
  657 Gujjar Singh   k 16 Sep 1897 Dabar, gs
 1587 Gurditt Singh   sl w 16 Sep 1897 Dabar, gs
  916 Harnam Singh   k 16 Sep 1897 Dabar, gs
  960 Hukam Singh   sl w 16 Sep 1897 Dabar, contusion from stone
  568 Indar Singh   dang w 16 Sep 1897 Dabar, gs left arm; sev w
                      18 Sep 1897 Damadolah, gs
 1116 Indar Singh   k 16 Sep 1897 Dabar, gs
 1543 Indar Singh   dang w 16 Sep 1897 Dabar, gs chest
  706 Jhanda Singh   k 16 Sep 1897 Dabar, gs
 1210 Jowahir Singh   sev w 16 Sep 1897 Dabar, gs forearm
  985 Karam Singh   sev w 16 Sep 1897 Dabar, sword cuts shoulder
                      & arm
 1240 Kehr Singh   sl w 14 Sep 1897 Markhanai, gs skull
 1251 Kesar Singh   sev w 16 Sep 1897 Dabar, gs thigh
 1435 Khewan Singh   sev w 16 Sep 1897 Dabar, gs thumb
 1070 Khushal Singh   k 16 Sep 1897 Dabar, gs
 1230 Kishan Singh   sev w 16 Sep 1897 Dabar, gs right hand;
                      sl w 18 Sep 1897 Damadolah, gs
 1573 Kishan Singh   k 18 Sep 1897 Damadolah, gs
 1605 Labh Singh   k 16 Sep 1897 Dabar, gs
 1081 Lal Singh   sev w 16 Sep 1897 Dabar, gs calf
 1526 Lal Singh   sl w 16 Sep 1897 Dabar, gs
  457 Lehna Singh   k 16 Sep 1897 Dabar, gs
 1428 Mangal Singh   sl w 16 Sep 1897 Dabar, gs
  473 Marya Singh   missing 16 Sep 1897 Dabar
 1371 Meka Singh   sev w 16 Sep 1897 Dabar, sword cut scapula

905 Mena Singh   sev w 16 Sep 1897 Dabar, gs
  514 Mit Singh   k 16 Sep 1897 Dabar, gs
 1501 Mulla Singh   k 16 Sep 1897 Dabar, gs
 1114 Nand Singh   sl w 21 Sep 1897 Bedmanai Pass, gs
 1372 Ochehra Singh sl w 22 Sep 1897 Bedmanai Pass, gs
 1328 Palla Singh   sl w 16 Sep 1897 Dabar, gs thigh
 1054 Partab Singh missing 16 Sep 1897 Dabar
  424 Ralla Singh   k 16 Sep 1897 Dabar, gs
 1049 Ralla Singh   sl w 16 Sep 1897 Dabar, gs
 1262 Ram Singh   k 16 Sep 1897 Dabar, gs
 1204 Roor Singh   sev w 16 Sep 1897 Dabar, gs shoulder
 1460 Rudh Singh   sl w 16 Sep 1897 Dabar, gs leg
 1131 Sawan Singh   sev w 16 Sep 1897 Dabar, gs leg
  851 Sundar Singh sev w 16 Sep 1897 Dabar, gs forearm
 1194 Sundar Singh sl w 16 Sep 1897 Dabar, gs leg
 1297 Sundar Singh sev w 16 Sep 1897 Dabar, gs mouth
 1417 Sundar Singh k 16 Sep 1897 Dabar, gs
  993 Sundur Singh k 16 Sep 1897 Dabar, gs
  322 Tara Singh   sev w 18 Sep 1897 Damadolah, gs
  342 Tara Singh   sev w 16 Sep 1897 Dabar, gs right hand & thigh
 1098 Teja Singh   sev w 16 Sep 1897 Dabar, gs wrist
  543 Uday Singh   sl w 16 Sep 1897 Dabar, gs leg
 1410 Uttam Singh   sev w 16 Sep 1897 Dabar, gs thigh
  198 Warriam Singh sl w 16 Sep 1897 Dabar, contusion from stone
 1003 Warriam Singh sl w 16 Sep 1897 Dabar, contusion from stone
 1203 Warriam Singh sl w 16 Sep 1897 Dabar, gs left hand
  999 Wazir Singh   dang w 16 Sep 1897 Dabar, gs clavicle

38th (DOGRA) REGIMENT OF BENGAL INFANTRY

Captain
Tomkins, William Edward   k 14 Sep 1897 Markhanai, gs head

Lieutenants
Bailey, Arthur Wellesley   k 14 Sep 1897 Markhanai, gs chest
Harington, Henry Andrew (attchd from 28th Bengal Inf)   dang w 14 Sep 1897 Markhanai, gs head

Naiks
 295 Bhagat Singh   k 3 Oct 1897 Badalai, gs
 175 Mahant   sev w 30 Sep 1897 nr Inayat Kili, gs elbow joint

Bugler
 892 Raghubir   sl w 3 Oct 1897 Badalai, gs finger

Sepoys
 541 Badri   dang w 30 Sep 1897 nr Inayat Kili, gs chest
  93 Baragi   k 18 Sep 1897 Damadolah, gs
1110 Beli   sev w 3 Oct 1897 Badalai, gs leg

```
639 Bhagel Singh    sl w 30 Sep 1897 nr Inayat Kili, gs arm
435 Billo    sev w 30 Sep 1897 nr Inayat Kili, gs hip
984 Fakiria    sev w 18 Sep 1897 Damadolah, gs
1017 Lakha    sl w 3 Oct 1897 Badalai, gs chest
389 Mehar Singh    k 14 Sep 1897 Markhanai, gs head
388 Musaddi    dang w 20 Sep 1897 Zagai, gs
994 Musaddi    sl w 3 Oct 1897 Badalai, gs elbow
844 Parma    sev w 23 Sep 1897 Bedmanai Pass, gs hand
230 Rupa    sev w 20 Sep 1897 Zagai, gs
775 Sagrim    sev w 3 Oct 1897 Badalai, gs wrist
```

39th (GARHWAL RIFLE) REGIMENT OF BENGAL INFANTRY

<u>Riflemen</u>
```
1381 Amar Singh Rawat    sl w 20/21 Sep 1897 Bedmanai Pass, gs
1432 Barina Gasain    sl w 20/21 Sep 1897 Bedmanai Pass, gs
 766 Doulati Rawat    dang w 20/21 Sep 1897 Bedmanai Pass, gs
 258 Gagaru Kaintura    sl w 20/21 Sep 1897 Bedmanai Pass, gs
```

45th (RATTRAY'S SIKH) REGIMENT OF BENGAL INFANTRY

<u>Sepoy</u>
```
3747 Harnam Singh    sl w 17 Aug 1897 Landakai, gs heel
```

2nd Btn 1st GURKHA (RIFLE) REGIMENT

<u>Lance-Naik</u>
```
 159 Karkia Thapa    dang w 27 Sep 1897 Khudokhe, gs left arm,
                     bone fractured
```

<u>Sepoys</u>
```
1663 Barjbahadur Gurung    sev w 27 Sep 1897 Khudokhe, gs right knee
 952 Dalbir Thapa    k 23 Sep 1897 Bedmanai Pass, bullet in brain
1593 Deoman Gharti    sev w 27 Sep 1897 Khudokhe, gs right thigh
1388 Jasbir Thapa    sev w 27 Sep 1897 Khudokhe, gs foot
1603 Narbir Thapa    sev w 23 Sep 1897 Bedmanai Pass, gs arm
1213 Srikishan Gurung    sev w 27 Sep 1897 Khudokhe, gs right thigh
```

CORPS OF GUIDES CAVALRY, PUNJAB FRONTIER FORCE

Captain
Palmer, Henry Ingham Evered   sev w 17 Aug 1897 Landakai, gs wrist

Lieutenant
MacLean, Hector Lachlan Stewart   k 17 Aug 1897 Landakai, gs; awarded posthumous VC

Daffadar
1087 Nanak Chand   sl w 6 Oct 1897, gs thigh

Farrier
1338 Sharif   sl w 30 Sep 1897 nr Inayat Kili, gs shoulder blade

Sowars
1531 Ata Mahomed   sev w 30 Sep 1897 nr Inayat Kili, gs thigh
1352 Fatteh Khan   sev w 20 Oct 1897, gs foot
1435 Mahomed Afzal   sl w 3 Oct 1897 Badalai, gs contusion
1512 Mahommed Khan   sev w 3 Oct 1897 Badalai, gs fracture
1091 Safiullah   sl w 30 Sep 1897 nr Inayat Kili, gs right shoulder

CORPS OF GUIDES INFANTRY, PUNJAB FRONTIER FORCE

Subadar
Shahi Jan   dang w 16 Sep 1897 Dabar, gs neck

Havildars
2471 Amur Ali   sev w 16 Sep 1897 Dabar, contusion from stone
2204 Baksh Singh   sev w 16 Sep 1897 Dabar, gs foot
2108 Joti   dang w 3 Oct 1897 Badalai, gs knee joint

Naik
2747 Mat Khan   k 16 Sep 1897 Dabar, gs

Lance-Naiks
3397 Naiz Mir   sev w 16 Sep 1897 Dabar, gs leg
3412 Narain Singh   dang w 16 Sep 1897 Dabar, gs chest

Sepoys
4245 Abbas Khan   sev w 16 Sep 1897 Dabar, gs abdomen
3954 Ahmad Ali   k 16 Sep 1897 Dabar, gs
4027 Ahmed Khan   sl w 16 Sep 1897 Dabar, sword cut foot
4139 Azam Khan   sl w 16 Sep 1897 Dabar, gs shoulder
4065 Badshah Gul   dang w 16 Sep 1897 Dabar, gs chest
4213 Chait Singh   sev w 16 Sep 1897 Dabar, gs right buttock
4213 Chet Singh   sev w 18 Sep 1897 Damadolah, gs
4236 Darweza Khan   sev w 16 Sep 1897 Dabar, gs thigh; awarded IOM 3rd Class

3909 Khawajur Nur   sev w 3 Oct 1897 Badalai, gs leg
3815 Lal Singh   sev w 14 Sep 1897 Markhanai, gs buttock
4187 Suleman   dang w 22 Sep 1897 Dag, gs
4228 Zamrud   k 22 Sep 1897 Dag, gs

1st REGIMENT OF PUNJAB CAVALRY, PUNJAB FRONTIER FORCE

Sowar
2185 Karimdad Khan   sl w 12 Oct 1897 nr Charmina, gs head

1st REGIMENT OF SIKH INFANTRY, PUNJAB FRONTIER FORCE

Lieutenant-Colonel
Bunny, Arthur Cautley   k 10 Jun 1897 Maizar, gs through body

Lieutenant
Higginson, Archibald James Macaulay   sev w 10 Jun 1897 Maizar, gs twice, left arm

Surgeon-Captain
Cassidy, Christopher Clemons   sev w 10 Jun 1897 Maizar, gs knee

Subadars
Gulfaraz   sev w 22 Jul 1897 nr the Tochi, gs left shoulder
Nawab Khan   sl w 10 Jun 1897 Maizar, gs twice in leg; awarded IOM 3rd Class

Jemadar
Najja Khan   sl w 10 Jun 1897 Maizar, gs rib

Havildars
3659 Gurmukh Singh   sl w 10 Jun 1897 Maizar, gs foot
3991 Nawab Khan   sl w 10 Jun 1897 Maizar, gs foot

Naik
4116 Ganda Singh   sev w 10 Jun 1897 Maizar, contusion knee

Lance-Naiks
3992 Achhar Singh   k 10 Jun 1897 Maizar; awarded IOM 3rd Class pension
4411 Atar Singh   k 10 Jun 1897 Maizar, gs; awarded IOM 3rd Class pension
4281 Karm Singh   sev w 10 Jun 1897 Maizar, gs buttock
3872 Kesar Singh   k 10 Jun 1897 Maizar, gs; awarded IOM 3rd Class
4474 Sawan Singh   k 10 Jun 1897 Maizar, gs

Sepoys

```
 209 Bir Singh      sev w 10 Jun 1897 Maizar, gs hip
 157 Bisa Singh     k 10 Jun 1897 Maizar, gs
4613 Bishen Singh   k 10 Jun 1897 Maizar, gs
4776 Ganda Singh    sl w 10 Jun 1897 Maizar, gs neck
4706 Ganesha Singh  sev w 10 Jun 1897 Maizar, gs thigh
 369 Hasham Khan    sl w 10 Jun 1897 Maizar, gs chest
 227 Hazura Singh   sev w 10 Jun 1897 Maizar, gs right shoulder
4990 Imam Ali       sev w 10 Jun 1897 Maizar, gs hand
4877 Kharak Singh   sl w 4 Oct 1897 Charmina, gs head
3767 Labh Singh     sl w 10 Jun 1897 Maizar, gs thigh
 183 Lal Singh      sev w 10 Jun 1897 Maizar, gs heel
  38 Makhmud        sev w 10 Jun 1897 Maizar, gs arm
4759 Muhammad Khan  k 10 Jun 1897 Maizar, gs; awarded IOM 3rd
                    Class pension
 384 Prem Singh     sev w 10 Jun 1897 Maizar, gs neck
 274 Roshan Khan    k 10 Jun 1897 Maizar, gs; awarded IOM 3rd
                    Class pension
4918 Sahib Singh    sev w 10 Jun 1897 Maizar, gs thigh
 446 Saidullah      sev w 10 Jun 1897 Maizar, gs thigh & chest
4583 Sant Singh     k 10 Jun 1897 Maizar, gs
4814 Sawan Singh    k 10 Jun 1897 Maizar, gs
4497 Shankar Khan   k 10 Jun 1897 Maizar, gs; awarded IOM 3rd
                    Class pension
4647 Sukha Singh    sev w 10 Jun 1897 Maizar, gs right thigh &
                    left knee
4595 Sundar Singh   k 10 Jun 1897 Maizar, gs
4879 Sundar Singh   sl w 4 Oct 1897 Charmina, gs face
 405 Tika Khan      sl w 10 Jun 1897 Maizar, gs shoulder
```

1st REGIMENT OF PUNJAB INFANTRY, PUNJAB FRONTIER FORCE

Lieutenant
Seton-Browne, Clement Lawrence Seton   sev w 10 Jun 1897 Maizar, gs thigh; awarded DSO

Subadar
Sundar Singh   k 10 Jun 1897 Maizar, gs; awarded IOM 2nd Class pension

Naik
295 Bur Singh   k 10 Jun 1897 Maizar, gs; awarded IOM 3rd Class pension

Lance-Naik
4663 Kanaiya Singh   k 10 Jun 1897 Maizar, gs; awarded IOM 3rd Class pension

Sepoys
```
 993 Alla Singh     sl w 10 Jun 1897 Maizar, gs back
 245 Dalel Singh    k 10 Jun 1897 Maizar, gs
1026 Dhulip Singh   sl w 10 Jun 1897 Maizar, gs back
 809 Dyal Singh     k 10 Jun 1897 Maizar, gs
 651 Fakir Khan     sl w 10 Jun 1897 Maizar, gs leg
1025 Indar Singh    k 10 Jun 1897 Maizar, gs; awarded IOM 3rd
                       Class pension
1031 Nand Singh     k 10 Jun 1897 Maizar, gs
 774 Nur Dad        sev w 10 Jun 1897 Maizar, gs calf; awarded IOM
                       3nd Class
 654 Rassul Khan    sev w 10 Jun 1897 Maizar, gs thigh
1004 Shamsher Khan  k 1897 Tochi, gs thigh
1022 Shere Singh    sl w 10 Jun 1897 Maizar, gs hand
1027 Wariam Singh   k 10 Jun 1897 Maizar, gs
```

No 6 (BOMBAY) MOUNTAIN BATTERY

Captain
Browne, James Frederick RA k 10 Jun 1897 Datta Khel, artery severed right arm

Lieutenant
Cruickshank, Hugh Alexander RA k 10 Jun 1897 Datta Khel, gs left arm & breast

Havildar
2438 Umar Din k 10 Jun 1897 Datta Khel, gs through forehead & left shoulder; awarded IOM 3rd Class pension

Lance-Naik
2432 Utam Chand sev w 10 Jun 1897 Datta Khel, gs right elbow & right thigh, dow; awarded IOM 3rd Class pension

Gunner
2530 Chet Singh sev w 10 Jun 1897 Datta Khel, gs nose, upper portion of bone shot away

Drivers
766 Alif Khan   k 10 Jun 1897 Datta Khel, gs stomach
796 Gurdit Singh sl w 10 Jun 1897 Datta Khel, gs right upper arm

BOMBAY SAPPERS & MINERS

<u>Jemadar</u>
Mahadeo Singh   3rd Co   sl w 20/21 Sep 1897 Bedmanai Pass, gs thigh

<u>Naik</u>
1439 Rammonohar Chobe   3rd Co   sl w 20/21 Sep 1897 Bedmanai Pass, gs left hand

28th REGIMENT OF BOMBAY INFANTRY (PIONEERS)

<u>Havildar</u>
 847 Niamatali Khan   sev w 25 Sep 1897 Jarobi, contusion

<u>Lance-Havildar</u>
2537 Shunker Nalowday   sl w 25 Sep 1897 Jarobi, gs

<u>Naik</u>
1919 Jai Singh   sev w 25 Sep 1897 Jarobi, gs

<u>Privates</u>
2564 Dhondoo Jadow   sl w 25 Sep 1897 Jarobi, gs
2244 Govind Bargay   sl w 25 Sep 1897 Jarobi, gs
2587 Govind Moray   sev w 25 Sep 1897 Jarobi, gs
2237 Govind Patanker   sev w 25 Sep 1897 Jarobi, gs
2253 Kalnak Ramnak   sl w 25 Sep 1897 Jarobi, gs
2511 Karamali Khan   sl w 25 Sep 1897 Jarobi, gs
2371 Rao Kirdak   sl w 25 Sep 1897 Jarobi, gs
2551 Sucaram Ghatgay   sl w 25 Sep 1897 Jarobi, gs

MALAKAND 1897

From Brig-Gen W H Meiklejohn, commanding Malakand Brigade, dated Malakand 13 August 1897

I have the honour to submit, for the information of His Excellency the Commander-in-Chief, my report of the fighting that took place at Malakand between the dates of 26th July and 1st August.

2. I have kept you informed by telegram of the events of each day, but I have been prevented from sending any detailed report before by the incessant nature of the fighting.

3. On the afternoon of the 26th, I was informed by Major H. A. Deane, Political Agent, who had previously warned me of possible trouble, that matters had assumed a very disquieting aspect, reports having reached him of the entire failure of the residents of the Swat Valley to stop the advance of a fanatical Fakir, who had gained immense influence on the superstitious and religious feelings of the people, and that he thought that the Guides should be called up, and arrangements made for the Brigade to turn out. The Guides were consequently wired for at once, and all Officers Commanding Regiments and Adjutants were ordered to meet me immediately.

4. At 7 P.M. I saw these officers and gave them instructions to be prepared to turn out at any moment. These instructions had hardly been given when Major Deane joined me, and informed me that news has just come in that the Fakir was moving towards Aladand, and that in his opinion the Brigade should turn out at once and prevent his seizing the Amandara Pass. Orders were consequently issued by me for the Officer Commanding, 45th Sikhs, with 2 guns of No. 8 Bengal Mountain Battery, 2 companies, 31st Punjab Infantry, and the Squadron, XIth Bengal Lancers, to start at midnight and seize the Amandara Pass. The remainder of the column to start at 3 A.M. under my own command.

5. All officers were recalled from leave and orders given that all regimental baggage was to be stored under guards in their own camps, there being no time to strike tents and carry them away to the fort.

6. At 9-45 P.M. a telegram was received from the Officer Commanding, Chakdarra, saying that two forces of Pathans were marching towards Chakdarra from the east along both banks of the river, and at 10 P.M. Major Deane arrived at the Brigade Office with the news that a Levy Jemadar had just arrived, giving information that the Fakir had passed Khar and was advancing on Malakand, and that neither levies nor people would act against him, and that the hills to the east of the camp were covered with Pathans. It was at once seen that a night-attack on the camp was intended, and the "alarm" was immediately sounded, the troops moving at once to their posts.

7. This had just been completed when the first shots were fired and a general attack was made on the camp by the Buddhist and Graded Roads. At the same time firing from the direction of the North Camp, and the glow of star shells showed that the North Camp was also threatened.

8. In the first rush the enemy succeeded in over-powering the picquet on the Graded Road, and penetrated into the camp behind the enclosure in which were the camps of the Sappers and Miners and Field Engineer Park.

9. On the right flank the Buddhist Road had been secured by the 45th Rattray's Sikhs under Lieutenant-Colonel McRae, who had, on the first alarm being sounded, despatched Major Taylor with a party to secure the gorge where the road reaches the top of the pass. Lieutenant-Colonel McRae, followed immediately with 30 men, caught up Major Taylor, and they together advanced to the gorge, and almost immediately encountered the head of the enemy's column, numbering several hundred men who were creeping silently up the Buddhist Road. They opened a very hot fire on them and the enemy at once broke into yells and screams and tried to rush them.

10. The small party held on to their position manfully till the enemy clambered up on to the rocks that overlooked the gorge on both sides, and from this position rolled down rocks and fired on them. Lieutenant Barff and some more men of the 45th Sikhs had by this time arrived

and been sent by Lieutenant-Colonel McRae to protect his right flank round which the enemy were trying to make a way. The remainder of the regiment now came up, and Lieutenant-Colonel McRae retired to a more defensible position about 50 yards in rear in which he remained and defied the enemy all night. Just before he retired Major Taylor was mortally wounded.

11. There is no doubt that the gallant resistance made by this small body in the gorge, against vastly superior numbers, till the arrival of the rest of the regiment, saved the camp from being rushed on that side, and I cannot speak too highly of the behaviour of Lieutenant-Colonel McRae and Major Taylor on this occasion.

12. On the left, on the alarm being sounded, the picquets supplied by the 24th Punjab Infantry had been doubled, one company of the same regiment under Lieutenant Costello was sent to line the walls of the enclosure facing the gorge through which the road to the North Camp passes, and another company under Lieutenant Climo was sent to line the wall of the Bazaar facing the gorge up which the Graded Road passes. The remainder of the regiment being held in readiness to support any part of the line that required it.

13. The central position, *viz.*, the enclosure in which were the Sappers and Miners Camp, the Commissariat Godown and the Field Engineer Park was occupied by No. 5 Company, Queen's Own Madras Sappers and Miners.

14. I ordered Lieutenant-Colonel Lamb to bring one company of his regiment into this enclosure, and I also withdrew the company lining the Bazaar wall into this enclosure, as the enemy were getting round their flank, and in their former position they ran a risk of being fired into by the company lining the enclosure facing the gorge leading to the North Camp. There were thus in this enclosure—

No. 5 Company, Madras Sappers and Miners, and
2 Companies, 24th Punjab Infantry.

15. The enemy having over-powered the picquet on the Abbott (Graded) Road got on to the high ground in rear of the position from which they kept up a heavy fire all night, periodically charging with great determination right up to the Abattis which was lined by the Sappers and Miners. Twice they penetrated, once capturing the Quarter Guard, in which was all the ammunition of the company. It was in trying to stop this charge that Lieutenant Watling, temporarily in command of the company, was wounded by a man whom he ran through with his sword. The enemy over-powered the guard, and for a time held the guard-room, but were eventually driven out by a party of the 24th Punjab Infantry under Lieutenant Climo. Some of the enemy penetrated into the Commissariat Godown, and here they killed Honorary Lieutenant Manley, my Brigade Commissariat Officer.

16. In the enclosure the fighting was very severe, for the enemy were on three sides of it, and fought with great determination, bringing a heavy cross fire on the defenders, and continually charging right up to the breast-works.

17. Lieutenant-Colonel Lamb, 24th Punjab Infantry, Major Herbert, my Deputy Assistant Adjutant-General, and Captain Holland, 24th Punjab Infantry, were all shot in this enclosure. The attack had been carried on with great vigour from 10-30 P.M. till 2-30 A.M. when the sounds of tomtoms and pipes approaching up the Graded Road indicated reinforcements coming to the enemy. The garrison of the enclosure was already hard pressed, and so I sent Lieutenant Rawlins, 24th Punjab Infantry, up to the fort to bring down 100 men from there. The enemy were all round the enclosure and there was every chance of his having to fight his way. He went with three orderlies and arrived back safely with the reinforcements. The fight lasted till 4-30 A.M., when the enemy withdrew.

18. At daybreak it was ascertained that the North Camp had not been seriously attacked and that all was well there. I consequently ordered the 31st Punjab Infantry with the Squadron, XIth Bengal Lancers, and 2 guns, supported by a wing of the 24th Punjab Infantry to pursue the enemy, the majority of whom had withdrawn in the direction of Khar and Butkheyla.

19. They pursued for a short distance up the valley when they came across a very large gathering of the enemy, and as it was evident that this attempt on our camp had been the signal for a large tribal gathering, I ordered Major Gibbs, who was in charge of the pursuit, to retire and bring up all the stores, ammunition and treasure of the troops in North Camp to the Kotal, and concentrate all his force before dark in that place.

20. The Squadron, XIth Bengal Lancers, under Captain Wright, which had covered the advance of Major Gibbs' force, had pushed right on to Chakdarra, being fired on the whole way, and Captain Wright wisely determined to stop at that place, where his party has proved a useful reinforcement to the two companies, 45th Sikhs, under Lieutenant Rattray and Lieutenant Wheatley, forming the garrison of the post.

21. The rest of the force retired to their respective camps. The manner in which Lieutenant Climo, on whom the command of the 24th Punjab Infantry devolved when Lieutenant-Colonel Lamb and Captain Holland were wounded, covered this retirement is most praiseworthy, and I shall have again to draw attention to the good work done by this officer on subsequent occasions.

22. The withdrawal of all baggage and stores, from North Camp to the Kotal, was commenced at once, there being no transport, however, to bring up the E. P. tents, all the camels being at Dargai, the camp equipage was left by my order, and was burnt by the enemy in the night. Almost every tent had been struck by Major Gibbs' force, but there was no time to do more. All day large bodies of the enemy were seen coming from different directions in the valley, and joining the enemy who were visible all over the hill tops, and it was certain that last night's fight was not merely an attempt to do as much harm as possible and then clear off, but the beginning of an important movement to try and turn us out of the valley and regain possession of the Pass, and that we must prepare for another attack in the night.

23. They did not wait till night, however, for, while the stores, etc., from North Camp were being sent up to the Kotal, the troops in North Camp were threatened by the enemy on the hills to the west, and the retirement was completed under cover of fire from the 24th Punjab Infantry and the Guides Cavalry, who had arrived in camp at 8-30 A.M. that morning.

24. At about 6-45 P.M., as the 31st Punjab Infantry were arriving in the Kotal Camp, a body of the enemy about 1,000 strong made a sudden attack down from the hills on the west, and driving in No. 2 Picquet of the 24th Punjab Infantry tried to rush the camp. Lieutenant Climo with two companies, 24th Punjab Infantry, at once went up the hill to meet them, and aided by 2 guns, No. 8 Bengal Mountain Battery, drove them back with loss towards the North Camp.

25. The Guides Cavalry arrived at 8-30 A.M. this morning (27th). The Guides Infantry arrived at 7-30 P.M. I would like to call His Excellency's attention to the march of this regiment. The Officer Commanding Guides received my telegram calling him to Malakand at 9 P.M. on the 26th, the Cavalry of the Corps left Mardan at 12-30 A.M. and arrived at Malakand at 8-30 A.M., *i.e.*, a distance of 32 miles in 8 hours, and the Infantry left Mardan at 2 A.M., arriving at Malakand at 7-30 P.M., *i.e.*, in 17½ hours. The heat on the road between here and Mardan was intense and the march reflects great credit on the regiment.

27. At 8-30 P.M. the enemy attacked with their whole force all along the line, but were repulsed everywhere. The force in the Kotal this night was composed of—

    24th Punjab Infantry,
    6 Companies, 45th Sikhs,
    Guides Infantry,
    Guides Cavalry,
    No. 5 Company, Queen's Own Sappers and Miners,
    No. 8 Bengal Mountain Battery,

and was disposed as follows:

On the Right Flank.—Holding a position about 50 yards in a rear of that which they finally held on the night of the 26th were the 45th Sikhs, with 2 guns, and supported by 100 of the Guides Infantry under Lieutenant McCaskill.

In the centre.—Holding the top of the Graded Road and the enclosures occupied by the Sappers Camp, Commissariat and Field Engineers Park were the—

    31st Punjab Infantry.
    No. 5 Company, Queen's Own Sappers and Miners.

The Guides.
2 guns.

On the Left.—Holding the hill to the north of camp and overlooking the short road to North Camp were the 24th Punjab Infantry and 2 guns.

28. The 31st Punjab Infantry being short of officers, Lieutenant Maclean was sent from the Guides to assist Major Gibbs. The position on the right and the centre enclosure were hardly pressed the whole night.

29. About 100 yards in advance of the north-east corner of the central enclosure was a fortified serai, and, in order to check the advance of the enemy along the Graded Road, a party of 25 men, 31st Punjab Infantry, under Subadar Syed Ahmed Shah was sent to occupy it with orders to block up the only entrance to the Serai. The enemy made a most determined attack on this Serai, but the garrison defended it gallantly from the commencement till 3 A.M. when the enemy succeeded in setting fire to it, and broke through one wall through which opening they rushed. The garrison now could hold on no longer, and with the aid of a ladder let themselves down over the wall nearest the camp, and retired to the enclosure, bringing their wounded with them. Nine of their number, I regret to say, were killed and ten wounded.

31. The darkness and the noise of firing all round prevented their condition being appreciated by the troops behind the breast-work, otherwise assistance would most surely have been sent them. Nothing could have been finer than the way these few men stuck to their post till it was made absolutely untenable.

32. The 24th Punjab Infantry were also hotly engaged all night, and in the early morning the enemy began to press close upon them from the heights on the west, whereupon Lieutenant Climo advanced up the spur to meet them with 2 companies, covered by the fire of the 2 guns attached to his position and 1 other company. The enemy stuck determinedly to their ground. They had many Martinis with them and kept up a heavy fire on Lieutenant Climo's force, at the same time rolling stones down on them. Lieutenant Climo, however advanced, driving the enemy before him from position to position, and pursuing them for some two miles. He estimates the enemy's loss at 40. This counter-attack was excellently executed and is one more proof of the soldierly ability and dash displayed by Lieutenant Climo ever since the outbreak of hostilities.

33. *28th July.*—During the day desultory firing was going on into the camp. On the night of the 28th the attack was renewed with the same energy as on the two previous nights and on all sides of the camp, the brunt of the fighting falling on the central position and on the right flank.

34. *29th July.*—On the morning of the 29th July signalling communication was re-established with Chakdarra, and it was learned that the fort had been attacked on the night of the 26th by a force, 1,000 strong, who had been repulsed without any loss to the garrison, and that they had since been attacked twice by day and twice by night.

35. At 4 P.M. this day (29th) one squadron, 11th Bengal Lancers, 88 strong, marched into Malakand under command of Major Beatson. In the evening the 38th Dogras and 35th Sikhs and details of the Guides arrived at Dargai under Colonel Reid. The heat on the road had been intense and 21 men of the 35th Sikhs died of heat apoplexy. I ordered Colonel Reid to halt at Dargai the next day in order to give these regiments a rest. During the day the Bazaar and Serai were levelled, trees were cleared away, abattis and breast-works strengthened, and in the evening large bonfires were lighted up in front of the central position, so that the enemy advancing by the Graded Road to the attack should be obliged to cross a line of light. The result was that the central position did not have such a severe time of it this night. It was known that the enemy had been largely reinforced during the day, and a vigorous attack was anticipated.

36. It commenced at 9-30 and was perhaps more vigorously and more fiercely pushed than on any previous night. It was principally delivered on the two flanks. At 2 A.M. a tremendous assault was made and at 2-30 A.M. suddenly ceased, and the enemy withdrew having been repulsed everywhere. The loss inflicted on them must have been very great, and as day broke they could be seen dragging away the bodies of their dead over the hills.

It was reported that in the morning the mad Fakir had personally led this attack, had been wounded and had fled to Landakai, and that his second-in-command and companion had been killed.

37. *30th July.*—At about 10 A.M. on the 30th a heliogram was received from Chakdarra that the fort had been attacked from 2 P.M. on the 29th till 8 A.M. that day, that the attack had been repulsed with great loss to the enemy, and that the casualties among the garrison were 1 sepoy dangerously wounded. Later in the day I received intimation that their supplies and ammunition were running short.

38. During the day a large organised body joined the enemy, showing that, although the two Fakirs were *hors-de-combat,* they were still determined to carry on the fight. The attack was commenced again at 9-30 P.M., but there was not the same spirit in the fighting that there had been before. Once during a thunderstorm that broke over the camp during the night the enemy charged the 45th Sikhs position, but were repulsed with the bayonet. Our casualties on the night of the 30th were—

British officers . . . . *Nil.*
Native ranks . . . . 2 wounded.

39. *31st July.*—At 7 A.M. on the 31st July the 35th Sikhs and 38th Dogras marched into camp having had a most trying march. The telegraph wire had been cut in the night on both sides of Dargai and 1,200 yards of wire had been carried away from opposite Shergarh. It was, however, repaired on the 31st, and news was received in the evening that Dargai was going to be attacked that night. It, however, was not attacked, nor, except a certain amount of sniping, did anything happen at Malakand on the night of the 31st.

40. *1st August.*—On the 1st August, my troops having had a quiet night and been able to get a little rest. I decided to try and relieve Chakdarra at once, taking with me the 45th Sikhs, 24th Punjab Infantry, Guides Cavalry and Infantry, the squadron, XIth Bengal Lancers, 4 guns, No. 8 Bengal Mountain Battery, and No. 5 Company, Queen's Own Madras Sappers and Miners.

41. At 11 A.M. I sent the Cavalry under Lieutenant-Colonel Adams of the Guides, down into the plain, by the short road into North Camp, with orders to make a dash for the Amandara Pass, to seize it if not held, and if it was held to send me back word of the strength and position of the enemy. Before the Cavalry had reached the plain, however, the enemy saw what was going to happen, and assembled in great numbers from every direction to oppose them. The Cavalry charged them once and slew a great number of them, but the broken nature of the ground cramped their action, and, as the enemy were gradually working round their left flank to cut them off from their only line of retreat, I sent Major E. Hobday, R.A., then Staff Officer to Colonel Reid, to order Lieutenant-Colonel Adams to withdraw, being convinced that, with the opposition that the force was certain to receive, they would not, starting so late, reach Chakdarra that night. I determined therefore to put off the attempt till the morning of the 2nd, when I should have the whole day before me.

42. Such is the narrative of the events which took place here between the 26th July and the 1st August. Of the behaviour of the troops of all ranks, I cannot speak too highly. The courage with which they have faced overwhelming odds night after night, the endurance with which they have stood and fought with next to no sleep for 5 days and 5 nights has been beyond all praise. The trial has been a very severe one, and I trust that His Excellency will agree that they have come out of it honourably.

Unless stated, casualties at Malakand occurred between 26 July and 1 August 1897, and at Chakdarra between 26 July and 2 August 1897.

STAFF

Major
Herbert, Lionel   Depy Asst Adjt-Gen   sev w 27 Jul Malakand, gs

No 8 (BENGAL) MOUNTAIN BATTERY

Lieutenant
Wynter, Francis Arthur   sev w Malakand, gs ankle

Gunners
- 340 Fateh Ali   sl w Malakand, contusion
- 368 Kala Khan   sl w Malakand, contusion
- 83 Sharif   sl w Malakand, gs

Drivers
- 112 Achchar Singh (Naik)   sl w Malakand, contusion
- 130 Naid Jandu   dang w 2 Aug Chakdarra, gs
- 243 Sohan Singh   sl w Malakand, contusion

11th REGIMENT OF BENGAL LANCERS

Daffadar
2125 Narain Singh   dang w 2 Aug Chakdarra, bullet in head, dow

Lance-Daffadars
- 1674 Wasawa Singh   dang w 2 Aug Chakdarra, bullet stomach, dow
- 2436 Wasawa Singh   sl w Malakand, bullet head

Sowars
- 2460 Dhona Singh   sl w Malakand, bullet calf
- 2449 Kesar Singh   sev w 27 Jul Chakdarra, gs neck
- 2070 Lalah Din   sev w 2 Aug Chakdarra, bullet thigh; awarded IOM 3rd Class
- 1929 Natta Singh   k 2 Aug Chakdarra, bullet chest
- 2424 Shanka   sev w 2 Aug Chakdarra, bullet hand
- Saudagar Singh   sl w 2 Aug Chakdarra, bullet foot
- 2279 Sujan Singh   sev w 27 Jul Chakdarra, gs thigh
- 2334 Surain Singh   sev w Malakand, bullet buttock

BENGAL COMMISSARIAT - TRANSPORT DEPARTMENT

<u>Honorary Lieutenant</u>
Manley, Leonard   k 27 Jul Malakand, gs & sword cuts

24th (PUNJAB) REGIMENT OF BENGAL INFANTRY

<u>Lieutenant-Colonel</u>
Lamb, John   dang w 27 Jul Malakand, bullet right thigh

<u>Captain</u>
Holland, Harry Franc   sev w 27 Jul Malakand, bullet twice in back

<u>Lieutenant</u>
Costello, Edmond William   (attchd from 22nd Punjabis)   w 27 & 30 Jul Malakand; awarded VC

<u>Subadar-Major</u>
Yasin Khan   sl w Malakand, bullet foot; awarded IOM 3rd & 2nd Class

<u>Subadars</u>
Gopala   sl w Malakand, sword cut left shoulder
Lal Singh   sl w Malakand, bullet ear

<u>Pay Havildar</u>
2617 Harnam Singh   sev w Malakand, bullet right elbow, arm amputated, dow

<u>Lance-Havildars</u>
2427 Narain Singh   sev w Malakand, bullet shoulder, sword cut neck & thigh, dow
2698 Prem Singh   sev w Malakand, two bullets shoulder & groin

<u>Lance-Naiks</u>
2828 Rangila Singh   sl w Malakand, bullet finger
4125 Thakur Singh   sl w 2 Aug Chakdarra, splinter finger

<u>Sepoys</u>
2542 Achchar Singh   sl w Malakand, sword cut shoulder
3310 Ain Khan   sl w Malakand, splinter shoulder
3263 Ala Singh   sl w Malakand, bullet hand
2267 Attar Singh   sl w Malakand, splinter finger
3586 Basawa Singh   sev w 2 Aug Chakdarra, bullet right arm
3389 Ganga Singh   sev w Malakand, sword cut arm
3408 Guldast   sl w Malakand, splinter neck
3815 Kushal Singh   sl w 2 Aug Chakdarra, bullet foot
3674 Mand Singh   sl w Malakand, bullet neck
3655 Mauja Singh   sev w Malakand, bullet shoulder
3678 Narain Singh   sev w Malakand, bullet hand

3396 Nur Gada   sl w 2 Aug Chakdarra, bullet arm
3970 Pal Singh   sl w Malakand, bullet face
3852 Sharam Singh   sev w 2 Aug Chakdarra, bullet stomach
3283 Wazira   sl w Malakand, bullet wrist

31st (PUNJAB) REGIMENT OF BENGAL INFANTRY

Lieutenant
Ford, Henry Burroughes   dang w 28 Jul Malakand, gs

Second-Lieutenant
Swinley, George Dighton Probyn   sev w 28 Jul Malakand, gs

Subadar
Syed Ahmed Shah   sl w 27 Jul Malakand, gs; awarded IOM 3rd Class

Lance-Havildar
1700 Ahmad Khan   sev w Malakand, sword cut; awarded IOM 3rd Class

Lance-Naiks
1629A Abdul Karim   sev w Malakand, gs
1983 Fateh Khan   sev w Malakand, gs
2145 Khiwa Khan   sev w Malakand, sword cut
2581 Kishn Singh   sev w Malakand, gs
2491 Malang Singh   k Malakand, gs

Sepoys
2707 Ahmad Khan   k Malakand, sword cut
2613 Akhmad Khan   k Malakand, gs
2311 Amir Ali   sev w Malakand, sword cut
3179 Bagga Singh   dang w Malakand, gs
2425 Bashakha Singh   sev w Malakand, gs
2202 Bhana   dang w Malakand, gs & sword cut
2121 Bhikham Singh   dang w Malakand, gs
2687 Bhikham Singh   k Malakand, sword cut
1997 Bhola   k Malakand, sword cut
2582 Bishn Singh   sev w Malakand, gs
2176 Buta Khan   k Malakand, gs
2080 Chanda   k Malakand, sword cut
2818 Dewa Singh   sev w Malakand, gs
1727 Dhajja   sl w Malakand, contusion from stone
2335 Dharam Singh   dang w Malakand, gs
2382 Dhian Singh   sev w Malakand, gs
2253 Dulo   sl w Malakand, gs
1697 Farid Bakhsh   sev w Malakand, gs; awarded IOM 3rd Class
1912 Gurditta   sl w Malakand, contusion from stone
3338 Hari Singh   sl w Malakand, sword cut shoulder
2389 Ilahie Bakhsh   k Malakand, sword cut
2742 Jai Karan   sev w Malakand, gs
2747 Kala Singh   k Malakand, sword cut

2571 Lachhman   sl w Malakand, contusion from stone
2060 Malo   sl w Malakand, gs
2828 Maru   sl w Malakand, contusion from stone
2015 Mathra   sl w Malakand, contusion from stone
2795 Moda Singh   sev w Malakand, gs
2062 Nagina   dang w Malakand, gs
2505 Nand Singh   sev w Malakand, gs
2812 Narain Singh   k Malakand, gs
2422 Nihala   k Malakand, gs
1923 Palin   k Malakand, gs
2537 Phuman Singh   sev w Malakand, gs
1783 Ram Dayal   sl w Malakand, gs
2027 Ram Singh   sl w Malakand, contusion from stone
1978 Sundar   sev w Malakand, gs
2447 Sundar Singh   sev w Malakand, sword cut
2344 Umar Bakhsh   sev w Malakand, gs

35th (SIKH) REGIMENT OF BENGAL INFANTRY

Attached to 45th Sikhs

Havildar
80 Prem Singh   sev w 2 Aug Chakdarra, gs

Sepoys
1031 Baddan Singh   sev w 2 Aug Chakdarra, gs
1392 Bhola Singh   k 2 Aug Chakdarra, gs
844 Harnam Singh   k 2 Aug Chakdarra, gs
882 Harnam Singh   sev w 2 Aug Chakdarra, gs

38th (DOGRA) REGIMENT OF BENGAL INFANTRY

Sepoy
718 Shams Din   sev w Malakand, gs ankle

45th (RATTRAY'S SIKH) REGIMENT OF BENGAL INFANTRY

Major
Taylor, William Willoughby   dang w 27 Jul Malakand, gs right side, dow

Lieutenant
Rattray, Haldane Burney   sev w 2 Aug Chakdarra, gs neck

Havildars
2636 Jawala Singh   sl w Malakand, gs right foot; awarded IOM 3rd Class
2533 Kala Singh   sev w Malakand, bullet right shoulder
2807 Kishen Singh   k Chakdarra, gs
2075 Rupal Singh   sl w 2 Aug Chakdarra, sword cut hand & forehead

Naiks
2631 Chanda Singh   sev w Malakand, gs right arm & sword cut face; awarded IOM 3rd Class
2870 Sant Singh   sev w 30 Jul 1897 Chakdarra; awarded IOM 3rd Class

Lance-Naiks
2993 Gulab Singh   sl w Malakand, gs face
3029 Natha Singh   sev w Malakand, gs right thigh; awarded IOM 3rd Class

Drummer
3553 Bhola Singh   dang w Malakand, gs abdomen

Sepoys
3797 Atma Singh   sev w Chakdarra, gs back
3318 Badan Singh   sev w Chakdarra, gs right hand
3401 Baggat Singh   sev w Chakdarra, gs back
3807 Basant Singh   sev w 2 Aug Chakdarra, gs right wrist
2784 Bhagwan Singh   sev w Malakand, gs right leg
3813 Bhola Singh   k Malakand, bullet in head
3250 Bishan Singh   sl w Malakand, contusion foot
3485 Bishen Singh   dang w 2 Aug Chakdarra, gs right thigh
3659 Boor Singh   sl w 2 Aug Chakdarra, gs left forearm
2973 Chattar Singh   sev w Malakand, gs left arm
3737 Dewa Singh   sl w Chakdarra, gs head
3576 Dharm Singh   sl w Malakand, gs finger
3344 Ganaya Singh   k Chakdarra, gs
3561 Gurmakh Singh   sl w Malakand, gs face
3287 Harnam Singh   sl w Chakdarra, gs chest
3643 Harnam Singh   sev w Malakand, gs left thigh
3806 Harnam Singh   sl w Malakand, gs right hand
2489 Hernam Singh   sev w 2 Aug Chakdarra, gs shoulder
3330 Hira Singh   sl w Malakand, gs left foot
3521 Jaggat Singh   sev w Chakdarra, gs both hands
 313 Jaimal Singh   sl w Chakdarra, gs leg
2523 Jawala Singh   k Chakdarra, gs
3075 Kehar Singh   k Chakdarra, gs
3234 Kehar Singh   sev w Malakand, gs back
3337 Lal Singh   sl w Malakand, sword cut hand
3722 Mal Singh   sev w Malakand, gs back
3322 Mangal Singh   k Malakand, gs
3759 Mogh Singh   sev w 2 Aug Chakdarra, gs thigh
2294 Mool Singh   dang w 2 Aug Chakdarra, gs right thigh

3551 Nand Singh   sl w Malakand, sword cut face
3510 Narain Singh   k Malakand, bullet
3488 Nihal Singh   sev w Malakand, gs right thigh
3434 Phuman Singh   sl w Malakand, gs left leg
3353 Prem Singh   sl w Malakand, contusion chest
2716 Ranga Singh   sev w Malakand, gs leg & thigh
3698 Shibba Singh   k Malakand, bullet
3561 Sowan Singh   sev w Chakdarra, gs right arm
3501 Sundar Singh   sev w Malakand, bullet right thigh
3595 Sundar Singh   sev w twice Malakand, bullets right thigh & left knee joint
3605 Uttam Singh   sl w Malakand, gs forehead
3515 Warriam Singh   sl w Malakand, sword cut face
3791 Warriam Singh   sev w Malakand, bullet right shoulder

CORPS OF GUIDES CAVALRY, PUNJAB FRONTIER FORCE

Captain
Baldwin, Guy Melfort DSO   sev w 1 Aug Malakand, sabre cut head

Lieutenant
MacLean, Hector Lachlan Stewart   sev w 28 Jul Malakand, gs face

Ressaidar
Tirath Ram   sl w Malakand, knife cut hand; awarded IOM 3rd Class

Sowars
1471 Abdul Hanam   sev w Malakand, gs thigh
1201 Ali Raza   sl w Malakand, gs back
1543 Bela Singh   sev w Malakand, gs thigh
1300 Dhanna Singh   dang w Malakand, gs chest
1523 Gulab Khan   sl w Malakand, gs abdominal wall
1292 Gurdit Singh   sl w Malakand, sword cut leg
1178 Hawas   dang w Malakand, gs head
1298 Hosein Shah   sl w Malakand, gs thigh
1125 Ishar Singh   k Malakand, gs
1171 Jagal Singh   sev w Malakand, gs thigh
1397 Kala Singh   dang w Malakand, gs abdomen
1486 Mahboob Shah   sl w Malakand, gs abdomen
1503 Mir Beg   sl w Malakand, gs graze chest
1420 Shadi Khan   dang w Malakand, gs buttock & groin, dow

CORPS OF GUIDES INFANTRY, PUNJAB FRONTIER FORCE

Second-Lieutenant
Keyes, Charles Valentine   sl w 1 Aug Malakand, contusion back

Subadar-Major
Sarfaraz Khan   sev w 2 Aug Chakdarra, sword cut thigh; awarded IOM 3rd Class

Jemadar
Khazan Singh   sl w Malakand, by stones

Havildar
2212 Daswanda Singh   sl w Malakand, by stones
2736 Senu   sev w Malakand, bullet knee

Lance-Naik
3757 Sher Mahommed   k 2 Aug Chakdarra, gs

Sepoys
3980 Ahmad Shah   sl w Malakand, bullet arm
2814 Akhmad   sl w Malakand, bullet contusion leg
3650 Bagga Singh   sl w Malakand, bullet thigh
4152 Bahu Singh   sev w 2 Aug Chakdarra, gs thigh
4141 Basant Singh   sl w 2 Aug Chakdarra, gs calf
3770 Bela Singh   sev w Malakand, sword cut left hand, spear chest & right arm
3421 Dharam Singh   k Malakand, gs
4046 Gopal Singh   sev w Malakand, bullet neck
3601 Hamid Gul   sl w 2 Aug Chakdarra, bayonet chest
3823 Hazara Singh   sl w 2 Aug Chakdarra, gs thigh
3686 Kaka Singh   k Malakand, gs
3774 Karm Singh   sev w Malakand, bullet right chest
3489 Kesar Singh   sev w Malakand, bullet right shoulder
4072 Mahommed Hassan   sev w 2 Aug Chakdarra, bullet foot
3927 Mir Mahomed   sev w Malakand, bullet left shoulder & neck
4066 Nekibulla   k 2 Aug Chakdarra, gs
2764 Ram Singh   sl w Malakand, by stone
3907 Sirdara Singh   sev w Malakand, bullet neck & shoulder
3946 Sohbat   sl w Malakand, bullet arm
3830 Sultan Shah   sl w 2 Aug Chakdarra, gs foot
3934 Sundar Singh   sl w Malakand, bullet elbow
3321 Warriam Singh   sev w Malakand, bullet left arm

No 5 CO, MADRAS SAPPERS & MINERS

Lieutenant
Watling, Francis Wyatt RE   sev w 27 Jul Malakand, sword cut leg

Sergeant
2300 Byrne, F.   RE   k Malakand, sword cuts

Jemadar
Chinna Sami   sev w Malakand, gs thigh

Naiks
1450 Azhagari   dang w Malakand, gs chest; awarded IOM 3rd Class
1616 Venkatosami   sl w Malakand, sword cut chin

Lance-Naiks
1698 Gorindaraju   sev w Malakand, spear leg
1849 Virasami   sev w Malakand, stone on forehead

Sappers
1086 Arulappan   sl w Malakand, leg
1334 Durgan   k Malakand, gs
1467 Durgan   sl w Malakand, spear thigh
 575 Madurai   sl w Malakand, contusion back
1386 Madurai   dang w Malakand, fractured femur
1324 Maduranayagam Perumal   sev w Malakand, stone contusion back
1972 Munisami   dang w Malakand, gs chest
1114 Narasinga Perumal   sev w Malakand, sword cut back
1638 Ponna Sami   k Malakand, gs
2115 Ponusami   sl w Malakand, stone on forehead
1424 Raman   sl w Malakand, stone contusion chest
 815 Ramosami   sl w Malakand, stone on head
1680 Ramosami   sev w Malakand, sword cut arm & shoulder
1474 Tulukkanam   sl w Malakand, stone contusion chest
1330 Verabhadran   sl w Malakand, stone contusion chest
1671 Virasami   sev w Malakand, gs heel

SAMANA 1897

From Maj-Gen A G Yeatman-Biggs, CB, commanding the Kohat Field Force, dated Fort Lockhart 21 September 1897

I have the honour to report, for the information of His Excellency the Commander-in-Chief, that news was received by me from reliable sources at Hangu on the 8th instant, to the effect that the Afridis had decided to come and assist the Orakzais in attacks on Hangu and on the Samana posts on Friday, the 10th instant.

Having on the same day received reports that the necessary amount of transport and supplies for putting thirty days' supplies into the Samana posts had been collected, I gave orders to start that night with a column, strength as per margin. The ammunition supply had, ten days previously, been sent up by me to the Samana, making up the total number of rounds to four hundred per rifle, 36th Sikhs.

4 guns, 9th Field Battery, R. A.   ⎫ To Pat Dar-
2 squadrons, 3rd Bengal Cavalry. ⎬ band only.
1 squadron, 3rd Punjab Cavalry. ⎭
4 companies, Royal Irish Regt., 300.
1-2nd Gurkhas, 500.
1-3rd Gurkhas, 500.
2nd Punjab Infantry, 500.
Half company, No. 4 Co., Bombay S. and M.
Sect. No. 8 British Field Hospital.
Sect. No. 42 Native Field Hospital.

Concentrating at Pat Darband at 1-30 A.M. on the 9th instant, the 1-2nd Gurkhas moved up the road as advanced guard, and occupied the plateau on which Dhar is situated, before daylight. At 4 A.M. the remainder of the column started. No enemy were reported in sight, and the road was found too bad for guns. So I sent the cavalry and artillery back to Hangu, and the convoy proceeded up the road, arriving at Fort Lockhart about mid-day.

On the 10th I sent the half company of the Bombay Sappers and Miners to improve the defences of Gulistan.

Hearing that the whole of the Afridi *lashkar* had arrived at Karappa during the night, I sent a few scouts of the 1-3rd Gurkhas down the spurs towards the Khanki valley, to ascertain if the information was correct, as Karappa cannot be seen from the Samana plateau. These scouts were supported by the 1-3rd Gurkhas and two companies of the 2nd Battalion of the Royal Irish Regiment.

About 10 A.M. large numbers of the enemy could be seen marching down the Khanki valley. I at once recalled the troops by heliograph. Just before receiving the order to retire the 1-3rd Gurkhas fired a few long range volleys into a party of the enemy, and three were seen to drop. At 1 P.M. Major Bewicke-Copley reported to me from Crag Picquet that 22 standards and about 10,000 men had passed down the valley.

It seemed probable that the tribesmen intended to carry out their threat of attacking Hangu, or perhaps Shahu Khel, a small post guarding the Khanki valley, about four miles north-west of the point where it is crossed by the Kohat-Hangu road.

This post had been reinforced by me with one company of the Royal Irish and 61 rifles of the 15th Sikhs, under command of Major Forster, Royal Irish Regiment.

I ordered the 2nd Punjab Infantry to seize Gogra Hill, supported by the 1-2nd Gurkhas.

The Commandant of the Border Militia Police, Mr. D. Donald, informed me that a large number of the enemy were making for the Darband Kotal, and the officer commanding the 1-2nd Gurkhas reported to me (7 P.M.) that seven standards and a considerable number were retracing their steps up the valley.

A convoy with two days' supplies had been ordered out from Hangu to meet me at the Pat Darband Kotal, where I found them when I advanced with the remainder of the column. The supplies had been sent up on 51 camels, as no mules were available.

The advanced guard and main column halted for the night at 9 P.M., on the hill marked in the accompanying sketch. A few shots were fired at the rear guard from Gogra Hill, and the whole of the *sarwans*, except one, bolted, and the camels, being left without drivers and without nose-strings, stampeded. The rear guard, consisting of a wing of the 1-3rd Gurkhas, under Lieutenant-Colonel Pulley, and two companies of the 1-2nd Gurkhas, under Captain Robinson, withstood several determined attacks, and did their utmost to save the convoy. At midnight I sent out two companies of the 2nd Punjab Infantry, under Lieutenant Elsmie, accompanied by Captain Scudamore, Deputy Assistant Quarter Master-General, to assist in bringing the camels in. All but two were found to have thrown their loads, so it was useless, and by 2 A.M. the rear guard had taken up the position assigned to them in the bivouac. The enemy consisted of Sheikhans, Mishtis, Mallakhels and Alikhels, and they admit to their losses being over 100 killed and wounded. A leading *malik* of the Sheikhans was wounded, and five leading Mallakhels killed.

When morning broke (12th), I sent out Colonel Lawrence, Royal Irish Regiment, with two companies of his battalion and five companies of each of the remaining corps, to endeavour to recover the camels and stores, but only thirteen camels were recovered, and of these only two had loads. The Royal Irish fired long-range volleys to keep the tribesmen at a respectful distance. On the return of Colonel Lawrence's reconnaissance, I set the column once more in motion towards Lakka, as being the best position from which both Hangu and Shahu Khel could be protected. I arrived there at 1 P.M., but finding no water, and having lost our food, I issued orders to commence the march to Hangu at 3 P.M. At 3-30 P.M. I received a message by helio. from Fort Lockhart that Saragarhi was hard pressed, and at 4-30 P.M. it was helioed that Saragarhi had fallen, and that Gulistan was hard pressed.

The troops after their hard day without food or water had earned a rest, but about 3.30 P. M., on the 13th, a letter was brought me from Major Des Vœux, 36th Sikhs, commanding at Gulistan, urgently asking for help. I immediately despatched two guns of the 9th Field Battery, and the 3rd Bengal Cavalry with their signallers to gallop along the road at the foot of the hills as far towards Gulistan as they could go, and sent a wire to Doaba to despatch two more guns of the 9th Field Battery and the squadron of the 3rd Punjab Cavalry to join in the demonstration.

The guns from Hangu were accompanied by Mr. D. Donald, who knows the country well, and he was able to show them a position from which they could fire a few rounds to encourage the garrison, and Major Middleton, commanding the 3rd Bengal Cavalry, sent through by helio., just before sunset, a message to assure the garrison that they would be relieved by mid-day on the 14th.

The four guns of the Derajat Mountain Battery had reached Hangu the previous day, having marched 35 miles in under thirteen hours, so they were added to our column, and we set out at midnight for Lakka.

At 4 A.M., on the 14th instant, I arrived at Lakka, and sent on two companies of the 1-3rd Gurkhas to occupy the hill on which we had bivouacked on the night of the 11th.

At 5 A.M. we marched for Gulistan. On arrival opposite Tsalai (7 A.M.) the advanced guard of the 1-3rd Gurkhas was assailed with a heavy fire. I brought up the guns and shelled the enemy's marksmen out of Tsalai tower at a range of 900 yards, and at once ordered the 1-3rd Gurkhas to attack the enemy's position on Gogra, the 1-2nd Gurkhas following in support. Gogra Hill was quickly taken, under cover of the fire of the guns, and one company of the Royal Irish fired long-range volleys at the Orakzais retreating down the Sarmela spur. The strength of the enemy was estimated at about 4,000.

The 2nd Punjab Infantry pressed on, followed by the guns, and the Gurkhas held the position until they had passed through.

As we neared Sangar the garrison of that post displayed a white standard which they had captured from the enemy. Sangar and Dhar had been attacked all night, but a sortie had been made from the first-named as soon as our guns opened fire, and Lieutenant-Colonel Haughton, commanding the 36th Sikhs, had joined the party with 12 men of the Royal Irish and 35 Sikhs, and had poured long-range volleys into the foe as they retreated down the Sarmela.

At 10 A.M. I reached Fort Lockhart and reconnoitred the enemy's position from a bastion of the fort, and found about 8,000 to 10,000 Afridis holding a strong position, which was skilfully occupied with lines of *sangars* on Saragarhi ridge.

I ordered up the guns, and by 10-30 A.M. they were playing on the enemy's position with shrapnel, whilst the 36th Sikhs from Fort Lockhart advanced to turn the Afridi right, and the 2nd Punjab Infantry made a frontal attack on their position, supported by the two Gurkha battalions as they arrived on the ground. The Afridis did not wait for the infantry, but fled from their position and made for the Khanki valley. I pressed on with all possible speed, as I did not know whether Gulistan was holding out or not. On reaching the high ground overlooking Gulistan, I found that the fort was invested by about 6,000 Orakzais, but they did not wait for the attack of the 2nd Punjab Infantry and 36th Sikhs, which was made under an accurate fire of the guns of the mountain battery, and by 1 P.M. they were in full retreat down the Khandartang spur, and Gulistan was relieved, after having been hard pressed by some 7,000 to 8,000 Afridis and Orakzais since the 12th instant.

1st Btn ROYAL SCOTS FUSILIERS

Captain
Smith, Arthut George Baird   sev w 27 Aug 1897 Ublan Pass, gs right leg

Lieutenant
North, Louis Aylmer   sev w 27 Aug 1897 Ublan Pass, gs thorax

Private
4196 Crain, Philip   missing 27 Aug 1897 Ublan Pass

36th (SIKH) REGIMENT OF BENGAL INFANTRY

The widows of the men killed were awarded the pension of the Indian Order of Merit 3rd Class.

Lieutenant
Blair, Arthur Kennedy   dang w 27 Aug 1897 Samana, gs left side chest, penetrating lung

Jemadar
Jawala Singh   sl w 13 Sep 1897 Samana, bullet splash left hand & left side neck

Havildars
 52 Bishen Singh   sl w 27 Aug 1897 Samana, bullet graze nose
165 Ishar Singh   k 12 Sep 1897 Saragarhi
 63 Kala Singh   dang w 13/14 Sep 1897 Gulistan, bullet right side & abdomen, dow 15 Sep; awarded IOM 3rd Class
755 Sundar Singh   dang w 13/14 Sep 1897 Gulistan, bullet pelvis & scrotum; awarded IOM 3rd Class

Naiks
332 Lal Singh   k 12 Sep 1897 Saragarhi
353 Ran Singh   sl w 12 Sep 1897 Samana, bullet left thumb

Lance-Naiks
546 Chanda Singh   k 12 Sep 1897 Saragarhi
874 Jamit Singh   sl w 13/14 Sep 1897 Gulistan, bullet face & neck
807 Sadda Singh   sev w 13/14 Sep 1897 Gulistan, bullet right thigh

Sepoys
1369 Badan Singh   sl w 13/14 Sep 1897 Gulistan, bullet right upper arm; awarded IOM 3rd Class
 907 Bassawa Singh   dang w 13 Sep 1897 Gulistan, right knee joint, dow 14 Sep; awarded IOM 3rd Class
 904 Bela Singh   sl w 13/14 Sep 1897 Gulistan, bullet left wrist & hand

1257	Bhagwan Singh	k 12 Sep 1897 Saragarhi
1265	Bhagwan Singh	k 12 Sep 1897 Saragarhi
1588	Bhagwan Singh	sev w 13/14 Sep 1897 Gulistan, bullet right forearm; awarded IOM 3rd Class
791	Bhola Singh	k 12 Sep 1897 Saragarhi
1606	Bhoop Singh	sev w 13/14 Sep 1897 Gulistan, bullet right ear & nose
715	Bishn Singh	sl w 13/14 Sep 1897 Gulistan, bullet left side chest
1140	Boor Singh	sl w 13/14 Sep 1897 Gulistan, bullet left forearm
875	Budha Singh	sl w 13/14 Sep 1897 Gulistan, bullet right hand & forearm
1374	Buta Singh	sev w 12 Sep 1897 Samana, bullet left fingers
1556	Buta Singh	k 12 Sep 1897 Saragarhi
1735	Dalel Singh	dang w 13 Sep 1897 Gulistan, bullet right side abdomen, dow 14 Sep
216	Dalip Singh	sl w 13/14 Sep 1897 Gulistan, bullet right hand
687	Daya Singh	k 12 Sep 1897 Saragarhi
1146	Ghula Singh	dang w 13/14 Sep 1897 Gulistan, bullet right side face; awarded IOM 3rd Class
693	Gurditt Singh	dang w 13/14 Sep 1897 Gulistan, bullet right shoulder & left side chest
1690	Gurditt Singh	sl w 13 Sep 1897 Samana, bullet left side face
814	Gurmukh Singh	k 12 Sep 1897 Saragarhi
1201	Gurmukh Singh	sl w 13/14 Sep 1897 Gulistan, bullet forehead; awarded IOM 3rd Class
1733	Gurmukh Singh	k 12 Sep 1897 Saragarhi
927	Harnam Singh	sl w 3 Sep 1897 Samana, bullet middle forehead
1573	Harnam Singh	dang w 13/14 Sep 1897 Gulistan, bullet pelvis & right thigh
1589	Harnam Singh	sl w 13/14 Sep 1897 Gulistan, bullet forehead; awarded IOM 3rd Class
359	Hira Singh	k 12 Sep 1897 Saragarhi
1183	Hira Singh	sev w 13/14 Sep 1897 Gulistan, bullet right thigh; awarded IOM 3rd Class
1716	Indar Singh	sl w 13/14 Sep 1897 Gulistan, bullet left side face & neck
760	Jiwan Singh	k 12 Sep 1897 Saragarhi
871	Jiwan Singh	k 12 Sep 1897 Saragarhi
1623	Jiwan Singh	sl w 13/14 Sep 1897 Gulistan, bullet right upper arm
1651	Jiwan Singh	k 12 Sep 1897 Saragarhi
812	Jwala Singh	sl w 13/14 Sep 1897 Gulistan, bullet left hand
1123	Kala Singh	sl w 13/14 Sep 1897 Gulistan, bullet right side face; awarded IOM 3rd Class
1153	Kishn Singh	sl w 13/14 Sep 1897 Gulistan, bullet right hand & neck
1225	Kishn Singh	dang w 4 Sep 1897 Samana, bullets right shin & right side abdomen, dow 5 Sep
1686	Lal Singh	sl w 13/14 Sep 1897 Gulistan, bullet right side face
1221	Nand Singh	k 12 Sep 1897 Saragarhi

```
 834 Narayan Singh    k 12 Sep 1897 Saragarhi
1586 Narayan Singh    sl w 13/14 Sep 1897 Gulistan, bullet left
                        side chest
1539 Natha Singh      sl w 13/14 Sep 1897 Gulistan, bullet forehead;
                        awarded IOM 3rd Class
 163 Ram Singh        k 12 Sep 1897 Saragarhi
 287 Ram Singh        k 12 Sep 1897 Saragarhi
 180 Rur Singh        sl w 13 Sep 1897 Samana, bullet face & neck
 182 Sahib Singh      k 12 Sep 1897 Saragarhi
1066 Sawan Singh      sev w 13/14 Sep 1897 Gulistan, bullet right
                        upper arm; awarded IOM 3rd Class
1375 Sham Singh       sev w 3 Sep 1897 Samana, bullet middle right
                        upper arm
1288 Sobha Singh      sl w 3 Sep 1897 Samana, bullet middle right
                        shin; awarded IOM 3rd Class
1321 Sundar Singh     k 12 Sep 1897 Saragarhi
1741 Thaman Singh     dang w 13/14 Sep 1897 Gulistan, bullet pelvis
                        & hip joint; awarded IOM 3rd Class
 492 Uttam Singh      k 12 Sep 1897 Saragarhi
1577 Uttam Singh      dang w 12 Sep 1897 Samana, bullet nose
1590 Uttam Singh      sl w 13/14 Sep 1897 Gulistan, bullet face &
                        neck
2040 Uttam Singh      sl w 13/14 Sep 1897 Gulistan, bullet left hand
                        & face
1216 Wariam Singh     sl w 13/14 Sep 1897 Gulistan, bullet left cheek
1380 Wariam Singh     sl w 3 Sep 1897 Samana, bullet hand; dang w 13
                        Sep 1897 Gulistan, bullet right jaws, dow 14
                        Sep; awarded IOM 3rd Class
```

1st Btn 2nd GURKHA (RIFLE) REGIMENT (SIRMOOR RIFLES)

<u>Captain</u>
Robinson, John Graham   sl w 11/12 Sep 1897 Gogra, gs

<u>Naiks</u>
```
1462 Balbir Burathoki    dang w 11/12 Sep 1897 Gogra, gs left
                           knee joint
1369 Rajman Gurung       sl w 11/12 Sep 1897 Gogra, gs left arm
```

<u>Riflemen</u>
```
1979 Dattu Sonar         sl w 11/12 Sep 1897 Gogra, gs left thigh
2504 Deobir Gurung       sl w 11/12 Sep 1897 Gogra, gs left arm
1614 Gangea Thapa        k 11/12 Sep 1897 Gogra, gs
 817 Kishenbahadar Sahai k 11/12 Sep 1897 Gogra, gs
2926 Ranbahadar Thapa    k 11/12 Sep 1897 Gogra, gs
2523 Surbir Rana         sl w 11/12 Sep 1897 Gogra, gs scalp
```

1st Btn 3rd GURKHA (RIFLE) REGIMENT

Naik
1450 Moti Gurung   k 14 Sep 1897 Gogra, Snider bullet abdomen

Riflemen
2424 Bhajir Gurung   sev w 14 Sep 1897 Gogra, bullet lower left knee
1805 Dhana Gurung   sev w 14 Sep 1897 Gogra, Snider bullet left calf
1646 Kehir Singh   sev w 11/12 Sep 1897 Gogra, bullet through lower jaw
1664 Motilal Kan   sl w 11/12 Sep 1897 Gogra, bullet right ear lobe
2072 Narpati Rana   k 11/12 Sep 1897 Gogra, bullet through chest nr heart
2321 Singjit Gurung   sl w 11/12 Sep 1897 Gogra, bullet inner left foot nr heel

2nd REGIMENT OF PUNJAB INFANTRY, PUNJAB FRONTIER FORCE

Subadar
Akbar Khan   sev w 27 Aug 1897 Ublan Pass, gs arm; awarded IOM 3rd Class

Jemadar
Attru   sl w 27 Aug 1897 Ublan Pass, gs abrasion

Naiks
4049 Mewa Singh   sl w 27 Aug 1897 Ublan Pass, gs contusion
4327 Saif Ali   sev w 27 Aug 1897 Ublan Pass, gs hand

Lance-Naiks
336 Nyaz Ali   dang w 27 Aug 1897 Ublan Pass, gs base of skull, dow same day

Sepoys
330 Achchar Singh   dang w 27 Aug 1897 Ublan Pass, gs abdomen
115 Farman Ali   sl w 27 Aug 1897 Ublan Pass, gs graze neck
64 Harnam Singh   dang w 14 Sep 1897 Gulistan, gs shoulder blade
142 Karm Singh   k 27 Aug 1897 Ublan Pass, gs centre forehead
71 Khan Zaman   k 11/12 Sep 1897 Darband Kotal, gs abdomen
4505 Nawais Ali   k 11/12 Sep 1897 Darband Kotal, gs abdomen
49 Partab Singh   sev w 27 Aug 1897 Ublan Pass, gs buttock
4839 Shakir Singh   sev w 27 Aug 1897 Ublan Pass, gs arm

TIRAH 1897-98

From Gen Sir W S A Lockhart, KCB, KCSI, Commanding Tirah Expeditionary Force, dated camp Rawalpindi 26 January 1898

2. As previously reported, on October 31st, I entered Afridi Tirah and encamped in Maidan with the 2nd Division and the 2nd Brigade of the 1st Division, the 1st Brigade being left in Mastura to dominate that valley and to hold the Sampagha Pass. At this time the troops at my disposal in Maidan numbered 9,700, and in Mastura 2,330.

3. On November 1st, I directed a reconnaissance to be made to Bagh with the object of visiting the mosque which was notorious as the spot where the Afridi rising originated, and as the focus of political intrigue and fanaticism. The force employed consisted of No. 8 Mountain Battery, Royal Artillery, the 2nd Battalion, King's Own Scottish Borderers, and the 1st Battalion, 3rd Gurkhas, under the command of Lieutenant-Colonel H. G. Dixon, C.B. Some opposition was met with, Captain T. G. Maclaren, King's Own Scottish Borderers, and three men of the 3rd Gurkhas being wounded, and one man of the 3rd Gurkhas being killed. The mosque was found to be an open wooden shed situated at the confluence of the streams which drain the Maidan valley. No documents were discovered either in the mosque, or in the houses in its vicinity.

On November 1st and 2nd, the Zakka Khels on either flank of the northern slope of the Arhanga Pass attacked convoys proceeding to camp in Maidan, and succeeded in capturing 60 transport animals, with 13 boxes of Lee-Metford ammunition, and a number of kits belonging to the 1st Battalion, Royal West Surrey Regiment, and the 15th Sikhs.

On November 3rd, the 3rd Brigade under Brigadier-General Kempster reconnoitred up to Tseri Kandao, whence the upper part of the Waran valley was seen and sketched. The troops were followed up by the enemy with a loss of five native soldiers wounded.

On November 8th, a picquet of the 2nd Battalion, 1st Gurkhas, guarding the southern slopes of the Arhanga Pass, surprised an ambush of the enemy lying in wait to attack convoys near the village of Unai, and inflicted heavy loss on them.

On November 9th, I made a reconnaissance in force to the crest of the Saran Sar, 5 miles east of camp. The force, under the command of Brigadier-General Westmacott, consisted of—

      No. 8 Mountain Battery, Royal Artillery.
      No. 5 Bombay Mountain Battery.
      1st Battalion, Dorsetshire Regiment.
      1st Battalion, Northamptonshire Regiment.
      15th Sikhs.
      36th Sikhs.
      No. 4 Company, Madras Sappers and Miners.

During the advance but few of the enemy showed themselves, but in the retirement, which began at 2 P.M., the Northamptonshire Regiment forming the rear-guard was closely pressed. Its movement from the crest into the valley, which was much delayed by the steepness of the descent and by the number of wounded men who had to be carried by their comrades, was covered by the guns, the flanks being held by the two Sikh regiments. Eventually a portion of the Northamptonshire Regiment became entangled in a deep ravine, where they were fired into at close quarters by the tribesmen. The 36th Sikhs were sent back to extricate them, but evening was coming on, and before assistance could be rendered a party consisting of an officer and 12 men was cut off and shot down. Had the battalion kept to the high ground where its flanks were protected by the two Sikh regiments, its loss would probably have been small; but unfortunately a route was chosen which offered every tactical advantage to the enemy, the result being that some of our troops became isolated, and were then attacked by overwhelming numbers. Our casualties were 2 British officers and 17 British soldiers killed; and 3 British officers, 35 British soldiers, 1 Native officer, and 6 Native soldiers wounded.

On November 11th, I again visited the Saran Sar with the force noted in the margin, under the command of Brigadier-General Gaselee. The object of the second reconnaissance was to complete the survey of the eastern section of the Maidan valley, to destroy the defences of the remaining Zakka Khel villages which there had been no time to deal with on the 9th, and to collect forage. This having been successfully accomplished, the force returned to camp. Heavy loss was inflicted on the enemy, who as usual pressed closely on the rear guard. Owing, however, to Brigadier-General Gaselee's skilful dispositions and the effective fire of the mountain guns, our losses were slight, comprising one British soldier killed, and one British officer and one Native soldier wounded.

Gurkha Scouts.
No. 1 Mountain Battery, Royal Artillery.
No. 2 Derajat Mountain Battery.
1st Battalion, Royal West Surrey Regiment.
2nd Battalion, Yorkshire Regiment.
2nd Battalion, 4th Gurkhas.
3rd Sikhs.

On November 13th, the 3rd Brigade under Brigadier-General Kempster, strengthened by No. 8 Mountain Battery, Royal Artillery, No. 5 Bombay Mountain Battery, No. 4 Company, Madras Sappers and Miners, No. 4 Company, Bombay Sappers and Miners, and the 36th Sikhs, proceeded at daybreak over the Tseri Kandao into the Waran Valley, the object being to reconnoitre and survey the valley, destroy the defences of the Zya-ud-din sub-section of the Zakka Khels, and provide the brigade with forage which was becoming scarce in the vicinity of Camp Maidan. The march was unopposed, and the troops camped three miles east of the crest of the Tseri Kandao.

On November 14th and 15th, the defences of a number of Zakka Khel villages in Waran were demolished, and the house of the notorious Mullah Saiad Akbar was levelled to the ground.

On November 16th, Brigadier-General Kempster's force returned to camp Maidan. Before the rear-guard reached the Tseri Kandao several casualties occurred, and after crossing the crest of the pass and suffering more loss, it was greatly delayed by the number of wounded to be carried. The tribesmen, Zakka Khels and Aka Khels, followed close on our troops and had to be driven back at the point of the bayonet. Encumbered by their wounded and their ammunition running short, the 15th Sikhs were unable to retire from a height which they were holding on the northern flank of the main body, and the 36th Sikhs, with two companies of the 1st Battalion, Dorsetshire Regiment, had to be sent back to their assistance. Being thus reinforced our troops attacked and drove off the tribesmen, inflicting heavy loss, which is reported on reliable authority to have amounted to at least 300 killed and wounded. Lieutenant-Colonel Haughton, 36th Sikhs, withdrew the force at his disposal, under cover of darkness, to some villages where he remained until the next morning, being attacked at intervals throughout the night. Unfortunately a party of the Dorsetshire Regiment lost their way in the dark, and were overwhelmed and killed by the enemy. Our casualties were 4 officers killed and 3 wounded. Of other ranks 26 were killed and 42 wounded. At daybreak on November 17th, Lieutenant-Colonel Haughton withdrew his force to camp Maidan without opposition, meeting on his way three battalions and one mountain battery which I had sent out under Brigadier-General Gaselee to cover his retirement.

The three days from November 18th to November 20th, were occupied in shifting the camp of the force to Bagh. The 2nd Brigade moved on the 18th, the 4th Brigade with my head-quarters on the 19th, and the 3rd Brigade on the 20th. The enemy attacked both the old and the new camp while the movement was going on, but were repulsed without difficulty, although I regret to say that as many as 24 casualties were reported.

On November 20th, the 15th Sikhs, whose strength had been gravely diminished by hard work, fighting and exposure, first in the Kurram valley and afterwards in Tirah, were ordered back to Shinaori, their place in the 3rd Brigade being subsequently filled by the 2nd Punjab Infantry from Karappa.

On November 22nd, I marched to Dwatoi with the force noted in the margin, which was under the command of Brigadier-General Westmacott. The high hills commanding the defile through which the troops moved were held by the 2nd Battalion, Yorkshire Regiment, and the 1st Battalion, 2nd Gurkhas, the positions thus taken up being occupied until the return of the force to Bagh on the 24th. The road through the defile was an exceedingly difficult one, the path in places being along the face of precipitous cliffs of slippery limestone, and the icy water of the stream, which averaged two feet in depth, having to be repeatedly forded. The march was opposed throughout the day, and as the ground was generally unsuitable for the employment of artillery, the successive positions taken up by the enemy's sharpshooters had to be carried by the advance guard. In consequence of this and the badness of the road, the movement through the defile was slow, and the rear-guard did not reach camp at Dwatoi until 11-30 A.M. on the 23rd. The night of the 22nd, which was passed by the troops at Dwatoi without blankets or great-coats, was an exceptionally cold one. On the 23rd, the defences of the Kuki Khel villages in the lower part of the Rajgal valley were destroyed, a portion of the valley was surveyed, and the road through the defile improved. On the 24th, the force returned to Bagh, leaving Dwatoi before daybreak. The enemy closely followed the rear-guard, and endeavoured at a difficult point in the defile to break in on the baggage. The tribesmen were, however, driven back at the point of the bayonet by the 36th Sikhs, who killed and wounded a large number of them. The rear-guard reached camp at Bagh at 5 P.M. Our loss during the three days amounted to 3 men killed, and 1 British officer and 31 men wounded.

No. 5 Bombay Mountain Battery.
2nd Battalion, King's Own Scottish Borderers.
2nd Battalion, Yorkshire Regiment.
36th Sikhs.
1st Battalion, 2nd Gurkhas.
1st Battalion, 3rd Gurkhas.
28th Bombay Pioneers.
Gurkha Scouts.
No. 4 Company, Madras Sappers and Miners.
No. 3   ,,   Bombay Sappers and Miners.

On November 24th, the head-quarters and four companies of the 1st Battalion, Royal Scots Fusiliers, joined the Main Column at Bagh, having been ordered up as a reinforcement from Kohat.

On November 25th, a reconnaissance was made by the 1st Brigade under Brigadier-General Hart from his camp in Mastura to the crest of the Torsmats Pass, 8,000 feet above sea-level.

On November 26th, the period granted to the Mamuzai and Massozai sections of the Orakzais, and to the Khani Khel Chamkannis, for compliance with the terms prescribed by the Government of India had expired, and I accordingly arranged to move a force against them from Bagh, to act in co-operation with the Kurram Moveable Column which I directed to march from Sadr through the Khurmana defile and meet me on November 29th at Hissar in the Massozai country. The force from Bagh under Brigadier-General Gaselee's command moved on November 26th and 27th, I myself leaving on the latter date. It consisted of the following troops:—

- No. 1 Kohat Mountain Battery.
- No. 2 Derajat „ „
- 1st Battalion, Royal West Surrey Regiment.
- 2nd „ Yorkshire Regiment.
- Wing of 1st Battalion, Royal Scots Fusiliers.
- 2nd Battalion, 4th Gurkhas.
- 3rd Sikhs.
- Gurkha Scouts.
- Nos. 3 and 4 Companies, Bombay Sappers and Miners.

On the 27th, the Kahu or Durbi Khel Pass into the Massozai country was seized, and on the 28th all the troops and baggage had crossed, the force concentrating the following day at Dargai.

On the 30th, I moved to Hissar, taking with me the troops noted in the margin under Brigadier-General Gaselee. The remainder of the force from Bagh remained in camp at Dargai under the command of Lieutenant-Colonel J. H. Spurgin, 1st Battalion, Royal Scots Fusiliers, who was directed to improve the road leading to Khanki Bazar, which I had arranged to visit on my return march for the purpose of coercing the Mamuzais and replenishing my supplies from the advanced depôt at Karappa.

Margin:
No. 1 Kohat Mountain Battery.
1st Battalion, Royal West Surrey Regiment.
2nd Battalion, 4th Gurkhas.
3rd Sikhs.
Gurkha Scouts.

On December 1st, a force under Colonel Hill consisting of—

- No. 1 Kohat Mountain Battery,
- 12th Bengal Infantry,
- 2nd Battalion, 4th Gurkhas,
- 200 men of the 1st Battalion, 5th Gurkhas,
- The Gurkha Scouts,
- 200 dismounted men, 6th Bengal Cavalry,
- 200 dismounted men, Central India Horse—

left Camp Hissar at an early hour to take punitive action against the Khani Khel Chamkannis. As the Chamkanni villages at Thabi are situated on the eastern slope of a deep valley surrounded by precipitous hills, it was no easy matter to dislodge the tribesmen who were holding the heights in force. This was eventually accomplished with some loss to our troops,* and heavy loss to the enemy from rifle and artillery fire; and a portion of the Chamkanni villages were destroyed. But before the work could be completed, it was time for the force to withdraw to camp, which it did without much opposition, the Massozais who had collected along the Makhmanghar crest to the north of the road observing the proceedings, but holding aloof.

* Killed—
  1 British officer.
  6 Native soldiers.
Wounded—
  2 British officers.
  1 Native officer.
  14 Native soldiers.
Total . 24

On December 2nd, the operations were resumed, and the remainder of the Thabi villages were destroyed in the face of obstinate resistance, the heights to the west of the villages having to be stormed at the point of the bayonet by the Gurkha Scouts under Captain F. G. Lucas. The enemy again suffered heavy loss, leaving 30 dead on the ground in addition to the large number of killed and wounded carried away. It has since been reported that several of their principal Maliks were among the killed. Our casualties were few.†

† Killed—
  2 Native soldiers.
Wounded—
  1 British officer.
  2 Native soldiers.
Total . 5

On December 1st and 2nd, Brigadier-General Gaselee with a small force visited the Gar Massozai villages in the Lozaka Toi, and, as the terms imposed by the Government of India had not been complied with by this section of the Orakzais, the village defences were destroyed. No opposition was met with.

On December 3rd, Colonel Hill returned with his column to Sadr, taking with him the sick and wounded of the force which had accompanied me from Bagh, and transferring to the wing of the Royal Scots Fusiliers the Maxim gun detachment of that regiment which had hitherto been attached to the Kurram Moveable Column.

The same day Brigadier-General Gaselee's force moved in two columns towards Khanki Bazar, which it reached on December 4th, and where it met a convoy of supplies from Karappa, escorted by a half squadron 18th Bengal Lancers, the 30th Punjab Infantry, the 2nd Punjab Infantry, No. 1 Company, Bengal Sappers and Miners, and the Kashmir Mountain Battery, under the command of Lieutenant-Colonel F. C. Maisey.

On December 5th, I proceeded with Brigadier-General Gaselee's force to the Chingakh Pass (7,700 feet in elevation), which I crossed the same day, reaching the camp at Bagh on the 6th. No opposition was met with while passing through the Mamuzai country, but on re-entering Afridi Tirah shots were exchanged with the Kambar Khels to the north of the pass.

4. Here I may mention that on November 7th, Colonel Hill made a reconnaissance in force from Sadr through the Khurmana defile to Hissar, in order to explore the ground through which his column would move in the event of operations being subsequently undertaken against the Chamkannis.

On the return of the column to Sadr on the afternoon of the same day, the enemy, who meanwhile had collected in considerable numbers, followed up the rear guard, but, being driven back with heavy loss by the 5th Gurkhas, discontinued their attack, and the last five miles were traversed without a shot being fired. Our casualties, so far as known at the time, consisted of 2 native soldiers killed and 4 wounded, but the next day the Officer Commanding the

Kapurthala Imperial Service Infantry reported that one native officer and 35 men of his regiment were missing. It appears that a picquet of the above strength had been directed to occupy a hill on the flank of the column, and when recalled by signal, which was duly acknowledged, it moved off to join the rear guard. Taking what the native officer must have believed to be a short cut, the men became entangled in difficult ground, and found their further progress blocked by a jungle fire which had been lighted early in the day. They turned back to regain the road by which they had ascended the hill, but the enemy had discovered their predicament, and assembling in strength succeeded in shooting down the whole party. Owing to the nature of the ground and the smoke of the burning grass, this unfortunate occurrence took place unseen and unheard by the rear guard; and as all were reported present to Colonel Hill, he knew nothing of what had happened until the following day.

On December 7th, I marched to Dwatoi with the 4th Brigade, the Gurkha Scouts, the divisional troops of the 2nd Division, except No. 9 Mountain Battery, Royal Artillery, which was attached to the 3rd Brigade, the divisional staff of the 2nd Division, and a portion of the army staff of the force.

The march was unopposed until we neared Dwatoi, where the advance guard was fired on from the heights to the north of the Rajgal stream; but the road had been cut away in several places by the tribesmen, and the water in the defile had risen nine inches, so that considerable delay occurred in the passage of the transport animals and field hospitals.

On December 8th, the 3rd Brigade followed the 4th Brigade to Dwatoi, but rain fell during the day and again damaged the road which had been repaired; and the stream continuing to rise, the rear guard did not reach camp until the morning of the 9th. On this day, I moved five miles up the Rajgal Valley with a mixed force of 1,000 rifles and No. 8 Mountain Battery, Royal Artillery, under Brigadier-General Westmacott's command, and destroyed a large number of village defences, besides collecting forage for the division. But slight opposition was encountered both going and returning, and there were only three casualties. The survey of the valley was completed, so far as the heavy mist and the time at my disposal would allow. On the 10th, the march was resumed, the 4th Brigade leading and encamping at Sandana, the 3rd Brigade following and encamping three miles in rear. The opposition met with during this day's march was slight, the Kamar and Sipah Khels, through whose country we were passing, being apparently disinclined to molest the movement of the force, in the hope that their village defences would be spared.

The march on December 11th was through Zakka Khel territory, and I anticipated that the enemy would oppose us every inch of the way. Accordingly, on the evening of the 9th, I ordered the two brigades to be closed up the next morning, the 4th Brigade forming a strong advance guard and the 3rd Brigade a strong rear guard, under whose protection the field hospitals, transport animals, and followers could move along in safety and under proper control. Rain fell during the night of the 10th and throughout the 11th. On the latter date the 4th Brigade marched to Sher Khel, a distance of ten miles, followed by the 3rd Brigade, which, though it started an hour and-a-half earlier, was unable to close up with the 4th Brigade as early as I had intended, owing to difficulty being experienced in leaving the camping ground. During the day the troops were harassed by a few sharpshooters armed with Lee-Metford rifles, but our casualties up to dusk were trifling. As evening came on, the number of the tribesmen rapidly increased, and the rear guard became heavily engaged. Eventually, being encumbered with a considerable number of killed and wounded, running short of ammunition, and finding that the enemy were endeavouring to intercept the baggage animals which had lagged behind, a portion of the rear guard under the command of Major G. T. F. Downman, 1st Battalion, Gordon Highlanders, occupied for the night some villages about two-and-a-half miles west of Sher Khel, the remainder of the 3rd Brigade camping with the 4th Brigade.

The following morning I sent two battalions and a mountain battery under Brigadier-General Kempster to extricate the rear guard, which had been attacked during the night and at daybreak. This was accomplished without further loss by 11 A.M., and I halted on December 12th at Sher Khel in order to give the troops a day's rest, and an opportunity of drying their clothes after the continuous rain of the previous thirty-six hours.

On December 13th the march was resumed. The 3rd Brigade, which hitherto had formed the rear guard, was in front, and leaving the Bara River at Gali Khel moved over the hills to the north, and encamped in the vicinity of Shinkamar, the 4th Brigade following and halting for the night two-and-a-half miles in rear. During this day's march the 4th Brigade was continuously attacked and at times severely pressed by the enemy, who towards the evening advanced boldly to close quarters in the open. Although our own loss was considerable, Brigadier-General Westmacott's able handling of his troops enabled him to inflict much heavier loss on the enemy, who, however, continued to fire into camp and attack the picquets at intervals throughout the night. On this date Brigadier-General Hammond, Commanding the Peshawar Column, reconnoitred from Swaikot towards Shinkamar, and meeting the advanced guard of the 3rd Brigade handed over 8 doolies with 300 kahars, which he had brought with him at my request to assist in carrying the sick and wounded of the 2nd Division into the next camp.

On December 14th the 2nd Division marched to Mamanai, three-quarters of a mile from the camp of the Peshawar column at Swaikot. The 4th Brigade again covered the rear of the division, and Brigadier-General Westmacott again succeeded in severely punishing the tribesmen who followed him up as on the previous day.

7. During the march from Bagh through Dwatoi down the Bara valley the troops of the 2nd Division were almost unceasingly engaged with the several sections of the Afridis, through whose country they passed, and towards the end of the march they were followed up by a large gathering representing every section. The flanking, picquet, and rear guard duties in the presence of such an active and enterprising enemy were exceedingly onerous, while the line of march was along the bed of a river, the water of which was of icy coldness and had to be repeatedly forded. The followers and kahars suffered most from the cold, and to assist the latter wounded men had to be frequently carried by their own comrades.

The 1st Division while moving from Mastura to Bara Fort met with slight opposition, but the march was an arduous one and in all respects was carried out in accordance with my wishes.

8. On December 15th and 16th, the Peshawar Column under Brigadier-General Hammond, left Swaikot for Jamrud, which was reached on the

17th. There it was joined on the 19th by the troops of the 1st Division, together with the Gurkha Scouts and the head-quarter wing of the 1st Battalion, Royal Scots Fusiliers.

The Peshawar Column and the 1st Division, Main Column, were halted at Jamrud from December 19th to 22nd, the troops which had returned from Tirah needing rest after their fatiguing march. At this time three British corps in the Main Column, which had been much weakened by losses in action or by sickness, were relieved by battalions from India, the 1st Battalion, Devonshire Regiment, being replaced by the 2nd Battalion, Royal Sussex Regiment, from Peshawar, the 1st Battalion, Dorsetshire Regiment, by the 1st Battalion, Duke of Cornwall's Light Infantry, from Rawal Pindi, and the 1st Battalion, Northamptonshire Regiment, by the 2nd Battalion, King's Own Yorkshire Light Infantry, also from Rawal Pindi. Shortly afterwards the same reason obliged me to dispense with the services of the head-quarter wing of the 1st Battalion, Royal Scots Fusiliers.

9. The plan of the operations now about to be undertaken comprised measures for re-opening the road through the Khyber Pass, for reconstructing the Khyber posts which had been destroyed by the Afridis in August last, including the defensible serai at Landi Kotal, for restoring the Landi Kotal water supply, and for destroying the defences of the Zakka Khel villages in the Khyber.

The Bazar valley had also to be visited in force, and the defences and towers of the principal Zakka Khel and Malikdin Khel villages destroyed.

On December 23rd, the Peshawar Column advanced unopposed to Ali Masjid and re-occupied the posts at that place and at Fort Maude, two guns of No. 3 Mountain Battery, Royal Artillery, and the 45th Sikhs being detailed as the garrison for Ali Masjid, and Fort Maude being held by a detachment of the Khyber Rifles.

On December 24th, the 1st Division, covered by the Peshawar Column, marched to Lala China, three-quarters of a mile below Ali Masjid. During the day I joined the 1st Division from Jamrud, escorted by two squadrons of the 4th Dragoon Guards, and accompanied by Lieutenant-General Sir Henry Havelock-Allan, V.C., G.C.B., M.P., who remained my guest while I was in the Bazar valley. A few shots were fired at night into camp, one British soldier being wounded.

On December 25th, the 1st Division advanced into the Bazar valley, its right being covered by the Peshawar Column which held the Aspoghar heights. I marched with the left column, consisting of the 2nd Brigade, No. 1 Mountain Battery, Royal Artillery, No. 2 Derajat Mountain Battery, No. 3 Company, Bombay Sappers and Miners, and the Gurkha Scouts, under the command of Brigadier-General Gaselee, and reached Chora unopposed. The road was comparatively easy, and but little labour was needed to render it passable by laden transport animals. The right column, which consisted of the 1st Brigade, No. 1 Kohat Mountain Battery, No. 1 Company, Bengal Sappers and Miners, and the 21st Madras Pioneers, under Brigadier-General Hart's command, was accompanied by Major-General Symons and the staff of the 1st Division. The road being bad, only a portion of the column reached Karamna, the remainder halting for the night at Alachi. Very slight opposition was met with. During the afternoon Major-General Symons reconnoitred the Bori Kandao from Karamna, and found the road extremely difficult.

On December 26th, the left column marched eleven miles from Chora to China, the principal Zakka Khel village in the Bazar valley, where it encamped. The tribesmen, though not in any considerable strength, molested our advance, the casualties for the day being one British and one Native soldier killed, and two British and two Native soldiers wounded.

On the same date the right column occupied Burg. The road between Karamna and Burg was found to be so bad that the 1st Brigade could not reach Bararkas, as had been at first intended. During the march to Burj opposition was met with, our casualties being one British soldier killed, and three British and two native soldiers wounded.

On December 27th, after destroying the defences and towers of China, I returned with the left column to Chora. The rear guard was followed up by the enemy who were repulsed with heavy loss to themselves, the notorious Mullah Idris being among the killed. Our casualties were one British soldier killed, and four British and two Native soldiers wounded. During this day's march I met Major-General Symons near the Palosi caves, and directed him to move the next day with the 1st Brigade to Karamna, and the day after to Lala China, destroying *en route* the defences of such villages as had not been dealt with during his advance.

Rain fell during the night of the 27th. On the 28th, after destroying the defences of Chora, I marched with the left column to Lala China, no opposition being met with, and returned thence to Jamrud under an escort of two squadrons, 4th Dragoon Guards. On the 29th and 30th the 1st Division concentrated at Jamrud. The right column was followed up by the enemy during its march from Burg to Lala China and suffered some loss, while inflicting much heavier loss on the enemy. The total casualties in the 1st Division during the operations in the Bazar valley were 1 British officer, 6 British soldiers, and 4 Native soldiers killed; and 1 British officer, 30 British soldiers, and 17 Native soldiers wounded.

10. Lieutenant-General Sir Henry Havelock-Allan left me at Lala China, and with my permission proceeded to Landi Kotal, arrangements being made to provide him with a sufficient escort. I deeply regret to report that on December 30th, as he was returning to Jamrud, he unfortunately left his escort near Ali Masjid, and riding down a ravine was shot dead by the enemy. Every precaution had been taken to ensure his safety, and on bidding him good-bye at Lala China I had impressed on him the necessity of invariably remaining with the troops detailed for his protection.

11. From December 30th up to the present date there is but little to record. The Peshawar Column met at first with considerable opposition in the Khyber, convoys and foraging parties being repeatedly fired on and followed up by the tribesmen, and the telegraph line interrupted daily between Ali Masjid and Landi Kotal. In view of the hostile attitude of the Zakka Khels in the Khyber, and the casualties resulting therefrom, I decided on January 3rd to strengthen the force occupying the pass by ordering the 1st Brigade from Jamrud to Ali Masjid, and by reinforcing the Landi Kotal garrison with the 45th Sikhs and 2nd Battalion, 4th Gurkhas. On these movements being carried out the tribesmen dispersed, but they have since resumed their guerilla warfare, though in smaller numbers than before.

STAFF

Maharaj Dhiraj Sir Pratap Singh, GCSI   w 29 Nov 1897 Lozaka Pass
extra ADC to Gen Lockhart

Captain
Badcock, Francis Frederick, DSO   Field Intelligence Officer, 2nd
    Division (1/5th Gurkhas)   sev w 25 Oct 1897 Karappa, gs,
    left arm amputated

Lieutenants
Crocker, George Delamain   Orderly Officer to Brig-Gen Kempster
    (2/Royal Munster Fus)   sl w 25 Oct 1897 Karappa, contusion
    left shoulder
Hammond, Harry Durham   Orderly Officer to Brig-Gen Hammond (RA)
    dang w 1 Jan 1898 Khyber Pass, gs spine, dow 8 Feb

COMMISSARIAT-TRANSPORT DEPARTMENT

Captains
Margesson, Evelyn William   (1/Norfolk Regt)   sev w 26 Mar 1898
                Mamanai-Barkai road, gs right arm
Watson, Edward Yerbury (Madras Staff Corps)   k 8 Nov 1897
                Maidan, gs head

Lieutenant
Williams, Weir de Lancey   (1/Hampshire Regt)   sev w 11 Dec 1897
                Bagh to Barkai march, gs leg

No 8 MOUNTAIN BATTERY, ROYAL ARTILLERY

Sergeant
38264 Williams, Henry John   sev w 7 Nov 1897 Maidan, gs chest

Corporal
61134 Wood, William Henry   sev w 29 Oct 1897 Samphaga Pass, gs
                right leg

Gunners
91295 Hammond, William   sev w 29 Oct 1897 Samphaga Pass, gs left
                leg
76938 McAuliffe, Aeneas   dang w 31 Jan 1898 Shinkamar, gs head,
                since dow
12541 Roberts, Joseph   sev w 31 Jan 1898 Shinkamar, gs right thigh

Drivers
333 Bahawal Khan   sev w 29 Oct 1897 Sampagha Pass, gs left leg
 37 Binda   sev w 16 Nov 1897 Waran (Tseri Kandao), gs left thigh
484 Kabut Khan   sev w 29 Oct 1897 Sampagha Pass, gs right leg
407 Mal Singh   sev w 13 Dec 1897 Bagh to Barkai march, gs foot
462 Wazira   k 31 Oct 1897 Arhanga Pass, gs axillary artery

No 9 MOUNTAIN BATTERY, ROYAL ARTILLERY

Driver
324 Ghulam Muhammad   dang w 12 Nov 1897 Maidan, gs hip & abdomen

No 5 Co, BENGAL SAPPERS & MINERS

Major
Bond, Francis George   RE   sl w 1 Jan 1898 Khyber Pass, by a stone
                    from a mine

Naik
3369 Wazir Singh   accidentally k 1 Jan 1898 Landi Kotal, by a
                    dynamite explosion

Sapper
4301 Dhan Singh   accidentally k 1 Jan 1898 Landi Kotal, by a
                    dynamite explosion

1st Btn ROYAL WEST SURREY REGIMENT

Major
Hanford-Flood, Robert Thomas   sl w 29 Oct 1897 Samphaga Pass, gs
                    left shoulder

Second-Lieutenant
Wright, Wallace Duffield   sev w 11 Nov 1897 Saran Sar, gs right arm

Lance-Corporal
3798 Roberts, Charles   sev w 27 Dec 1897 Khyber Pass, gs left leg

Drummer
4333 Ogden, William   sl w 27 Dec 1897 Khyber Pass, gs right shoulder

Privates
3320 Batchelor, Thomas   sev w 14 Dec 1897 Sappri Pass, gs left
                thigh
4468 Bateman, Frank   sev w 29 Oct 1897 Sampagha Pass, gs right leg
3353 Benning, Harry   sev w 27 Dec 1897 Khyber Pass, gs right chest
4697 Bushell, Christopher   k 26 Oct 1897 Karappa, gs skull
4118 Cobley, Edward   sev w 1 Nov 1897 Maidan, gs right thigh
3132 Eames, James   k 1 Nov 1897 Maidan, gs abdomen
3025 Edser, Charles   k 1 Nov 1897 Maidan, gs chest, sword cuts
                & skull fracture
4916 French, Charles   k 27 Dec 1897 Khyber Pass, gs back
2867 Gard, John   sev w 29 Oct 1897 Sampagha Pass, gs back
3559 Gray, Arthur   k 26 Nov 1897 west of Lozaka, gs abdomen
3240 Grover, Henry   k 29 Oct 1897 Sampagha Pass, gs skull
4562 Guntrip, Henry   sev w 1 Nov 1897 Maidan, gs left thigh
4445 Hartley, James   sev w 1 Nov 1897 Maidan, gs left hip
4064 Hooker, Arthur   sl w 29 Oct 1897 Sampagha Pass, gs left
                forearm
4679 Morritt, Frederick Henry   k 11 Nov 1897 Saran Sar, gs chest
3424 Page, Albert   sev w 1 Nov 1897 Maidan, gs scalp, left hand &
                arm
3766 Parsons, Hubert   sev w 29 Oct 1897 Sampagha Pass, gs right
                buttock
4034 Pope, James   sev w 18 Nov 1897 Bagh, gs left elbow
4580 Toomey, Edward   sev w 29 Oct 1897 Sampagha Pass, gs right hand
4603 Weedon, Arthur   sev w 18 Nov 1897 Bagh, gs fracture jaw
4030 White, George   sev w 29 Oct 1897 Sampagha Pass, gs left leg
4566 Williams, William   k 1 Nov 1897 Maidan, gs chest
4476 Worsley, Frederick   sev w 29 Oct 1897 Sampagha Pass, gs chest

1st Btn DEVONSHIRE REGIMENT

Sergeant
 829 Webb, William   sl w 29 Oct 1897 Sampagha Pass, gs right leg

Lance-Corporal
4403 Blackmore, John Thomas   sev w 25 Oct 1897 Karappa, gs left foot

Drummer
3077 Morgan, Frank   sev w 29 Oct 1897 Sampagha Pass, gs right arm

Privates
4041 Acland, William   sev w 13 Nov 1897 Mastura, gs right arm
 453 Butler, Alfred   sev w 25 Oct 1897 Karappa, gs thigh
3431 Cartwright, George   sl w 25 Oct 1897 Karappa, gs arm
3019 Chilcot, George   sl w 25 Oct 1897 Karappa, gs left thigh
4174 Collins, Walter Joseph   sl w 13 Nov 1897 Mastura, gs left thigh
4061 Hine, John   sev w 29 Oct 1897 Sampagha Pass, gs left shoulder
3710 Labram, John   dang w 25 Oct 1897 Karappa, gs thigh, fractured
2733 Norgate, Frederick   sl w 28 Oct 1897 Gandakai, gs left arm

```
3816 Norton, George    sl w 28 Oct 1897 Gandakai, gs hand
4118 Reed, Thomas      sev w 28 Oct 1897 Gandakai, gs back
3294 Shutts, Frederick    sl w 29 Oct 1897 Sampagha Pass, gs face
```

2nd Btn YORKSHIRE REGIMENT

Lieutenants
```
Caffin, Ernest Gregorie    sev w 1 Nov 1897 Maidan, gs right chest
Jones, David Edward Osborne    k 22 Nov 1897 Dwatoi, gs heart
Williams, Berkeley Cole Wilmot    sev w 29 Nov 1897 Lozaka Pass, gs
    left leg
```

Second-Lieutenant
```
Watson, Oliver Cyril Spencer    dang w 22 Nov 1897 Dwatoi, gs abdomen
```

Colour-Sergeant
```
4083 Wyatt, Benjamin    sev w 18 Nov 1897 Bagh, gs arm
```

Sergeants
```
1306 Calvert, William    sev w 27 Nov 1897 Lozaka Pass, gs groin
2443 Bromwich, Thomas    dang w 28 Oct 1897 Gandakai, gs chest,
    dow 29 Oct
2218 Harnby, John H.    sev w 16 Nov 1897 Maidan, gs right leg
3581 House, William    k 18 Nov 1897 Bagh, gs heart
3549 Richardson, Bedell    sev w 29 Nov 1897 Lozaka Pass, gs right
    foot
 168 Roche, Edward    dang w 26 Dec 1897 China,Bazar Valley, gs thigh
```

Lance-Corporals
```
4396 Brunton, Frank Arthur Willie    sev w 22 Nov 1897 Dwatoi, gs both
    buttocks; awarded DCM
4388 King, William    sev w 29 Nov 1897 Lozaka Pass, gs left leg
```

Privates
```
3134 Alton, Charles    sev w 15 Nov 1897 Maidan, gs chest
3761 Carling, John    dang w 27 Dec 1897 Khyber Pass, gs neck, dow
3255 Connell, William    sev w 29 Nov 1897 Lozaka Pass, gs left leg
3634 Cullum, George    sev w 29 Oct 1897 Sampagha Pass, gs leg
3950 Donovan, Edward    sev w 19 Nov 1897 between Maidan camp & Bagh,
    gs left thigh
3346 Elliot, John    sev w 19 Nov 1897 between Maidan camp & Bagh, gs
    lower extremity
1210 Feeney, Patrick    dang w 26 Dec 1897 China,Bazar Valley, gs skull
3523 Ferguson, Charles    sev w 25 Oct 1897 Karappa, gs tibia
4699 Hine, Alfred Thomas    k 26 Dec 1897 China,Bazar Valley, gs back
3919 Johnson, Frederick    sev w 18 Nov 1897 Bagh, gs chest
3040 Kent, William    sev w 29 Oct 1897 Sampagha Pass, gs left leg
3888 Kirk, Robert    sev w 16 Nov 1897 Maidan, gs right leg
4024 Mathews, Charles    k 27 Nov 1897 west of Lozaka, gs chest
3241 Mulroy, John    dang w 25 Oct 1897 Karappa, gs neck
4205 O'Brien, James    sev w 29 Nov 1897 Lozaka Pass, gs left shoulder
```

3746 Pawson, Henry   sev w 18 Nov 1897 Bagh, gs left arm
3710 Phillips, Edward   dang w 25 Oct 1897 Karappa, gs right thigh,
         compound fracture
4381 Poole, Arthur   sev w 18 Nov 1897 Bagh, gs ball of great toe
4728 Reardon, David   sev w 17 Nov 1897 Maidan, gs left leg, both
         bones broken
4709 Rex, Samuel Robert   sl w 29 Oct 1897 Sampagha Pass, gs left leg
3289 Scarborough, Henry   sl w 29 Oct 1897 Sampagha Pass, gs right
         thumb
4543 Simpson, David   sl w 29 Nov 1897 Lozaka Pass, gs left hand
4236 Smithson, Henry   k 18 Nov 1897 Bagh, gs head
3743 Tobin, John   sev w 25 Oct 1897 Karappa, gs right calf muscles
4185 Turner, James   sev w 29 Nov 1897 Lozaka Pass, gs right arm
3169 Watson, William   dang w 25 Oct 1897 Karappa, gs right thigh,
         compound fracture
3682 Wheatley, George   sev w 25 Oct 1897 Karappa, gs right leg
3504 Williams, Henry   sl w 28 Nov 1897 Lozaka Pass, gs right thigh
4141 Wright, John   sev w 18 Nov 1897 Bagh, gs left arm

1st Btn ROYAL SCOTS FUSILIERS

Captain
Shortt, Francis de Sausmarez   dang w 13 Dec 1897 Bagh to Barkai
         march, gs chest

Corporal
4301 Howard, Frederick   dang w 13 Dec 1897 Bagh to Barkai march,
         three sword cuts

Lance-Corporal
3890 McMurray, Joseph   k 13 Dec 1897 Bagh to Barkai march

Privates
3092 Ball, Michael   sl w 14 Dec 1897 Bagh to Barkai march, gs thigh
4871 Bryson, Robert   dang w 29 Nov 1897 Lozaka Pass, gs left arm
3768 Campbell, William   k 13 Dec 1897 Bagh to Barkai march
4337 Davis, Amos   sl w 13 Dec 1897 Bagh to Barkai march, gs head
3286 Drummond, Archibald   k 12 Dec 1897 Bagh to Barkai march, gs neck
1512 Fairbairn, George   k 13 Dec 1897 Bagh to Barkai march
3884 Greig, George   dang w 10 Dec 1897 Bagh to Barkai march, gs head,
         dow
4907 Gunning, James   dang w 11 Dec 1897 Bagh to Barkai march, gs
         groin
3940 Irvine, Robert   dang w 11 Dec 1897 Bagh to Barkai march, gs
         chest, dow
4433 King, David   sl w 11 Dec 1897 Bagh to Barkai march, gs face
3489 McFadin, Thomas   k 11 Dec 1897 Bagh to Barkai march
4164 McNulty, James   dang w 28 Nov 1897 Lozaka Pass, gs abdomen
3464 Mansell, John   sev w 12 Dec 1897 Bagh to Barkai march, gs face
4516 Phillips, William   sl w 29 Nov 1897 Lozaka Pass, gs left thigh

```
4595 Pooles, James      k 13 Dec 1897 Bagh to Barkai march
3562 Taylor, James      dang w 29 Nov 1897 Lozaka Pass, gs head
3283 Thompson, James    k 29 Nov 1897 Lozaka Pass, gs abdomen
4439 Vevers, Andrew     sl w 30 Dec 1897 Jamrud, gs face
```

2nd Btn KING'S OWN SCOTTISH BORDERERS

Captains
MacLaren, Thomas George   sl w 1 Nov 1897 Maidan, spent bullet
Sladen, David Ramsay   sl w 18 Oct 1897 Chagru Kotal, gs splinter face

Second-Lieutenant
Keys, Terence Humphrey   sl w 18 Oct 1897 Chagru Kotal, spent bullet chest

Colour-Sergeant
1350 Cross, Thompson   sev w 13 Dec 1897 Bagh to Barkai march, gs right leg; awarded DCM

Sergeants
2747 Jackman, Harry   sl w 18 Oct 1897 Dargai, gs right hand
1761 Martin, William   sl w 13 Dec 1897 Bagh to Barkai march, gs left arm

Lance-Corporals
5343 Hinchcliffe, George   sev w 7 Dec 1897 Bagh to Barkai march, gs foot
3744 Meikle, Adam   sev w 22 Nov 1897 Dwatoi, gs right thigh
4151 Reynolds, Thomas   sev w 25 Oct 1897 Karappa, gs back

Privates
5129 Barney, Andrew   sev w 25 Oct 1897 Karappa, gs leg
4683 Barton, Andrew   sl w 25 Oct 1897 Karappa, gs thigh
3673 Boocock, George   sev w 8 Nov 1897 Maidan, gs left leg
3599 Borthwick, Robert   k 18 Oct 1897 Dargai
4546 Cairney, Patrick   dang w 22 Nov 1897 Dwatoi, gs knee
4348 Cockburn, James   sl w 13 Dec 1897 Bagh to Barkai march, gs right thigh
5170 Daubenay, Rich rd   dang w 13 Dec 1897 Bagh to Barkai march, gs chest
3725 Dunn, John   sev w 13 Dec 1897 Bagh to Barkai march, gs left thigh
4148 Forsyth, George   sev w 13 Dec 1897 Bagh to Barkai march, gs face, wrist & thigh
3911 Gartie, William   sl w 12 Nov 1897 Maidan, gs left thigh
3697 Gibb, Alexander   sl w 29 Oct 1897 Sampagha Pass, gs cheek
3877 Gowans, Stewart   dang w 22 Nov 1897 Dwatoi, gs foot
3537 Haywood, William   dang w 22 Nov 1897 Dwatoi, gs abdomen
4873 Hull, Tom   sl w 18 Oct 1897 Dargai, gs right hand
5377 Johnson, James   sev w 13 Dec 1897 Bagh to Barkai march, gs right thigh
4506 Kenny, Thomas   dang w 21 Nov 1897 Bagh, gs right arm

```
4190 Knowles, William    k 21 Nov 1897 Bagh, gs body
5118 Lennox, George      k 23 Nov 1897 Dwatoi, gs abdomen
5000 McLauglin, Patrick   sl w 13 Dec 1897 Bagh to Barkai march, gs
                            left elbow
4289 McLeod, Robert      dang w 23 Nov 1897 Dwatoi, gs chest
4510 McRae, Charles      k 13 Dec 1897 Bagh to Barkai march, gs spine
5073 Marshall, John      sl w 24 Nov 1897 Dwatoi, gs body
3336 Menzies, Robert Kerr   sl w 18 Oct 1897 Dargai, gs left thumb
4055 Miller, Isaac       sev w 13 Dec 1897 Bagh to Barkai march, gs
                            right leg
5289 Morris, William     sev w 12 Nov 1897 Maidan, gs left leg
5312 Purcell, George     sev w 21 Nov 1897 Bagh, gs right leg
4410 Ross, James         sev w 13 Dec 1897 Bagh to Barkai march, gs
                            right thigh
5244 Russell, John       k 13 Dec 1897 Bagh to Barkai march, gs head
5057 Ryan, Robert        dang w 13 Dec 1897 Bagh to Barkai march, gs
                            left th gh
1650 Stewart, John       dang w 19 Nov 1897 Bagh, gs abdomen, dow
3017 Trenham, Richard    sl w 24 Nov 1897 Dwatoi, gs leg
5611 Waits, Thomas       k 7 Dec 1897 Bagh to Barkai march, gs head
3254 Welland, William    sl w 14 Dec 1897 Bagh to Barkai march, gs
                            thigh
5350 Wilson, Samuel      sev w 13 Dec 1897 Bagh to Barkai march, gs chest
3841 Young, William      k 7 Dec 1897 Bagh to Barkai march, gs head
```

2nd Btn ROYAL INNISKILLING FUSILIERS

<u>Sergeant</u>
3896 Smith, Thomas   sev w 1 Jan 1898 Khyber Pass, gs left leg

<u>Lance-Corporal</u>
4224 Patrick, James   dang w 7 Dec 1897 nr Swaikot, Bara Valley,
                         sword cuts head

<u>Private</u>
4521 Logan, John   k 7 Dec 1897 nr Swaikot, Bara Valley, gs head

1st Btn DUKE OF CORNWALL'S LIGHT INFANTRY

<u>Second-Lieutenant</u>
De la Condamine, Harry John   sev w 11 Mar 1898 Barkai, gs left
                                 patella; sl w right knee & nose

<u>Private</u>
3520 Curtis, Francis John   sl w 11 Mar 1898 Barkai, gs splinter
                               left knee

2nd Btn ROYAL SUSSEX REGIMENT

Lieutenant
Julius, Stanley de Vere Alexander   sl w 27 Dec 1897 Barg, gs knee

Colour-Sergeant
1669 Fisk, George   k 27 Dec 1897 Barg, gs abdomen

Lance-Corporals
4418 Gold, William   sev w 25 Dec 1897 Khyber Pass, gs both buttocks
4352 Lydiard, Arthur   k 27 Dec 1897 Barg, gs heart

Privates
3746 Budd, Oliver   sev w 27 Dec 1897 Barg, gs left arm, dow
3863 Croft, Charles   k 27 Dec 1897 Barg, gs heart
4386 Harman, William   sl w 27 Dec 1897 Barg, gs left foot
4444 King, James   sev w 27 Dec 1897 Barg, gs abdomen
4084 Knee, Walter   sev w 27 Dec 1897 Barg, gs right shoulder
4591 Maudling, Thomas (Frederick?)   sl w 27 Dec 1897 Barg, gs
    thigh; awarded DCM
4759 Miles, James   k 15 Jan 1898 Ali Masjid, gs head
5011 Newbury, William   sev w 8 Feb 1898 Ali Masjid, gs shoulder
4443 Tree, Robert   sev w 28 Dec 1897 Barg, gs right buttock

1st Btn DORSETSHIRE REGIMENT

Captain
Arnold, William Reginald   dang w 20 Oct 1897 Chagru Kotal, gs right
    groin & both legs

Lieutenants
Crooke, George Douglas (attchd from Suffolk Regt)   k 16 Nov 1897
    Waran
Fowke, Francis   dang w 10 Dec 1897 Bagh to Barkai march, gs thigh
Hales, Reginald Evelyn Atherstone (attchd from East Yorks Regt)
    k 16 Nov 1897 Waran
Ingham, Oliver Philip Stanhope   sev w 9 Nov 1897 Saran Sar, gs
    right thigh
Mercer, Archibald Ariel   sev w 9 Nov 1897 Saran Sar, gs left hand

Sergeants
1135 Bennett, Henry   k 16 Nov 1897 Waran (Tseri Kandao), gs
 763 Carver, Joseph   sev w 20 Oct 1897 Dargai, gs buttock
1745 Dalton, Alfred   dang w 10 Dec 1897 Bagh to Barkai march, gs
    abdomen
2706 Ellis, Harry   dang w 20 Oct 1897 Dargai, gs right leg, neck
    & shoulder
2417 Hodgkinson, William   sev w 20 Oct 1897 Dargai, gs hand
1240 Morgan, Frank   sev w 16 Nov 1897 Waran (Tseri Kandao), contusions
1395 White, William Thomas   sev w 9 Nov 1897 Saran Sar, gs right thigh

Lance-Sergeants
1802 Andrews, Thomas   sev w 20 Oct 1897 Dargai, gs back
1233 Ford, John William   k 20 Oct 1897 Dargai
3276 Mallord, Albert   sev w 20 Oct 1897 Dargai, gs left leg
2191 Troke, Frederick   sev w 20 Oct 1897 Dargai, gs left arm

Corporals
3761 Baker, Frederick   k 20 Oct 1897 Dargai
4010 Green, Charles Edwin   dang w 20 Oct 1897 Dargai, gs right knee
3350 Griffin, George Edward   sev w 20 Oct 1897 Dargai, gs ankle
3237 Lester, Philip   sev w 20 Oct 1897 Dargai, gs left elbow
3745 Southwell, Frank   k 20 Oct 1897 Dargai
2987 Woodhouse, William   sev w 20 Oct 1897 Dargai, gs leg

Lance-Corporals
3404 Bowditch, George   dang w 7 Nov 1897 Maidan, gs buttock
4062 Doggett, Albert   dang w 20 Oct 1897 Dargai, gs groin
4003 Fitch, Christian   sl w 20 Oct 1897 Dargai, gs right foot
2009 Gard, Caleb   sev w 20 Oct 1897 Dargai, gs right leg
3130 Ryall, William   k 16 Nov 1897 Waran (Tseri Kandao), gs
3962 Spooner, Frederick   dang w 20 Oct 1897 Dargai, gs back & shoulder
3357 Wakely, Henry   sev w 20 Oct 1897 Dargai, gs left leg
3577 Woods, William   sev w 20 Oct 1897 Dargai, gs right foot

Drummer
2449 Cook, Alfred   dang w 20 Oct 1897 Dargai, gs ankle & thigh

Privates
3816 Andrews, Albert   sev w 20 Oct 1897 Dargai, gs right leg
3397 Antell, Harry   sev w 20 Oct 1897 Dargai, gs right wrist
1701 Anthony, George   sev w 20 Oct 1897 Dargai, gs right arm; awarded DCM
3481 Baker, Charles   sl w 20 Oct 1897 Dargai, gs right ear
3547 Bennett, George   k 7 Nov 1897 Maidan, gs
4061 Betts, George   sev w 20 Oct 1897 Dargai, gs left ankle
4060 Borland, George   k 20 Oct 1897 Dargai
4605 Chant, John   dang w 20 Oct 1897 Dargai, gs right thigh
3634 Croghan, William Henry   k 16 Nov 1897 Waran (Tseri Kandao), gs
3274 Curtis, Walter   sev w 20 Oct 1897 Dargai, gs elbow
3812 Dempsey, James   sev w 16 Nov 1897 Waran (Tseri Kandao), gs left arm
4511 Desert, George   sev w 7 Nov 1897 Maidan, gs arm
3326 Domoney, William   sl w 7 Nov 1897 Maidan, gs thigh
4267 Drake, Frederick   k 16 Nov 1897 Waran (Tseri Kandao), gs
4452 Drury, Walter   dang w 7 Nov 1897 Maidan, gs abdomen, dow
3267 Elford, Herbert William   k 16 Nov 1897 Waran (Tseri Kandao), gs
4440 Foulkes, Alfred   sev w 20 Oct 1897 Dargai, gs right arm
4045 Green, Charles   sev w 9 Nov 1897 Saran Sar, gs thigh
2969 Gregory, Walter   dang w 9 Nov 1897 Saran Sar, gs chest, dow
4271 Guy, Charles   dang w 9 Nov 1897 Saran Sar, gs genitals
4072 Hartop, George   dang w 20 Oct 1897 Dargai, gs shoulder
3336 Hewlett, Frederick   dang w 7 Nov 1897 Maidan, gs right buttock
4301 Jones, Alfred   dang w 20 Oct 1897 Dargai, gs left thigh
3849 Jones, Frederick   sev w 20 Oct 1897 Dargai, gs jaw & back

```
3673 Jones, George     dang w 20 Oct 1897 Dargai, gs groin
3846 Kellaway, Charles   sev w 20 Oct 1897 Dargai, gs ankle
3517 Keohane, Timothy    sev w 9 Nov 1897 Saran Sar, gs left arm
3204 Kerley, Frederick   sev w 7 Nov 1897 Maidan, gs thigh
4046 Kirby, Levi    k 20 Oct 1897 Dargai
4600 McCarthy, William Henry    k 16 Nov 1897 Waran (Tseri Kandao), gs
4589 Macey, Harry    k 16 Nov 1897 Waran (Tseri Kandao), gs
4156 Merrick, Frederick    k 20 Oct 1897 Dargai
3772 Miles, Frederick    k 16 Nov 1897 Waran (Tseri Kandao), gs
3750 Miller, Samuel    sev w 16 Nov 1897 Waran (Tseri Kandao), gs
          right forearm
4443 Millie, George    k 16 Nov 1897 Waran (Tseri Kandao), gs
3804 Moores, Isaiah    dang w 20 Oct 1897 Dargai, gs right ankle &
          left arm
4044 Nicholls, Henry    k 20 Oct 1897 Dargai
3824 Nicholson, Thomas    sev w 16 Nov 1897 Waran (Tseri Kandao),
          contusion head
2345 Pope, Charles    sev w 16 Nov 1897 Waran (Tseri Kandao), gs hand
4353 Pope, Robert    dang w 20 Oct 1897 Dargai, gs left thigh
3473 Prentis, Frederick    dang w 20 Oct 1897 Dargai, gs left shoulder
3127 Read, Alfred    sev w 7 Nov 1897 Maidan, gs left arm
4195 Rees, John    sev w 16 Nov 1897 Waran (Tseri Kandao), gs forearm
          & hip
3708 Salvage, William    sev w 7 Nov 1897 Maidan, gs hip
4578 Sawyer, George    sev w 16 Nov 1897 Waran (Tseri Kandao), gs foot
4459 Sheen, Albert    dang w 20 Oct 1897 Dargai, gs left eye
3966 Sims, Albert Charles    k 20 Oct 1897 Dargai
4123 Smyth, Ernest    dang w 20 Oct 1897 Dargai, gs both legs
4118 Soames, John    dang w 20 Oct 1897 Dargai, gs right thigh
3655 Spencer, Jowett    dang w 20 Oct 1897 Dargai, gs both thighs
4620 Strickland, James    sev w 9 Nov 1897 Saran Sar, gs foot
3251 Tapper, Walter    sev w 16 Nov 1897 Waran (Tseri Kandao),
          contusions
3542 Thomas, Henry    sl w 20 Oct 1897 Dargai, gs foot
4447 Thompson, Edward    sev w 20 Oct 1897 Dargai, gs back
3937 Vickery, Samuel    sev w 16 Nov 1897 Waran (Tseri Kandao),
          sword cut left arm; awarded VC
4347 Wakeley, Benjamin    k 20 Oct 1897 Dargai
3711 Webb, James    sev w 16 Nov 1897 Waran (Tseri Kandao), sword
          cut right side
4259 White, John James    dang w 8 Dec 1897 Bagh to Barkai march, gs
          left thigh
4418 Woodham, Walter    sev w 10 Dec 1897 Bagh to Barkai march, gs
          right arm
```

2nd Btn OXFORDSHIRE LIGHT INFANTRY

Lieutenant-Colonel
Plowden, Francis Hugh   sev w 30 Dec 1897 Khyber Pass, gs abdomen

Captain
Parr, Clements   dang w 30 Dec 1897 Khyber Pass, gs right leg

Lieutenant
Owen, Roger Carmichael Robert   sev w 30 Dec 1897 Khyber Pass, gs right arm

Sergeant-Major
1150 Dempsey, Harry Hamilton   dang w 30 Dec 1897 Khyber Pass, gs abdomen, dow; awarded DCM

Colour-Sergeant
2433 Jones, John   sev w 30 Dec 1897 Khyber Pass, gs right leg

Sergeants
 552 Gaskin, Thomas   sev w 30 Dec 1897 Khyber Pass, gs left elbow
1764 Hopkins, John   k 30 Dec 1897 Khyber Pass, gs hand
3258 Horseman, George   sl w 30 Dec 1897 Khyber Pass, gs left foot
3555 Smith, William   dang w 30 Dec 1897 Khyber Pass, gs left arm

Lance-Corporals
3482 Bell, William   k 30 Dec 1897 Khyber Pass, gs head
3940 Luckett, William   sev w 30 Dec 1897 Khyber Pass, gs left shoulder

Privates
4974 Betterton, William   sev w 30 Dec 1897 Khyber Pass, gs right foot
4952 Butler, William   k 30 Dec 1897 Khyber Pass, gs head
4704 Fountain, Richard   sl w 30 Dec 1897 Khyber Pass, gs right shoulder
3481 Smith, Ernest   dang w 30 Dec 1897 Khyber Pass, gs left elbow joint
4520 Surman, Thomas   sev w 30 Dec 1897 Khyber Pass, gs left elbow joint
5042 Warner, John   sev w 30 Dec 1897 Khyber Pass, gs both thighs

2nd Btn DERBYSHIRE REGIMENT

Captains
Bowman, Henry James   sev w 13 Nov 1897 Mastura, gs scapula
Smith, William Edward Clifton   k 20 Oct 1897 Chagru Kotal, gs forehead

Sergeants
 579 Keeling, Joseph   sev w 20 Oct 1897 Dargai, gs shoulder; awarded DCM
2839 Parr, John   sev w 20 Oct 1897 Dargai, gs back

Lance-Sergeant
3421 Sanworth, Jonas   dang w 25 Dec 1897 Khyber Pass, gs right knee

Corporal
3156 Bull, Frederick   sl w 25 Dec 1897 Khyber Pass, gs right cheek

Lance-Corporals
3976 Allsopp, John   sl w 29 Dec 1897 Karamna, gs left shoulder
3480 Barnes, Robert   sl w 25 Oct 1897 Karappa, gs
1773 Broadhurst, Daniel   sl w 29 Dec 1897 Karamna, gs left hand
3272 Cooper, Herbert   sl w 29 Dec 1897 Karamna, gs right thigh
4606 Fasham, Charles   sl w 29 Dec 1897 Karamna, gs right knee & left hand
4461 Morgan, Samuel   sev w 29 Dec 1897 Karamna, gs left knee
3549 Orton, Charles   dang w 25 Oct 1897 Karappa, gs abdomen, dow
3400 Westerman, Edward   sl w 25 Oct 1897 Karappa, gs
3972 Young, Arthur   sev w 25 Oct 1897 Karappa, gs back

Privates
4482 Addinall, Thomas   sev w 25 Oct 1897 Karappa, gs chest
5592 Betts, Amos   k 25 Dec 1897 Khyber Pass, gs
3255 Carter, Frederick   sev w 29 Dec 1897 Karamna, gs testicle & Leg
5064 Cook, Arthur   sl w 20 Oct 1897 Dargai, gs right hip
2433 Cook, George   sl w 29 Dec 1897 Karamna, gs right arm
2424 Dalton, Edward   sl w 28 Dec 1897 Barg, gs left hand
4755 Dunn, William   k 20 Oct 1897 Dargai
4958 Edinborough, Edward   sev w 12 Dec 1897 Sappri Pass, gs buttock
3584 Eyre, Samuel   mort w 25 Oct 1897 Karappa, gs chest, d same day
4448 Gilder, Alfred   sl w 20 Oct 1897 Dargai, gs right elbow
3142 Green, Walter   sl w 29 Dec 1897 Karamna, gs right hand
4454 Hacklett, Ralph   sev w 25 Oct 1897 Karappa, gs right knee
4499 Holden, John   sev w 9 Dec 1897 Waran Valley, gs ankle
4190 Hucker, Willie   sev w 20 Oct 1897 Dargai, gs
3660 Hudson, Henry   sl w 29 Dec 1897 Karamna, gs left knee
2732 Ponberth, Richard   mort w 20 Oct 1897 Dargai, gs abdomen
3076 Redgate, Henry   sl w 9 Dec 1987 Waran Valley, gs cheek; sl w 29 Dec 1897 Karamna, gs right hand
4212 Renton, Thomas   k 20 Oct 1897 Dargai
4702 Sleight, Charles   sev w 25 Oct 1897 Karappa, gs foot
3392 Spick, John   sev w 20 Oct 1897 Dargai, gs fracture scapula; awarded DCM
3933 Turpie, Arthur   sl w 29 Dec 1897 Karamna, gs right hand
3355 Tweed, Frederick   k 20 Oct 1897 Dargai
3474 Tyson, Henry   sev w 29 Dec 1897 Karamna, gs chest
4232 Walters, Thomas   sl w 20 Oct 1897 Dargai, gs right fingers
4013 Warren, Albert   sl w 25 Dec 1897 Khyber Pass, gs left hand
4857 Wheat, John   sev w 29 Dec 1897 Karamna, gs left thigh
3571 Wood, Charles   sev w 28 Oct 1897 Gandakai, gs shoulder

1st Btn NORTHAMPTONSHIRE REGIMENT

Lieutenants
Giffard, Cecil Lerrier   k 6 Nov 1897 Maidan, gs cheek
Trent, George Alexander   sev w 9 Nov 1897 Saran Sar, gs right thigh
Waddell, John Tannoch   k 9 Nov 1897 Saran Sar, gs

Second-Lieutenant
MacIntire, Andrew Herbert   k 9 Nov 1897 Saran Sar, gs head

Colour-Sergeants
1420 Fairgrieves, William   sl w 13 Dec 1897 Bagh to Barkai march, gs ear
  25 Hull, Joseph   dang w 9 Nov 1897 Saran Sar, gs left ankle
4317 Luck, Robert   k 9 Nov 1897 Saran Sar, gs head
2313 Underdown, William   sl w 9 Nov 1897 Saran Sar, gs left ankle

Sergeants
2174 Anderson, William   dang w 1 Nov 1897 Maidan, gs left arm, fractured; awarded DCM
2396 Jackson, Herbert   k 20 Nov 1897 Arhanga Pass, gs head
3258 Lennon, Stephen   sl w 16 Nov 1897 Maidan, gs right hand
 978 Litchfield, Andrew   dang w 9 Nov 1897 Saran Sar, gs left thigh, fractured

Lance-Sergeant
2704 Goffey, Arthur   dang w 9 Nov 1897 Saran Sar, gs abdomen, dow

Corporals
3966 Ashwell, John   k 14 Dec 1897 Bagh to Barkai march, gs pelvis
3680 Pearshall, Frederick William   k 20 Nov 1897 Arhanga Pass, gs chest
3922 Roddy, James Morris   k 9 Nov 1897 Saran Sar, gs

Lance-Corporals
3966 Ashwell, John   sl w 9 Nov 1897 Saran Sar, gs scalp
3108 Cooper, William   sl w 28 Oct 1897 Gandakai, gs thigh
3918 Gardiner, Frederick   k 9 Nov 1897 Saran Sar, gs
3917 Griffith, John Thomas   sev w 1 Dec 1897 Arhanga Pass, gs chest
4360 Harvey, William   sev w 9 Nov 1897 Saran Sar, gs right thigh
2269 King, Thomas   dang w 14 Dec 1897 Bagh to Barkai march, gs scrotum
2989 Mason, James   dang w 10 Dec 1897 Bagh to Barkai march, gs right leg
4247 Oliver, John   sev w 9 Nov 1897 Saran Sar, gs fracture right hand

Drummers
2682 Little, Harry   k 9 Nov 1897 Saran Sar, gs
3460 Mason, Samuel (Sergeant)   dang w 13 Dec 1897 Bagh to Barkai march, gs throat
3053 Simpson, John Edward   k 9 Nov 1897 Saran Sar, gs chest

Privates
3329 Archer, William Charles   dang w 9 Nov 1897 Saran Sar, gs left leg, both bones fractured
2808 Auburn, Walter   sl w 9 Nov 1897 Saran Sar, gs right thigh

4664 Banks, George   sev w 18 Nov 1897 Maidan, gs chest
2932 Bland, Stephen   sev w 9 Nov 1897 Saran Sar, gs left leg
2899 Brown, John   sl w 9 Nov 1897 Saran Sar, gs left breast
3740 Bull, John   k 9 Nov 1897 Saran Sar, gs right groin
3933 Burgess, Harry   k 9 Nov 1897 Saran Sar, gs
4264 Burton, George   dang w 9 Nov 1897 Saran Sar, gs head & right wrist, dow
4490 Busby, David   dang w 14 Dec 1897 Bagh to Barkai march, gs left leg
3488 Dunn, James   sev w 9 Nov 1897 Saran Sar, gs right buttock, dow
4384 Foster, George   sev w 9 Nov 1897 Saran Sar, gs right hand
3854 French, William   dang w 16 Nov 1897 Maidan, gs fracture right arm
4037 Greenwood, James   dang w 13 Dec 1897 Bagh to Barkai march, gs arm
4085 Harris, George   sl w 9 Nov 1897 Saran Sar, gs right hand
3861 Harrison, Alfred   sl w 13 Dec 1897 Bagh to Barkai march, gs groin
2108 Hearne, Daniel   k 9 Nov 1897 Saran Sar, gs
3711 Kisbee, Frederick sev w 9 Nov 1897 Saran Sar, gs left shoulder
4443 Line, Arthur   k 10 Dec 1897 Bagh to Barkai march, gs head
3358 Newell, Garrett   k 9 Nov 1897 Saran Sar, gs
2659 Nibbs, Harry   sl w 9 Nov 1897 Saran Sar, gs left buttock
4142 Okey, George   k 16 Nov 1897 Maidan, gs head
3661 Packington, William k 9 Nov 1897 Saran Sar, gs
3709 Passingham, George k 9 Nov 1897 Saran Sar, gs
2864 Plummer, Robert   k 8 Nov 1897 Saran Sar, gs
3695 Pressman, Henry   sev w 9 Nov 1897 Saran Sar, gs left thigh & left thumb
4007 Prosser, George   k 9 Nov 1897 Saran Sar, gs
3914 Quinn, George Henry k 9 Nov 1897 Saran Sar, gs back & right breast
4312 Read, Frederick   dang w 9 Nov 1897 Saran Sar, gs back & right arm
4560 Robinson, John   sev w 9 Nov 1897 Saran Sar, gs right side
3977 Rumble, John   dang w 20 Nov 1897 Arhanga Pass, gs abdomen
3502 Shaughnessy, Michael sev w 9 Nov 1897 Saran Sar, gs chest
4249 Smart, Charles   sev w 20 Nov 1897 Arhanga Pass, gs left thigh
2950 Smith, Edward   sev w 9 Nov 1897 Saran Sar, gs left middle toe
3779 Smith, Frank   sev w 9 Nov 1897 Saran Sar, gs right forearm
2561 Sower, William   sev w 9 Nov 1897 Saran Sar, gs right knee
4506 Spicer, George   sl w 9 Nov 1897 Saran Sar, gs left thigh
4421 Stebbings, Thomas sev w 9 Nov 1897 Saran Sar, gs left thigh
4501 Underwood, Lewis   k 9 Nov 1897 Saran Sar, gs
2194 Vials, George William sl w 9 Nov 1897 Saran Sar, bayonet, accidental
3068 Warde, Charles   sev w 9 Nov 1897 Saran Sar, gs left groin & left forearm
3659 Willis, George   sev w 9 Nov 1897 Saran Sar, gs left thigh
3981 Woolford, John   k 9 Nov 1897 Saran Sar, gs
3841 Worth, David   k 9 Nov 1897 Saran Sar, gs abdomen

2nd Btn KING'S OWN YORKSHIRE LIGHT INFANTRY

Major
Earle, Henry   DSO   sev w 29 Jan 1898 Shinkamar, gs left forearm

Captain
Marrable, Arthur George   sev w 29 Jan 1898 Shinkamar, gs right thigh

Lieutenants
Dowdall, Thomas Percy   k 29 Jan 1898 Shinkamar, gs
Walker, Malcolm Reginald   k 29 Jan 1898 Shinkamar, gs

Second Lieutenants
Hall, Gordon Charles William Gordon   sev w 29 Jan 1898 Shinkamar, gs right leg
Hughes, Ernest St George   k 29 Jan 1898 Shinkamar, gs

Colour-Sergeants
 472 Guest, William   k 29 Jan 1898 Shinkamar
1395 Smith, William   sev w 29 Jan 1898 Shinkamar, gs right leg

Sergeant
3439 Boston, Charles   dang w 31 Jan 1898 Shinkamar, gs left arm

Lance-Sergeant
3463 Axleby, Walter Edgar   k 29 Jan 1898 Shinkamar

Corporals
3504 Dawes, George   k 29 Jan 1898 Shinkamar
2754 Johnson, Willie   k 29 Jan 1898 Shinkamar

Lance-Corporals
2907 Bedford, William   sev w 29 Jan 1898 Shinkamar, gs right arm
3966 Cantrill, Richard   k 29 Jan 1898 Shinkamar
4115 Darby, John   sev w 29 Jan 1898 Shinkamar, gs right thigh
4126 Miller, William   sl w 29 Jan 1898 Shinkamar, gs left hand
3898 Revitt, Hector   sl w 29 Jan 1898 Shinkamar, gs right hand
4064 Sawyer, John   k 29 Jan 1898 Shinkamar
4446 Singleton, William   sl w 29 Jan 1898 Shinkamar, gs face
3896 Wallace, James   sev w 29 Jan 1898 Shinkamar, gs chest & back
3612 Whitely, Arthur   k 29 Jan 1898 Shinkamar

Bandsman
3535 MacDonald, Edmund   sev w 29 Jan 1898 Shinkamar, gs arm

Privates
4997 Ablett, James   sl w 29 Jan 1898 Shinkamar, gs scalp
3046 Amery, John   k 29 Jan 1898 Shinkamar, gs head
3662 Ashby, Alfred Henry   k 29 Jan 1898 Shinkamar
3719 Bailey, John   k 29 Jan 1898 Shinkamar
3367 Barnes, John   sl w 29 Jan 1898 Shinkamar, gs left knee & right hand
4339 Beattie, David   k 29 Jan 1898 Shinkamar
4211 Beeley, Arthur   k 29 Jan 1898 Shinkamar

4886 Bend, Samson   dang w 29 Jan 1898 Shinkamar, gs., dow
3822 Birch, Thomas   dang w 29 Jan 1898 Shinkamar, gs left thigh
4483 Cook, William   dang w 29 Jan 1898 Shinkamar, gs face
4053 Cope, Charles   dang w 29 Jan 1898 Shinkamar, gs left thigh
3118 Corbidge, Harry   k 29 Jan 1898 Shinkamar
4520 Corrigan, William   k 29 Jan 1898 Shinkamar
3492 Deakin, William   k 29 Jan 1898 Shinkamar
4815 Dixon, William   k 29 Jan 1898 Shinkamar
3747 Dolophin, James   k 29 Jan 1898 Shinkamar
3752 Dutton, Walter   k 29 Jan 1898 Shinkamar
3765 Finn, John   sev w 29 Jan 1898 Shinkamar, gs both legs
4153 Hall, Alfred   dang w 29 Jan 1898 Shinkamar, gs right thigh
4928 Harris, William   k 29 Jan 1898 Shinkamar
3778 Harrison, William   dang w 29 Jan 1898 Shinkamar, gs left arm
4536 Heaps, James   sl w 29 Jan 1898 Shinkamar, gs right hand
4061 Hill, William   k 29 Jan 1898 Shinkamar
4481 Jackson, Joseph   dang w 29 Jan 1898 Shinkamar, gs right
                forearm
3578 Kaye, Dyson   sl w 29 Jan 1898 Shinkamar, gs left hand;
                awarded DCM
4145 Kerins, John   k 29 Jan 1898 Shinkamar
3867 Lambley, John   dang w 29 Jan 1898 Shinkamar, gs forearm
3770 Lawrence, John   sl w 29 Jan 1898 Shinkamar, gs chest
1101 Lloyd, Walter   sl w 29 Jan 1898 Shinkamar, gs left hand
4595 Lyons, Frederick William   sl w 29 Jan 1898 Shinkamar, gs
                sole of left foot
4274 Maddison, Isaac   k 29 Jan 1898 Shinkamar
3947 Moran, John   k 29 Jan 1898 Shinkamar, gs abdomen
3931 Morris, Richard   dang w 29 Jan 1898 Shinkamar, gs right forearm
3976 Moseley, Garbett   sev w 29 Jan 1898 Shinkamar, gs left thigh
4238 Rivett, Albert   dang w 29 Jan 1898 Shinkamar, gs, dow
3814 Ryan, John   dang w 29 Jan 1898 Shinkamar, gs left leg
4896 Thompson, Charles   sl w 29 Jan 1898 Shinkamar, gs left knee
3968 Tite, George Henry   k 29 Jan 1898 Shinkamar
3039 Turner, John George Jubb   k 29 Jan 1898 Shinkamar
4882 Warner, Arthur   k 29 Jan 1898 Shinkamar
3194 Watson, George   sl w 29 Jan 1898 Shinkamar, gs left hand
3963 Wilson, George   sl w 29 Jan 1898 Shinkamar, gs right hand
4410 Wright, William   dang w 29 Jan 1898 Shinkamar, gs left arm

1st Btn GORDON HIGHLANDERS

Lieutenant-Colonel
Mathias, Henry Harding   CB   sl w 20 Oct 1897 Chagru Kotal, gs
                right foot

Majors
Jennings-Bramly, Richard Dyneley   k 18 Oct 1897 Chagru Kotal, gs
                heart
MacBean, Forbes   sev w 20 Oct 1897 Chagru Kotal, gs left groin

Captain
Uniacke, Henry Percy   sl w 20 Oct 1897 Chagru Kotal, gs left wrist

Lieutenants
Cameron, George Ewen Eyre Gordon   sev w 10 Nov 1897 Maidan, gs (a bullet struck his revolver, causing it to go off)

Craufurd, George Standish Gage   sl w 20 Oct 1897 Chagru Kotal, gs left thigh

Dingwall, Kenneth   sev w 20 Oct 1897 Chagru Kotal, gs knee & stomach

Lamont, Alexander   k 20 Oct 1897 Chagru Kotal, gs head

Meiklejohn, Matthew Fontaine Maury   sl w 20 Oct 1897 Chagru Kotal, gs right hand

Pears, Maurice Loraine (attchd from 1/Scottish Rifles)   dang w 18 Oct 1897 Chagru Kotal, gs left leg

Colour-Sergeant
1276 Pickersgill, Eli   dang w 20 Oct 1897 Chagru Kotal, gs right thigh & wrist, dow

Sergeants
2401 Grassick, George L.   sev w 20 Oct 1897 Chagru Kotal, gs right knee

3128 Hickie, Henry George   sl w 20 Oct 1897 Dargai, gs right heel

2465 McKay, James   sl w 20 Oct 1897 Dargai, gs right side

3045 Mann, Alexander   sev w 18 Oct 1897 Dargai, gs right wrist

Corporals
1208 Bell, James   k 20 Oct 1897 Dargai

2029 Cooper, James   dang w 10 Nov 1897 Maidan, gs small of back

4430 Harding, Benjamin   k 12 Dec 1897 Bagh to Barkai march, gs head

3393 Ryan, James   dang w 20 Oct 1897 Dargai, gs left arm (fractured) & wrist

4770 Walker, James   dang w 12 Dec 1897 Bagh to Barkai march, gs left leg

Lance-Corporals
3662 Drummond, George   sl w 25 Oct 1897 Karappa, gs left leg

5714 Edwards, Alexander   sev w 20 Oct 1897 Dargai, gs left groin

3059 Freestone, William J.   sev w 20 Oct 1897 Dargai, gs right leg

3726 Howe, John B.   dang w 12 Dec 1897 Bagh to Barkai march, gs thigh

5202 Meck, David   sev w 20 Oct 1897 Dargai, gs right hip

Pipers
2951 Findlater, George   dang w 20 Oct 1897 Dargai, gs fracture left leg; awarded VC

4373 Fraser, James R.   sl w 20 Oct 1897 Dargai, gs thigh

3491 Kidd, John   dang w 15 Nov 1897 Waran, gs both thighs

3711 Milne, Patrick (Lance-Corporal)   dang w 20 Oct 1897 Dargai, gs chest; awarded DCM

4230 Will, George   sl w 20 Oct 1897 Dargai, gs buttock

Privates

3558	Anderson, William	sev w 20 Oct 1897 Dargai, gs right hand
5089	Bremner, William	dang w 18 Oct 1897 Dargai, gs right thigh
3811	Brown, George F.	dang w 18 Oct 1897 Dargai, gs left shoulder
5010	Burns, Frank	dang w 20 Oct 1897 Dargai, gs left shoulder
3868	Civil, Alfred	dang w 20 Oct 1897 Dargai, gs abdomen & left arm, dow
3411	Davie, John	dang w 20 Oct 1897 Dargai, gs neck, dow
4651	Dorman, Alexander H.	dang w 20 Oct 1897 Dargai, gs right thigh & hand
3866	Edmonds, Oliver	sl w 18 Oct 1897 Dargai, gs left side
4582	Farlie, Albert John	sev w 12 Dec 1897 Bagh to Barkai march, gs left forearm
5279	Flood, Peter	sev w 20 Oct 1897 Dargai, gs right arm
4461	Furniss, Harry	dang w 11 Dec 1897 Bagh to Barkai march, gs abdomen, dow
4627	Gordon, John Charles	sl w 12 Dec 1897 Bagh to Barkai march, gs left leg
4121	Hagan, George	k 18 Oct 1897 Dargai, gs chest
4095	Hammond, James	dang w 26 Mar 1898 Mamanai-Barkai road, gs left shoulder, arm amputated
4008	Hannan, James	dang w 20 Oct 1897 Dargai, gs left knee
3376	Heffern, Harry H.	dang w 20 Oct 1897 Dargai, gs groin
4908	Henderson, David	dang w 20 Oct 1897 Dargai, gs hip
4810	Hunter, Robert	dang w 18 Oct 1897 Dargai, gs right thigh
4110	Jackson, David	sl w 23 Oct 1897 Karappa, gs head
4571	Johnson, Robert J.	sl w 12 Dec 1897 Bagh to Barkai march, gs right leg
4867	Jones, John	dang w 20 Oct 1897 Dargai, gs left thigh
4726	Keith, William	sev w 20 Oct 1897 Dargai, gs thigh
4328	Langham, James	k 11 Dec 1897 Bagh to Barkai march, gs chest
4603	Laughland, Robert	sl w 20 Oct 1897 Dargai, gs right thigh & eye
3741	Lawrence, Henry	sev w 11 Dec 1897 Bagh to Barkai march, gs forearm
3456	Lawson, Edward	sl w 20 Oct 1897 Dargai, gs right arm; awarded VC
5003	McArdle, Patrick	dang w 20 Oct 1897 Dargai, gs right shoulder
5361	McFarlane, Walter	dang w 26 Mar 1898 Mamanai-Barkai road, gs right shoulder & knee
5489	McKelvie, Samuel	dang w 15 Nov 1897 Waran, gs left thigh
5047	McKinnon, John	sev w 20 Oct 1897 Dargai, gs back
3516	McMillan, William	sev w 20 Oct 1897 Dargai, gs both legs
4308	McPherson, Alexander	dang w 20 Oct 1897 Dargai, gs fracture left clavicle
3771	Miles, Thomas	dang w 18 Oct 1897 Dargai, gs left thigh
4413	Morley, George	k 11 Dec 1897 Bagh to Barkai march, gs stomach
4832	Neale, Joseph	dang w 11 Dec 1897 Bagh to Barkai march, gs right thigh & leg, dow
5287	Noddings, Thomas	dang w 20 Oct 1897 Dargai, gs right leg
4274	Pater, James	sev w 12 Dec 1897 Bagh to Barkai march, gs right arm
4299	Quinn, James Joseph	k 20 Oct 1897 Dargai

IGS - R

```
4069 Rennie, Peter     sev w 5 Dec 1897 Bagh, gs left shoulder
4790 Spark, William    sev w 20 Oct 1897 Dargai, gs right leg & arm
3780 Stone, Luke       sev w 15 Nov 1897 Waran, gs face
3241 Stott, John       dang w 10 Nov 1897 Maidan, gs abdomen, dow
4122 Taylor, Frederick    sl w 12 Dec 1897 Bagh to Barkai march, gs
                           right leg
3604 Tees, Robert      sl w 20 Oct 1897 Dargai, gs right knee
2733 Walker, Albert    sl w 18 Oct 1897 Dargai, gs back
4004 Warne, Joseph W.A.   dang w 20 Oct 1897 Dargai, gs right thigh
3501 Weight, Walter    sev w 20 Oct 1897 Dargai, gs fracture left foot
5093 Will, George      sev w 12 Dec 1897 Bagh to Barkai march, gs left
                           leg
4301 Wood, Charles     sl w 20 Oct 1897 Dargai, gs right knee
4361 Wright, Richard   sl w 12 Dec 1897 Bagh to Barkai march, gs
                           right side of neck
```

6th REGIMENT OF BENGAL CAVALRY

Lieutenants
Battye, Richmond Noffatt   k 1 Dec 1897 Hissar, gs head
Pennington, William Herbert (attchd from 12th Bengal Cavalry)
                sl w 1 Dec 1897 Thabai

Rissaldar
Mumtaz Husain Khan   sev w 1 Dec 1897 Thabai, gs hand

Daffadar
 869 Farzand Ali   sl w 1 Dec 1897 Thabai, gs

Sowars
1658 Abdul Hamid   sl w 1 Dec 1897 Thabai, gs leg
1657 Intikan Ali   sl w 1 Dec 1897 Thabai, gs right shoulder
 862 Mungli   sev w 1 Dec 1897 Thabai, gs right elbow joint
1365 Nana   sl w 1 Dec 1897 Thabai, gs thigh

9th REGIMENT OF BENGAL LANCERS

Jemadar
Sarwar Khan   k 18 Oct 1897 Mamanai, Bara Valley, gs head

Daffadars
1726 Abbas Khan   sl w 18 Oct 1897 Mamanai, Bara Valley, gs right
                       knee
1599 Fazal Rahman Khan   k 18 Oct 1897 Mamanai, Bara Valley, gs chest

Lance-Daffadar
1751 Nur Muhammad   sl w 18 Oct 1897 Mamanai, Bara Valley, gs right foot

Trumpeter
1914 Khan Muhammad Khan   k 18 Oct 1897 Mamanai,Bara Valley, gs chest

Sowars
2288 Elahi Bakhsh   sl w 18 Oct 1897 Mamanai,Bara Valley, gs scalp
1689 Hayat Khan   k 18 Oct 1897 Mamanai,Bara Valley, gs abdomen
2063 Muhammad Khan   sl w 5 Dec 1897 nr Gandao,Bara Valley,
                contusion leg
2171 Sahib Gul   sev w 18 Oct 1897 Mamanai,Bara Valley, gs right
                shoulder
2260 Taji Khan   k 5 Dec 1897 nr Gandao,Bara Valley
2137 Umardaraz Khan   missing 18 Oct 1897 Mamanai,Bara Valley

17th REGIMENT OF BENGAL CAVALRY

Daffadar
 438 Gulmir Khan   sev w 4 Nov 1897 Maidan, gs left leg

18th REGIMENT OF BENGAL LANCERS

Major
Money, George Alfred   sl w 13 Nov 1897 Mastura, gs

Sowar
1593 Ghulam Habib Khan   sev w 18 Nov 1897 Bagh, gs calf

9th GURKHA (RIFLE) REGIMENT OF BENGAL INFANTRY

Havildar
 243 Kesar Chand   dang w 3 Dec 1897 Gandao Pass, gs, dow 4 Dec

Riflemen
 733 Churamani Mahat   sev w 29 Dec 1897 Khyber Pass, gs thigh
 931 Karbir Kaurka   k 29 Dec 1897 Khyber Pass, gs abdomen
1014 Narbahadur Khatri   k 17 Jan 1898 Khyber Pass, gs chest
1274 Setu Rawat   sev w 29 Dec 1897 Khyber Pass, gs shoulder & arm

12th (KELAT-I-GHILZAI) REGIMENT OF BENGAL INFANTRY

Sepoys
942 Daulat Khan   k 1 Dec 1897 Thabai
936 Lal Muhammad Khan   k 1 Dec 1897 Thabai
446 Muhammad Khan   sev w 1 Dec 1897 Thabai, gs left hand
764 Shaikh Muhammad Shafi   k 1 Dec 1897 Thabai
379 Shaik Nabbi   sev w 1 Dec 1897 Thabai, gs arm
896 Sikandar Khan   sev w 1 Dec 1897 Thabai, gs right arm

15th (LUDHIANA SIKH) REGIMENT OF BENGAL INFANTRY

Lieutenant-Colonels
Abbott, Henry Alexius   sev w 16 Nov 1897 Waran, gs face & nose
Hadow, Reginald Campbell   DSO   sev w 26 Oct 1897 Khangarbur,
        gs right leg

Captain
Lewarne, Nicholas Albert   k 16 Nov 1897 Waran, gs

Subadars
Bhagat Singh   sev w 16 Nov 1897 Waran (Tseri Kandao), gs right
       arm; awarded IOM 3rd Class
Gurdatt Singh   sl w 16 Nov 1897 Waran (Tseri Kandao), gs back;
       awarded IOM 3rd Class

Jemadars
Chatar Singh   k 6 Nov 1897 Maidan, gs right groin, right thigh &
       right leg
Man Singh   sl w 9 Nov 1897 Saran Sar, gs right thigh
Pyara Singh   sev w 16 Nov 1897 Waran (Tser Kandao), gs neck
Waryam Singh   sev w 18 Oct 1897 Dargai, gs left thigh;
       awarded IOM 3rd Class

Havildars
2670 Bishan Singh   k 16 Nov 1897 Waran (Tseri Kandao)
2052 Isar Singh   dang w 16 Nov 1897 Waran (Tseri Kandao), gs right
       knee
2138 Sobha Singh   sev w 16 Nov 1897 Waran (Tseri Kandao), gs right
       forearm
2370 Suhel Singh   dang w 16 Nov 1897 Waran (Tseri Kandao), gs
       chest & right thumb

Lance-Havildar
2412 Hari Singh   sev w 16 Nov 1897 Waran (Tseri Kandao), gs chest

Lance-Naiks

2776	Bhola Singh	sev w 16 Nov 1897 Waran (Tseri Kandao), gs right forearm & hand
2683	Hazara Singh	sev w 6 Nov 1897 Maidan, gs left leg
2667	Jamit Singh	sev w 20 Nov 1897 Arhanga Pass, gs elbow joint, arm amputated
2744	Narayan Singh	missing 6 Nov 1897 Maidan
2818	Narayan Singh	sl w 16 Nov 1897 Waran (Tseri Kandao), gs right thigh

Sepoys

3379	Amar Singh	sev w 6 Nov 1897 Maidan, gs left thigh; awarded IOM 3rd Class
3016	Atar Singh	dang w 18 Oct 1897 Dargai, gs right thigh
2847	Bhola Singh	sev w 18 Oct 1897 Dargai, gs left tibia; awarded IOM 3rd Class
3738	Bishan Singh	sev w 6 Nov 1897 Maidan, gs buttock; awarded IOM 3rd Class
3552	Buta Singh	sev w 6 Nov 1897 Maidan, gs right arm & left hand
3691	Chanan Singh	sev w 16 Nov 1897 Waran (Tseri Kandao), gs left leg
3358	Gayan Singh	dang w 21 Nov 1897 Maidan, gs left knee
3825	Ghulla Singh	sev w 16 Nov 1897 Waran (Tseri Kandao), gs back
2869	Gopal Singh	k 18 Oct 1897 Dargai
3550	Gopal Singh	dang w 9 Nov 1897 Saran Sar, gs abdomen
3480	Hira Singh	k 9 Nov 1897 Saran Sar
3601	Hira Singh	dang w 16 Nov 1897 Waran (Tseri Kandao), gs left knee
3640	Hira Singh	sev w 9 Nov 1897 Saran Sar, gs buttock
3291	Indar Singh	sev w 16 Nov 1897 Waran (Tser Kandao), gs chest
3602	Indar Singh	sev w 16 Nov 1897 Waran (Tseri Kandao), gs chest
3553	Isar Singh	k 16 Nov 1897 Waran (Tseri Kandao)
3287	Jai Singh	k 18 Oct 1897 Dargai
3241	Jhanda Singh	missing 16 Nov 1897 Waran (Tseri Kandao)
3304	Jiwan Singh	sev w 6 Nov 1897 Maidan, gs left leg
3740	Jiwa Singh	k 16 Nov 1897 Waran (Tseri Kandao)
3599	Kahn Singh	sl w 20 Nov 1897 Arhanga Pass, gs left hand
2946	Kakar Singh	sl w 15 Nov 1897 Waran, gs knee
3586	Kapur Singh	k 16 Nov 1897 Waran (Tseri Kandao)
3621	Kishan Singh	k 16 Nov 1897 Waran (Tseri Kandao)
3315	Kishn Singh	sl w 18 Oct 1897 Dargai, gs face; awarded IOM 3rd Class
3680	Lal Singh	sev w 18 Oct 1897 Dargai, gs left shoulder
3581	Lehna Singh	k 16 Nov 1897 Waran (Tseri Kandao)
3010	Nand Singh	dang w 29 Oct 1897 Sampagha Pass, gs chest
3040	Nidhan Singh	sev w 15 Nov 1897 Waran, gs right thigh
2959	Ram Singh	sev w 16 Nov 1897 Waran (Tseri Kandao), gs right arm
3650	Ram Singh	sev w 18 Oct 1897 Dargai, gs right shoulder
3785	Sadhu Singh	sev w 16 Nov 1897 Waran (Tseri Kandao), gs nose & shoulder
2594	Sahib Singh	sev w 16 Nov 1897 Waran (Tseri Kandao), gs right thigh

3367 Sant Singh   sev w 16 Nov 1897 Waran (Tseri Kandao), gs right
                  thigh, sword cuts right elbow & scalp
3791 Sujjan Singh sl w 3 Nov 1897 Maidan, gs neck
3820 Sundar Singh k 16 Nov 1897 Waran (Tseri Kandao)
3487 Uger Singh   dang w 9 Nov 1897 Saran Sar, gs chest
3432 Waryam Singh k 6 Nov 1897 Maidan, gs head

22nd (PUNJAB) REGIMENT OF BENGAL INFANTRY

Sepoy
4072 Jasa Singh   sev w 2 Nov 1897 Kai, gs left radius

30th (PUNJAB) REGIMENT OF BENGAL INFANTRY

Naik
2152 Jowahir Singh   k 25 Dec 1897 Khyber Pass, gs

Sepoys
3343 Dogar Singh   sl w 14 Jan 1898 Khyber Pass towards Landi
                    Kotal, gs thigh
2810 Fateh Khan   sl w 13 Dec 1897 Kwaja Kiddar, gs right hand
3484 Hari Singh   sl w 16 Jan 1898 Khyber Pass between Ali Masjid
                    & Landi Kotal, gs contusion hand & foot
3246 Hira   k 14 Jan 1898 Khyber Pass towards Landi Kotal, gs chest
3049 Lachman Singh   sev w 27 Dec 1897 Barg, gs head
3130 Mal Singh   sl w 25 Dec 1897 Khyber Pass, gs contusion head
3389 Nand Singh   k 16 Jan 1898 Khyber Pass between Ali Masjid &
                   Landi Kotal, gs head
3598 Nihala sev w 25 Dec 1897 Khyber Pass, gs left foot
3541 Sher Singh   sl w 16 Jan 1898 Khyber Pass between Ali Masjid
                   & Landi Kotal, gs contusion hand
3136 Wazir Singh   sev w 29 Dec 1897 Karamna, gs head

34th (PUNJAB) REGIMENT OF BENGAL INFANTRY (PIONEERS)

Major
Hickman, Devereux Walter   k 3 Jan 1898 Khyber Pass, gs heart

Sepoys
1047 Isar Singh   sl w 1 Jan 1898 Khyber Pass, gs
1528 Sundar Singh   mort w 1 Jan 1898 Khyber Pass, gs

36th (SIKH) REGIMENT OF BENGAL INFANTRY

Lieutenant-Colonel
Haughton, John   k 29 Jan 1898 Shinkamar, gs

Captains
Custance, Hugh Lionel   sev w 16 Nov 1897 Waran, gs left thigh
Searle, Charles Thomas Arnaud   sev w 31 Oct 1897 Arhanga Kotal,
                                  gs right thigh
Sullivan, Edward Langford   sev w 6 Nov 1897 Maidan, gs left radius
Venour, Walter Edwin (attchd from 5th Punjab Inf)   sl w 24 Nov 1897
                                  Dwatoi, gs right leg

Lieutenants
Munn, Reginald George   sev w 16 Nov 1897 Waran, gs right hand
Turing, Arthur Henry   k 29 Jan 1898 Shinkamar, gs

Second-Lieutenant
Browne, David Stuart   sl w 31 Jan 1898 Shinkamar, gs contusion eye

Surgeon-Lieutenant
Dick, Maxwell   sl w 31 Jan 1898 Shinkamar, gs right ring finger

Havildars
 177 Badan Singh   sl w 24 Nov 1897 Dwatoi, gs right forearm
 168 Bhagwan Singh   dang w 8 Dec 1897 Bagh to Barkai march, gs chest
 888 Ishar Singh   sl w 29 Oct 1897 Sampagha Pass, gs thigh
 186 Lal Singh   sev w 8 Dec 1897 Bagh to Barkai march, gs right leg
 212 Narain Singh   dang w 29 Jan 1898 Shinkamar, gs head, dow
  69 Wariam Singh   dang w 16 Nov 1897 Waran (Tseri kandao), gs
                     right wrist, left thigh & hip; awarded IOM
                     3rd Class

Naiks
 352 Ishar Singh   sev w 14 Dec 1897 Bagh to Barkai march, gs right
                     forearm
 758 Jiwan Singh   k 29 Jan 1898 Shinkamar, gs
 775 Ram Singh   sev w 24 Nov 1897 Dwatoi, gs right upper arm

Lance-Naiks
 383 Bhola Singh   sl w 23 Nov 1897 Dwatoi, gs right leg
 849 Bhola Singh   dang w 16 Nov 1897 Waran (Tseri Kandao), gs
                     right wrist
 944 Chanan Singh   sev w 20 Nov 1897 Bagh, gs face & head
 398 Oudha Singh   sl w 18 Nov 1897 Maidan, gs left arm
1163 Sham Singh   sl w 10 Dec 1897 Bagh to Barkai march, gs left arm

Bugler
1462 Sher Singh   k 16 Nov 1897 Waran (Tseri Kandao)

Sepoys
1638 Attar Singh   sl w 13 Dec 1897 Bagh to Barkai march, gs right leg
1720 Basant Singh   sev w 24 Nov 1897 Dwatoi, gs right foot
 986 Basawa Singh   sev w 16 Nov 1897 Waran (Tseri Kandao), gs right thumb & neck
1508 Bhagat Singh   sl w 9 Nov 1897 Saran Sar, gs back & both knees
2061 Bhagwan Singh   sev w 16 Nov 1897 Waran (Tseri Kandao), gs right thigh
1550 Bhan Singh   k 16 Nov 1897 Waran (Tseri Kandao)
1434 Bir Singh   sl w 9 Nov 1897 Saran Sar, gs right thigh
1490 Bishan Singh   sl w 29 Oct 1897 Sampagha Pass, gs thigh
2010 Bishan Singh   sl w 24 Nov 1897 Dwatoi, gs right thigh
1694 Budh Singh   sev w 24 Nov 1897 Dwatoi, gs right arm
1594 Bur Singh   k 16 Nov 1897 Waran (Tseri Kandao)
1532 Chanda Singh   dang w 24 Nov 1897 Dwatoi, gs right arm
1115 Dayal Singh   sl w 13 Dec 1897 Bagh to Barkai march, gs right leg
1722 Dayal Singh   sl w 13 Dec 1897 Bagh to Barkai march, gs right leg
1281 Eshar Singh   k 28 Oct 1897 Gandakai, gs head
1975 Ganga Singh   sl w 16 Nov 1897 Waran (Tseri Kandao), gs right hand
 379 Gunga Singh   sl w 16 Nov 1897 Waran (Tseri Kandao), gs left thigh & leg
1112 Gurmuk Singh   k 13 Dec 1897 Bagh to Barkai march, gs head
1196 Hansa Singh   dang w 23 Nov 1897 Dwatoi, gs right forearm
 654 Harnam Singh   sev w 1 Nov 1897 Maidan, gs left thigh
 927 Harnam Singh   k 24 Nov 1897 Dwatoi, gs right hip & thigh
1392 Harnam Singh   dang w 10 Dec 1897 Bagh to Barkai march, gs both thighs
1891 Harnam Singh   sl w 16 Nov 1897 Waran (Tseri Kandao), gs left thigh
1316 Hazara Singh   dang w 29 Oct 1897 Sampagha Pass, gs abdomen, dow
1276 Hira Singh   sl w 13 Dec 1897 Bagh to Barkai march, gs right buttock
1333 Hira Singh   k 8 Nov 1897 Maidan, gs neck
1426 Hurdit Singh   dang w 24 Nov 1897 Dwatoi, gs right forearm
1352 Ishar Singh   dang w 24 Nov 1897 Dwatoi, gs left shoulder
1479 Ishar Singh   sev w 13 Dec 1897 Bagh to Barkai march, gs left arm
1532 Jiwan Singh   sev w 10 Dec 1897 Bagh to Barkai march, gs back
 648 Kala Singh   sev w 14 Dec 1897 Bagh to Barkai march, gs right thigh
 795 Kala Singh   sl w 13 Dec 1897 Bagh to Barkai march, gs buttock
 836 Kan Singh   sl w 10 Dec 1897 Bagh to Barkai march, gs back
1262 Kan Singh   k 16 Nov 1897 Waran (Tseri Kandao)
2074 Kartar Singh   sl w 13 Dec 1897 Bagh to Barkai march, gs right buttock

1692 Kesar Singh   k 9 Dec 1897 Bagh to Barkai march, gs left side chest
1689 Kishan Singh   dang w 10 Dec 1897 Bagh to Barkai march, gs loin
2018 Kishan Singh   k 13 Dec 1897 Bagh to Barkai march, gs left thigh & head
1991 Labh Singh   k 13 Dec 1897 Bagh to Barkai march, gs head
1105 Lehna Singh   sev w 8 Nov 1897 Maidan, gs right thigh & right hand
1236 Lehna Singh   dang w 29 Oct 1897 Sampagha Pass, gs head
1724 Nagina Singh   dang w 25 Oct 1897 Karappa, gs chest
1718 Natha Singh   dang w 9 Nov 1897 Saran Sar, gs right leg
1817 Natha Singh   sev w 14 Mar 1897 Bagh to Barkai march, gs right forearm
1519 Nidhan Singh   k 16 Nov 1897 Waran (Tseri Kandao)
 714 Partab Singh   sl w 24 Nov 1897 Dwatoi, gs left wrist
1448 Pula Singh   sev w 24 Nov 1897 Dwatoi, gs both legs
1084 Rattan Singh   sl w 13 Dec 1897 Bagh to Barkai march, gs left thigh
1360 Rattan Singh   sev w 12 Dec 1897 Bagh to Barkai march, gs left leg
1104 Sarwan Singh   sl w 13 Dec 1897 Bagh to Barkai march, gs left shoulder
1149 Sawan Singh   k 29 Jan 1898 Shinkamar, gs
1570 Sibba Singh   k 16 Nov 1897 Waran (Tseri Kandao)
1798 Teja Singh   sl w 24 Nov 1897 Dwatoi, gs left side neck
  20 Uttam Singh   sl w 8 Dec 1897 Bagh to Barkai march, gs face
 619 Uttam Singh   sev w 29 Jan 1898 Shinkamar, gs right arm

45th (RATTRAY'S SIKH) REGIMENT OF BENGAL INFANTRY

<u>Naik</u>
2531 Jhanda Singh   sev w 25 Dec 1897 Khyber Pass, gs left thigh

<u>Sepoys</u>
3582 Ram Singh   sev w 25 Dec 1897 Khyber Pass, gs back
3161 Kirpal Singh   dang w 25 Dec 1897 Khyber Pass, gs abdomen, dow

2nd Btn 1st GURKHA (RIFLE) REGIMENT

<u>Lieutenant-Colonel</u>
Sage, Charles Arthur Ross   sev w 28 Oct 1897 Gandaki, gs left thigh

<u>Naik</u>
 740 Tikaram Kumal   sl w 25 Oct 1897 Karappa, gs

Lance-Naik
 321 Balbir Gurung   sev w 8 Dec 1897 Arhanga Pass, gs right leg

Riflemen
 835 Bhagatbir Thapa   sl w 25 Oct 1897 Karappa, gs
1652 Dalbahadur Gurung   sev w 25 Oct 1897 Karappa, gs right buttock
1299 Gagan Sing Khattri sl w 28 Oct 1897 Gandakai, gs scalp
1690 Kharak Sing Rana   sev w 5 Nov 1897 Mastura, gs back
1537 Matbar Sing Thapa   dang w 29 Dec 1897 Karamna, gs chest

1st Btn 2nd GURKHA (RIFLE) REGIMENT (SIRMOOR RIFLES)

Captains
Judge, Charles Bellew   k 20 Oct 1897 Chagru Kotal, gs head, neck & chest
Norie, Charles Edward de Manley   sev w 11 Dec 1897 Bagh to Barkai march, gs left arm, amputated
Robinson, John Graham   dang w 20 Oct 1897 Chagru Kotal, gs abdomen, dow 23 Oct

Lieutenant
Wylie, George MacLeod (attchd from 2nd Btn)   k 16 Nov 1897 Waran, gs head

Subadars
Bahadur Sing Rana   dang w 20 Oct 1897 Dargai, gs right leg & back
Ranbir Thapa   k 20 Oct 1897 Dargai, gs abdomen

Jemadars
Birbal Sing Khattri   sl w 20 Oct 1897 Dargai; awarded IOM 3rd Class
Kalu Gurung   sev w 11 Dec 1897 Bagh to Barkai march, gs left leg

Havildars
1388 Arjun Gurung   k 20 Oct 1897 Dargai
1709 Birbal Gurung   dang w 20 Oct 1897 Dargai, gs right forearm, left side neck & leg
1659 Fateh Sing Newar   sev w 11 Dec 1897 Bagh to Barkai march, gs body
2163 Goba Rai   k 20 Oct 1897 Dargai
1575 Motiram Rana   sev w 3 Nov 1897 Maidan, gs right groin
1589 Nar Sing Thapa   sev w 11 Dec 1897 Bagh to Barkai march, gs left leg

Naiks
1676 Dirgmani Thapa   sl w 25 Oct 1897 Karappa, gs mouth & neck
1739 Garjmani Thapa   sl w 29 Nov 1897 Lozaka Pass, gs thigh
1606 Jai Bhan Bohra   k 20 Oct 1897 Dargai
2402 Kaman Sing Thapa   sl w 20 Oct 1897 Dargai, gs chest; awarded IOM 3rd Class
1732 Patiram Gharti   dang w 20 Oct 1897 Dargai, gs right shoulder
2392 Sher Sing Gharti   sev w 20 Oct 1897 Dargai, gs fracture tarsus

Lance-Naiks

1650 Chet Sing Khawas   sev w 20 Oct 1897 Dargai, gs right foot
1979 Gorea Gurung   sl w 13 Dec 1897 Bagh to Barkai march, gs neck
1348 Lall Sing Thapa   dang w 22 Nov 1897 Bagh, gs chest
 380 Sundar Gurung   sev w 16 Nov 1897 Waran (Tseri Kandao), gs
        lower body
 685 Sunjit Lama   sev w 3 Nov 1897 Maidan, gs right leg

Riflemen

2168 Badal Sing Limbu   sev w 20 Oct 1897 Dargai, gs back
2036 Bagbir Sarki   k 16 Nov 1897 Waran (Tseri Kandao)
2494 Bala Sing Thapa   sev w 20 Oct 1897 Dargai, gs right side
2917 Balesur Thapa   k 20 Oct 1897 Dargai
2761 Bhangu Ale   k 16 Nov 1897 Waran (Tseri Kandao)
2794 Bhim Sing Thapa   k 20 Oct 1897 Dargai
 965 Bhimsin Thapa   sev w 11 Dec 1897 Bagh to Barkai march,
        gs right ear
2679 Bishna Roka   sl w 20 Oct 1897 Dargai, gs left hand
2969 Budhir Gurung   sl w 20 Oct 1897 Dargai, gs right foot
2716 Chakrabir Thapa   k 20 Oct 1897 Dargai
2486 Chandarbir Gurung   sl w 20 Oct 1897 Dargai, gs right arm
1864 Chandarbir Rana   sev w 20 Oct 1897 Dargai, gs
2040 Dal Sing Rana   sl w 20 Oct 1897 Dargai, gs scalp
2812 Dalu Thapa   sev w 20 Oct 1897 Dargai, gs right hand
2863 Deoraj Thapa   sev w 11 Dec 1897 Bagh to Barkai march, gs
        right arm
2951 Dewan Sing Rana   k 13 Dec 1897 Bagh to Barkai march, gs
        forehead
1809 Dhanbir Basniat   dang w 20 Oct 1897 Dargai, gs left foot
2418 Dhanbir Pun   dang w 20 Oct 1897 Dargai, gs right knee
2791 Dhanea Thapa   k 20 Oct 1897 Dargai
2261 Dhojbir Limbu   sev w 20 Oct 1897 Dargai, gs left knee
2484 Durgamani Thapa   sev w 20 Oct 1897 Dargai, gs back
 595 Fatteh Sing Thapa   (attchd from 2nd Btn)   sl w 20 Oct 1897
        Dargai, gs
2824 Gagan Sing Gurung   sev w 20 Oct 1897 Dargai, gs both thighs
2082 Gamar Sing Gurung   sev w 11 Dec 1897 Bagh to Barkai march,
        gs right leg & shoulder
2516 Gambar Sing Gurung   sev w 20 Oct 1897 Dargai, gs left forearm
2411 Gangea Thapa   sl w 31 Jan 1898 Shinkamar, gs right fore-finger
2110 Ghanbir Sahi   dang w 10 Dec 1897 Bagh to Barkai march, gs
        left leg
2478 Goresar Thapa   sev w 20 Oct 1897 Dargai, gs right shoulder
2154 Harakbir Thapa   dang w 20 Oct 1897 Dargai, gs right thigh
2485 Harak Sing Gurung   sev w 18 Oct 1897 Dargai, gs right thigh
1840 Harku Gurung   sev w 20 Oct 1897 Dargai, gs thigh
2818 Hastea Ale   sev w 20 Oct 1897 Dargai, gs skull
2111 Jagbir Mangi   sev w 20 Oct 1897 Dargai, gs right leg
2903 Jagbir Thapa   sev w 25 Oct 1897 Karappa, gs chest
2588 Jangbir Gurung   sev w 20 Oct 1897 Dargai, gs forearm
1252 Jangbir Rana   sev w 20 Oct 1897 Dargai, gs left side of back
2203 Jangbir Rana   sev w 29 Nov 1897 Lozaka Pass, gs chest
2817 Jitbahadur Gurung   sev w 20 Oct 1897 Dargai, gs back

```
2815 Jitman Thapa       k 29 Nov 1897 Lozaka Pass, gs heart
2400 Judhbir Hamal      k 20 Oct 1897 Dargai
2718 Kaliram Pun        sl w 3 Nov 1897 Maidan, gs right foot
2894 Kalu Thapa         sev w 20 Oct 1897 Dargai, gs
 868 Karbir Thapa       sev w 11 Dec 1897 Bagh to Barkai march, gs
                        left wrist
1672 Karbir Thapa       sl w 20 Oct 1897 Dargai, gs
2517 Kulman Thapa       sev w 18 Oct 1897 Dargai, gs left thigh
2652 Lalbir Gurung      sev w 20 Oct 1897 Dargai, gs right thigh & leg
2477 Manbhadar Thapa    sev w 16 Nov 1897 Waran (Tseri Kandao), gs
                        left leg
2610 Manbir Gurung      sev w 22 Nov 1897 Bagh, gs right arm
2867 Manbir Gurung      sev w 13 Dec 1897 march from Bagh to Barkai,
                        gs left shoulder
1924 Manikharan Gharti  sl w 20 Oct 1897 Dargai, gs
2524 Manilal Gurung     k 16 Nov 1897 Waran (Tseri Kandao)
2962 Maniram Thapa      sev w 20 Oct 1897 Dargai, gs abdomen; k 11
                        Dec 1897 Bagh to Barkai march, gs body
1741 Nain Sing Rana     k 20 Oct 1897 Dargai
2052 Nain Sing Rawat    sl w 20 Oct 1897 Dargai, gs right leg
2871 Nandbir Thapa      sev w 20 Oct 1897 Dargai, gs right knee
2202 Nandlal Thapa      k 20 Oct 1897 Dargai
2848 Narbahadur Gurung  k 20 Oct 1897 Dargai
2628 Narbir Thapa       sev w 20 Oct 1897 Dargai, gs
1785 Narjit Gharti      k 20 Oct 1897 Dargai
2488 Nar Sing Thapa     sev w 20 Oct 1897 Dargai, gs right carpus
2062 Nayar Sing Gharti  sev w 20 Oct 1897 Dargai, gs right
                        shoulder
2623 Pahal Sing Gurung  k 15 Nov 1897 Waran, gs left leg
2764 Partiman Thapa     sl w 16 Nov 1897 Waran (Tseri Kandao), gs
                        left hand
2756 Pertap Sing Gurung sev w 20 Oct 1897 Dargai, gs right arm
2713 Puranbir Thapa     sev w 20 Oct 1897 Dargai, gs scalp
2773 Rabilal Thapa      dang w 20 Oct 1897 Dargai, gs chest
2836 Ran Bahadur Thapa  sev w 20 Oct 1897 Dargai, gs right hand
2626 Ranbir Gurung      k 18 Oct 1897 Dargai
2910 Ranbir Thapa       sl w 20 Oct 1897 Dargai, gs left shoulder
3121 Ransur Gurung      sev w 7 Nov 1897 Maidan, gs right arm
2117 Rithu Sing Khatri  k 11 Dec 1897 Bagh to Barkai march, gs head
2800 Saman Sing Ghale   sev w 20 Oct 1897 Dargai, gs right leg
2617 Sarabjit Gurung    sev w 16 Nov 1897 Waran (Tseri Kandao), gs
                        right leg
2879 Sarabjit Gurung    dang w 18 Oct 1897 Dargai, gs abdomen, dow
2915 Sarabjit Thapa     sl w 10 Dec 1897 Bagh to Barkai, gs right ear
2978 Sarabjit Thapa     sl w 20 Oct 1897 Dargai, gs left eyebrow
 787 Sirman Gurung      (attchd from 2nd Btn)   k 20 Oct 1897 Dargai
2360 Siupersad Khatri   sev w 20 Oct 1897 Dargai, gs right buttock
2581 Talbir Pun         sev w 20 Oct 1897 Dargai, gs right side chest
2873 Tikaram Gurung     sev w 15 Nov 1897 Waran, gs right leg
 388 Tularam Thapa      (attchd from 2nd Btn)   k 20 Oct 1897 Dargai
2020 Wazir Sing Gurung  k 20 Oct 1897 Dargai
```

1st Btn 3rd GURKHA (RIFLE) REGIMENT

Captain
Bateman-Champain, Arthur Patrick   (attchd from 2nd Btn)   sl w 13 Dec 1897 Bagh to Barkai march, gs chest

Lieutenant
West, George William Maxwell   k 13 Dec 1897 Bagh to Barkai march, gs chest

Jemadars
Harakbir Gurung   sev w 18 Oct 1897 Dargai, gs lumbar region
Tularam Mal   dang w 13 Dec 1897 Bagh to Barkai march, gs chest

Havildars
1109 Khimya Thapa   sl w 13 Dec 1897 Bagh to Barkai march, gs head
 438 Nand Ram Khattri   sl w 31 Jan 1898 Shinkamar, gs left shoulder
1041 Padam Sing Karki   sl w 13 Dec 1897 Bagh to Barkai march, gs right thigh
 102 Singbir Thapa   sev w 13 Dec 1897 Bagh to Barkai march, gs buttock

Naiks
1449 Dhokal Gurung   sl w 18 Oct 1897 Dargai, gs right ankle
1501 Nandbir Thapa   k 20 Oct 1897 Dargai
1422 Partiman Thapa   sl w 13 Dec 1897 Bagh to Barkai march, gs head

Lance-Naiks
1573 Dalbir Thapa   k 1 Nov 1897 Maidan, gs cardiac region
1491 Damar Sing Thapa   sev w 13 Dec 1897 Bagh to Barkai, gs left leg
1537 Karakbir Thapa   sev w 23 Oct 1897 Karappa, gs left wrist

Riflemen
2482 Amar Sing Gurung   dang w 25 Oct 1897 Karappa, gs left forearm
1423 Bakhat Bahadur Gurung   dang w 18 Oct 1897 Dargai, gs right thigh
1979 Bala Sing Gurung   k 27 Oct 1897 Karappa, gs chest
1644 Bhabesar Thapa   sev w 13 Dec 1897 Bagh to Barkai march, gs left forearm
2107 Bhairab Bahadur Gurung   sl w 13 Dec 1897 Bagh to Barkai march, gs neck & jaw
1918 Bhanbir Gurung   k 20 Oct 1897 Dargai
2047 Budhi Sing Gurung   sev w 7 Dec 1897 Bagh to Barkai march, gs left arm
2437 Chamar Sing Gurung   k 13 Dec 1897 Bagh to Barkai march, gs pelvis
2374 Chandarbir Rana   k 18 Oct 1897 Dargai
2439 Dalbahadur Gurung   sev w 13 Dec 1897 Bagh to Barkai march, gs left arm
2383 Dalu Thapa   sev w 8 Dec 1897 Bagh to Barkai march, gs left leg
2141 Dhojbir Thapa   sl w 18 Oct 1897 Dargai, gs right arm
2350 Dilaram Thapa   sl w 18 Oct 1897 Dargai, gs right thigh

2459 Gajbir Thapa   sev w 10 Dec 1897 Bagh to Barkai march, gs
                left thigh
1632 Gungadhar Thapa   sl w 18 Oct 1897 Dargai, gs head
1511 Harak Bahadur Thapa   sl w 1 Nov 1897 Maidan, gs right foot
2100 Harakbir Rana   sl w 24 Nov 1897 Dwatoi, gs chin & chest
2333 Hastbir Thapa   sev w 18 Oct 1897 Dargai, gs left leg
1899 Jangbir Sahi   sev w 1 Nov 1897 Maidan, gs left wrist
2407 Kalivraz Gurung   sev w 19 Nov 1897 Bagh, gs head
1869 Kalu Gurung   sev w 13 Dec 1897 Bagh to Barkai march, gs
                left arm
1709 Kalu Thapa   sl w 13 Dec 1897 Bagh to Barkai march, gs left leg
2401 Kalya Gurung   k 8 Dec 1897 Bagh to Barkai march, gs head
1934 Karbir Rana   k 18 Oct 1897 Dargai
1817 Karne Thapa   sl w 8 Dec 1897 Bagh to Barkai march, gs uttock
2405 Karn Pun   k 13 Dec 1897 Bagh to Barkai march, gs head
2252 Khagendra Thapa   sev w 13 Dec 1897 Bagh to Barkai march, gs
                right arm
2272 Kulbahadur Thapa   sev w 13 Dec 1897 Bagh to Barkai march, gs
                left shoulder
2364 Kulbir Gurung   dang w 12 Dec 1897 Bagh to Barkai march, gs
                left thigh
2227 Lalbir Thapa   sl w 20 Oct 1897 Dargai, gs face & neck;
            awarded IOM 3rd Class
1263 Lilaram Thapa   k 13 Dec 1897 Bagh to Barkai march, gs chest
2418 Manbir Thapa   k 13 Dec 1897 Bagh to Barkai march, gs head
2279 Maniraj Thapa   k 13 Dec 1897 Bagh to Barkai march, gs spine
2086 Nandkesar Rana   dang w 18 Oct 1897 Dargai, gs right arm
1905 Naresar Thapa   dang w 13 Dec 1897 Bagh to Barkai march,
            gs pelvis
2037 Narjit Thapa   k 20 Nov 1897 Bagh, gs head
2201 Pahalman Sahai   sl w 20 Oct 1897 Dargai, gs right lumbar
                muscles; awarded IOM 3rd Class
2275 Puran Ale   sev w 18 Oct 1897 Dargai, gs right foot
1758 Rajmani Gurung   sl w 23 Nov 1897 Dwatoi, gs right leg
2223 Ram Sing Sahi   k 27 Oct 1897 Karappa, gs right thigh,
                cutting artery
2069 Ran Sing Thapa   sev w 13 Dec 1897 Bagh to Barkai march, gs
                left thigh
2430 Ratanbir Ale   sev w 18 Oct 1897 Dargai, gs pelvis
1699 Sahabir Gurung   sl w 1 Nov 1897 Maidan, gs left shoulder
2396 Sarabjit Thapa   k 24 Nov 1897 Dwatoi
2431 Sarap Sing Rana   dang w 18 Nov 1897 Maidan, gs buttock
1811 Sher Bahadur Gurung   sl w 18 Oct 1897 Dargai, gs right ear
1643 Talbikram Rana   sev w 13 Dec 1897 Bagh to Barkai march, gs
                left arm

2nd Btn 4th GURKHA (RIFLE) REGIMENT

Havildar
 251 Birumal Thapa   sl w 8 Nov 1897 Maidan, gs right hand

Lance-Naik
 923 Dalbhim Thapa   sev w 28 Oct 1897 Gandakai, gs left upper arm

Musician
1509 Sher Sing Thapa   sev w 27 Nov 1897 Lozaka Pass, gs right hand

Riflemen
1257 Balbir Thapa   k 8 Nov 1897 Maidan, gs left leg
1637 Bhartbir Gurung   dang w 8 Nov 1897 Maidan, gs left elbow,
      arm amputated
1341 Bherab Sing Gurung   sev w 26 Nov 1897 Lozaka Pass, gs left
      thigh
1142 Bikram Thapa   k 28 Oct 1897 Gandakai, gs head
1076 Chandarbir Thapa   sev w 26 Dec 1897 Chura, gs right buttock
1335 Debu Rana   sev w 28 Oct 1897 Gandakai, gs thigh
1715 Dhansur Gurung   sl w 26 Dec 1897 Chura, gs back
1069 Jaman Sing Gurung   sl w 2 Dec 1897 Thabai, gs left cheek
 450 Jokhe Gurung   dang w 3 Nov 1897 Maidan, gs left upper arm
1289 Khabun Sing Gurung   sev w 26 Nov 1897 Lozaka Pass, gs left leg
1550 Kumb Sing Gurung   sev w 1 Dec 1897 Thabai, gs abdomen
1542 Lal Sing Thapa   dang w 26 Nov 1897 Lozaka Pass, gs neck
1093 Lilambur Ale   dang w 26 Nov 1897 Lozaka Pass, gs right thigh
1693 Mikhman Rana   sev w 27 Nov 1897 Lozaka Pass, gs abdomen
 794 Parbal Thapa   missing 1 Dec 1897 Thabai
 848 Puran Gharti   sev w 29 Oct 1897 Sampagha Pass, gs face
3693 Sante Rana   k 26 Dec 1897 Chura, gs chest
 591 Singbir Pun   sev w 25 Oct 1897 Karappa, gs left leg
1191 Tikaram Thapa   sev w 26 Nov 1897 Lozaka Pass, gs chest

No 1 (KOHAT) MOUNTAIN BATTERY, PUNJAB FRONTIER FORCE

Gunner
54 Maya Singh   sl w 25 Oct 1897 Karappa, gs wrist

Driver
21 Rustam Ali   sl w 9 Dec 1897 Waran Valley, gs right hand

No 2 (DERAJAT) MOUNTAIN BATTERY, PUNJAB FRONTIER FORCE

Lieutenant
Wyatt, Francis Ogilvy (attchd from No 23 Co, RA)   sl w 29 Nov 1897 Kahu, gs right arm

Gunner Naik
531 Muhammad Ali   k 18 Nov 1897 Bagh, gs left lung

Gunners
565 Daulat   dang w 18 Nov 1897 Bagh, gs thigh, dow
607 Lal Khan   sl w 28 Oct 1897 Gandakai, gs hand
426 Nand Singh   sl w 18 Nov 1897 Bagh, gs wrist

Driver Naik
269 Bhola Singh   sev w 29 Nov 1897 Kahu, gs left thigh

3rd REGIMENT OF SIKH INFANTRY, PUNJAB FRONTIER FORCE

Lieutenant
White, George Edmund (attchd from 1/Devonshire Regt)   dang w 20 Oct 1897 Chagru Kotal, gs chest

Subadars
Lehna Singh   sev w 20 Oct 1897 Dargai, gs left side chest; awarded IOM 3rd Class
Malu Singh   dang w 20 Oct 1897 Dargai, gs abdomen, dow 24 Oct

Jemadar
Beli Ram   sev w 20 Oct 1897 Dargai, gs back; awarded IOM 3rd Class

Havildars
 869 Gul Feroz   sev w 20 Oct 1897 Dargai, gs right foot
1630 Jan Muhammad   sev w 20 Oct 1897 Dargai, gs
 516 Lalit Singh   sev w 20 Oct 1897 Dargai, gs

Naiks
1436 Juma Khan   sev w 20 Oct 1897 Dargai, gs
1021 Lal Singh   dang w 18 Oct 1897 Dargai, gs left leg
1205 Suchet Singh   sev w 20 Oct 1897 Dargai, gs left forearm

Lance-Naiks
1427 Jai Singh   dang w 2 Dec 1897 Thabai, gs left thigh
1576 Pala Singh   sev w 29 Nov 1897 Dargai, gs leg

Buglers
2558 Bhagwan Singh   dang w 18 Nov 1897 Bagh, gs left arm
1857 Prem Singh   sev w 29 Nov 1897 Dargai, gs leg

Sepoys

2548	Bilanda Singh	sev w 20 Oct 1897 Dargai, gs right leg
1784	Chanan Singh	sev w 20 Oct 1897 Dargai, g right thigh
1908	Chet Singh	k 20 Oct 1897 Dargai
2634	Dalip Singh	k 20 Oct 1897 Dargai
2196	Devi Singh	dang w 20 Oct 1897 Dargai, gs left shoulder
2659	Ganda Singh	k 27 Nov 1897 Lozaka Pass, gs abdomen
2377	Ganga Singh	sl w 27 Dec 1897 Khyber Pass, gs face
2549	Ganga Singh	sl w 20 Oct 1897 Dargai, gs hand
2555	Gopi	sev w 20 Oct 1897 Dargai, gs left hand
2626	Gulzar Khan	sev w 27 Dec 1897 Khyber Pass, gs both thighs & right hand
1702	Hazara Singh	sl w 29 Oct 1897 Sampagha Pass, gs left thigh
2057	Kala Singh	sev w 2 Dec 1897 Thabai, gs left leg
1777	Karm Singh	sev w 20 Oct 1897 Dargai, gs
2663	Khani Sher	k 25 Oct 1897 Karappa, gs abdomen
2286	Khiyali	sev w 20 Oct 1897 Dargai, gs lumbar region
2456	Labh Singh	k 20 Oct 1897 Dargai
2069	Mangal Singh	k 18 Nov 1897 Bagh, gs abdomen
2396	Mehr Singh	dang w 20 Nov 1897 between Maidan camp and Bagh, gs chest
2468	Miran Baksh	sev w 9 Nov 1897 Saran Sar, gs left foot
2603	Nathu Singh	sev w 20 Oct 1897 Dargai, gs right leg
2422	Nur Shah Gul	sev w 20 Oct 1897 Dargai, gs
1374	Partab Singh	sl w 29 Oct 1897 Sampagha Pass, gs face
1699	Ranjha Singh	sev w 20 Oct 1897 Dargai, gs left thigh
2619	Sant Ram	sl w 20 Oct 1897 Dargai, gs
2484	Sohan Singh	sev w 31 Oct 1897 Arhanga Pass, gs neck

2nd REGIMENT OF PUNJAB INFANTRY, PUNJAB FRONTIER FORCE

Lance-Naik

3878	Waras Khan	sev w 13 Dec 1897 Bagh to Barkai march, gs thigh

Sepoys

403	Ali Muhammad	sev w 11 Dec 1897 Bagh to Barkai march, gs shoulder
483	Biru	dang w 11 Dec 1897 Bagh to Barkai march, gs chest
141	Ghazi Khan	sev w 12 Dec 1897 Bagh to Barkai march, gs right thigh
215	Hamidulla	k 10 Dec 1897 Bagh to Barkai march, gs head
4640	Ishar Singh	sev w 12 Dec 1897 Bagh to Barkai march, gs right thigh
4508	Jawala Singh	sl w 11 Dec 1897 Bagh to Barkai march, gs hand
588	Jiwand Singh	sev w 11 Dec 1897 Bagh to Barkai march, gs back
435	Kala Singh	k 14 Dec 1897 Bagh to Barkai march, gs chest
4309	Karm Khan	sev w 12 Dec 1897 Bagh to Barkai march, gs right thigh

```
 137 Labh Singh     k 27 Oct 1897 Karappa, gs neck
 528 Miraj Gul      dang w 12 Dec 1897 Bagh to Barkai march, gs chest
 151 Muhammad Azim  k 27 Oct 1897 Karappa, gs chest
 314 Mutsadi       sev w 13 Dec 1897 Bagh to Barkai march, gs forearm
                      & hips
 125 Narayan Singh  dang w 10 Dec 1897 Bagh to Barkai march, gs
                      chest, dow
 742 Nur Din        dang w 8 Feb 1898 Gandao, gs chest
  77 Partab Singh   sev w 11 Dec 1897 Bagh to Barkai march, gs
                      both hands
4263 Payanda Singh  sev w 10 Dec 1897 Bagh to Barkai march, gs leg
4795 Ram Dyal       dang w 18 Dec 1897 Bara, sword cut head
 173 Sher Ali       sev w 11 Dec 1897 Bagh to Barkai march, gs leg
4897 Talo Singh     sev w 11 Dec 1897 Bagh to Barkai march, gs leg
```

1st Btn 5th GURKHA (RIFLE) REGIMENT, PUNJAB FRONTIER FORCE

Major
Vansittart, Eden   sl w 2 Dec 1897 Thabai, gs

Lieutenant
Villiers-Stuart, William Desmond   dang w 1 Dec 1897 Thabai,
                                      gs thigh, fractured

Havildar
1846 Bir Sing Gurung   sev w 1 Dec 1897 Thabai, gs thorax;
                          awarded IOM 3rd Class

Riflemen
```
2240 Dhanbir Ran       k 7 Nov 1897 Karmana Darra
2390 Drig Sing Satu    k 2 Dec 1897 Thabai
3399 Jit Sing Gurung   dang w 7 Nov 1897 Karmana Darra, gs left
                         shoulder
3404 Kumar Sing Gurung sev w 1 Dec 1897 Thabai, gs thigh
2836 Lachman Thapa     k 1 Dec 1897 Thabai
2908 Mansbir Thapa     k 1 Dec 1897 Thabai
2880 Mohan Sing Gurung sl w 7 Nov 1897 Karmana Darra, gs
                         left foot
2697 Ranbir Thapa      k 2 Dec 1897 Thabai
```

5th GURKHA SCOUTS

Havildar
 161 Bidan Sing   sev w 26 Nov 1897 west of Bagh, gs leg

Riflemen
```
3247 Dhanbar Gurung   k 15 Nov 1897 Maidan, gs head
3112 Dhanraj Gurung   sev w 26 Nov 1897 west of Bagh, gs thigh
3442 Kasiram Thapa    sl w 29 Oct 1897 Sampagha Pass, gs chin
```

21st REGIMENT OF MADRAS INFANTRY (PIONEERS)

<u>Jemadar</u>
Inayat Khan   dang w 23 Oct 1897 Karappa, gs abdomen, dow 24 Oct

<u>Sepoys</u>
2399 Arogyam   sev w 6 Nov 1897 Maidan, gs left thigh
1543 Gooranah   sev w 28 Dec 1897 Barg, gs left arm
1857 Ismail Khan   sev w 28 Dec 1897 Barg, gs left foot
2512 Kalashah   sev w 23 Oct 1897 Karappa, gs left shoulder
1733 Kappalswamy   sl w 28 Dec 1897 Barg, gs neck
1499 Lutchimi Naryanswamy   sev w 28 Dec 1897 Barg, gs back
1141 Permalloo   sev w 28 Dec 1897 Barg, gs left shoulder
1730 Seetanah   k 28 Dec 1897 Barg, gs head

No 5 (BOMBAY) MOUNTAIN BATTERY

<u>Captain</u>
De Butts, Frederick Robert McCrea   RA   k 29 Oct 1897 Sampagha Pass, gs femoral artery

<u>Naik</u>
2465 Sadda Singh   sl w 16 Nov 1897 Waran (Tseri Kandao), gs right hand

<u>Gunner</u>
2325 Ismail   sl w 30 Oct 1897 Arhanga Pass, gs

<u>Drivers</u>
 630 Achhar Singh   dang w 15 Nov 1897 Waran, gs back & stomach, dow
 913 Buta Khan   sl w 7 Dec 1897 Bagh to Barkai march, gs head
 711 Jiwa Singh   sev w 13 Dec 1897 Bagh to Barkai march, gs thigh

No 3 Co, BOMBAY SAPPERS & MINERS

<u>Naik</u>
1437 Rammanobar Chaube   dang w 18 Nov 1897 Bagh, gs forehead & right wrist

<u>Nalband</u>
 506 Sooklal Mohipati   sev w 26 Nov 1897 west of Lozaka Pass, gs right hand

<u>Muleteer</u>
 444 Shaba Khandoo   sev w 26 Nov 1897 west of Lozaka Pass, gs leg

No 4 Co, BOMBAY SAPPERS & MINERS

Lieutenant
Tonge, Cecil Richard RE k 28 Dec 1897 Karamna, by explosion of a mine

Sergeant
22673 Clarke, Alfred John RE sl w 23 Nov 1897 Dwatoi, gs right calf

Colour-Havildar
618 Dharamgir sl w 28 Dec 1897 Karamna, contusions

Lance-Naik
1979 Sobha Singh k 28 Dec 1897 Karamna, by an explosion

Bugler
723 Saknak Ramnac sl w 28 Dec 1897 Karamna, right elbow dislocated

Sappers
1995 Dulaji Gowli dang w 25 Dec 1897 Khyber Pass, gs right shoulder
2000 Narain Singh dang w 26 Nov 1897 Kahu, gs right shoulder & face
1886 Sundar Singh sl w 8 Nov 1897 Maidan, gs right calf
2044 Utman Singh sl w 26 Nov 1897 Kahu, gs right hand

28th REGIMENT OF BOMBAY INFANTRY (PIONEERS)

Subadar
Muhammad Khan sl w 18 Nov 1897 Bagh, gs contusion foot

Hospital Assistant 2nd Grade
144 Shaik Ommer k 10 Jan 1898 Gandao, gs

Naik
2402 Baboo Sinday k 18 Jan 1898 Gandao Pass, gs

Lance-Naiks
859 Narna Pawar k 16 Jan 1898 Gandao Pass, gs
2161 Shirpatti Jadow dang w 9 Dec 1897 Bagh to Barkai march, gs pelvis

Privates
2182 Aba Nimbalkar k 16 Jan 1898 Gandao Pass, gs
2503 Ahmed Khan sev w 10 Dec 1897 Bagh to Barkai march, gs thigh
2477 Bahadur Khan sev w 13 Dec 1897 Bagh to Barkai march, gs thigh
1878 Dhondi Ghotgayker dang w 18 Nov 1897 Bagh, gs chest
1795 Govind Baney sev w 10 Dec 1897 Bagh to Barkai march, gs foot
1631 Govind Bardarey dang w 18 Jan 1898 Gandao Pass, gs neck & left leg

1963 Gul Akhmad Khan   sl w 22 Nov 1897 Raj-Gul, gs right arm
2579 Kondie Dhangar   sev w 22 Nov 1897 Raj-Gul, gs shoulder &
                            thigh
2497 Krishna Morey   k 7 Nov 1897 Maidan, gs brain
2108 Luknak Bhagnak   sl w 22 Nov 1897 Raj-Gul, gs right iliac
                            region
 541 Mahadoo Sirdourey sev w 18 Jan 1898 Gandao Pass, gs both
                            thighs
 536 Maroti Baber   k 18 Jan 1898 Gandao Pass, gs
2493 Rama Sinday   dang w 16 Jan 1898 Gandao Pass, gs right leg
2399 Sileman   sl w 22 Nov 1897 Raj-Gul, gs left hand
2100 Sitaram Chipkar   k 22 Nov 1897 Raj-Gul, gs head
 540 Tukaram Kesre   k 18 Jan 1898 Gandao Pass, gs

Driver
1957 Mehta Singh   dang w 9 Dec 1897 Bagh to Barkai march, gs
                            pelvis, dow

CENTRAL INDIA HORSE

Trumpeter
1493 Ahmad Khan   sl w 1 Dec 1897 Thabai, gs abdomen

JEYPORE IMPERIAL SERVICE TRANSPORT TRAIN

Daffadar
Nur Muhammad   sev w 1 Nov 1897 Maidan, gs left thigh

Saddler
Dulia   sl w 1 Nov 1897 Maidan, gs

Drivers
    Abdula   sev w 1 Nov 1897 Maidan, gs leg
    Karam Elahi   k 1 Nov 1897 Maidan, gs chest
    Pima   k 1 Nov 1897 Maidan, gs chest
 53 Sirdar Singh   dang w 15 Jan 1898 Jamrud, gs right side, dow

JHIND IMPERIAL SERVICE INFANTRY

Kot Havildar
 91 Sundar Singh   missing 13 Dec 1897 Bagh to Barkai march

Havildars
- 529 Kishan Singh sev w 13 Dec 1897 Bagh to Barkai march, gs right arm
- 695 Niamat Khan sev w 13 Nov 1897 Mastura, gs left arm

Naiks
- 367 Bodal sev w 13 Dec 1897 Bagh to Barkai march, gs left foot
- 191 Prem Singh k 13 Dec 1897 Bagh to Barkai march, cut up
- 764 Sobha Singh sev w 16 Nov 1897 Maidan, gs left thigh

Lance-Naik
- 298 Shima sev w 3 Nov 1897 Maidan, gs right leg

Sepoys
- 1135 Bassant Singh sev w 13 Dec 1897 Bagh to Barkai, gs right hand
- Chabar Singh sl w 12 Oct 1897 Chagru Kotal, gs
- 786 Gul Khan sev w 8 Nov 1897 Karappa, gs back
- 373 Hoshiyara sev w 13 Dec 1897 Bagh to Barkai march, gs left thigh
- 875 Imam Din sl w 8 Nov 1897 Karappa, gs hip
- 1207 Jaimal Singh sev w 10 Dec 1897 Bagh to Barkai march, gs arm
- 795 Jewa sev w 19 Nov 1897 Bagh, gs neck
- 301 Kala Singh sev w 16 Nov 1897 Maidan, gs left foot
- 785 Khair Din sl w 8 Nov 1897 Karappa, gs hand
- 1141 Kishan Singh sl w 14 Dec 1897 Bagh to Barkai march, gs right knee
- 724 Mehar Khan sev w 18 Nov 1897 Mastura, gs hand
- 1176 Mota Singh sev w 25 Oct 1897 Karappa, gs left foot
- 1162 Natha Singh sev w 13 Dec 1897 Bagh to Barkai march, gs left thigh
- 1220 Phuman Singh sl w 13 Dec 1897 Bagh to Barkai march, gs buttock
- 1222 Rulia sl w 13 Nov 1897 Mastura, gs right thigh
- 876 Sundar Khan sl w 8 Nov 1897 Karappa, gs shoulder
- 1181 Umra Khan sev w 12 Oct 1897 Chagru Kotal, gs
- 1195 Wazir Singh sev w 16 Nov 1897 Maidan, gs left arm
- 1106 Yusuf Ali sev w 25 Oct 1897 Karappa, gs right leg

KAPURTHALLA IMPERIAL SERVICE INFANTRY

Subadar
Dewa Singh k 7 Nov 1897 Karmana Darra

Kot Havildar
312 Sant Ram k 7 Nov 1897 Karmana Darra

Havildar
59 Uttam Singh k 7 Nov 1897 Karmana Darra

Naiks
```
 407 Gopal Singh     k 7 Nov 1897 Karmana Darra
 637 Hukam Singh     k 7 Nov 1897 Karmana Darra
 478 Nabi Bakhsh     k 7 Nov 1897 Karmana Darra
 599 Narain Singh    k 7 Nov 1897 Karmana Darra
 590 Sundar Singh    k 7 Nov 1897 Karmana Darra
```

Lance-Naiks
```
 697 Bhagat Singh    k 7 Nov 1897 Karmana Darra
 552 Jawala Singh    k 7 Nov 1897 Karmana Darra
 873 Khushal Singh   k 7 Nov 1897 Karmana Darra
```

Sepoys
```
1025 Badam Singh     k 7 Nov 1897 Karmana Darra
 469 Bagga Singh     k 7 Nov 1897 Karmana Darra
 815 Bhagwan Singh   k 7 Nov 1897 Karmana Darra
 617 Bhan Singh      k 7 Nov 1897 Karmana Darra
 791 Bir Singh       k 7 Nov 1897 Karmana Darra
 710 Chanda Singh    dang w 1 Dec 1897 Thabai, gs pelvis, dow
 544 Chundar Singh   k 7 Nov 1897 Karmana Darra
 615 Dyal Singh      k 7 Nov 1897 Karmana Darra
 995 Ganesh Singh    k 7 Nov 1897 Karmana Darra
 498 Hira Singh      k 7 Nov 1897 Karmana Darra
 641 Ishar Singh     k 7 Nov 1897 Karmana Darra
 978 Jawala Singh    k 7 Nov 1897 Karmana Darra
1067 Jawala Singh    k 7 Nov 1897 Karmana Darra
 958 Jawan Singh     k 7 Nov 1897 Karmana Darra
 960 Jawan Singh     k 7 Nov 1897 Karmana Darra
 565 Kharak Singh    k 7 Nov 1897 Karmana Darra
1011 Labh Singh      k 7 Nov 1897 Karmana Darra
 798 Lukha Singh     sev w 1 Dec 1897 Thabai, gs arm
 953 Miran Baksh     k 7 Nov 1897 Karmana Darra
 677 Nand Singh      sev w 7 Nov 1897 Karmana Darra, gs forehead
 918 Nant Singh      k 7 Nov 1897 Karmana Darra
 665 Nizamdin        k 7 Nov 1897 Karmana Darra
 934 Puran Singh     k 7 Nov 1897 Karmana Darra
 569 Ram Singh       k 7 Nov 1897 Karmana Darra
 700 Roor Singh      k 7 Nov 1897 Karmana Darra
 198 Saij Singh      k 7 Nov 1897 Karmana Darra
 869 Sewa Singh      sl w 1 Dec 1897 Thabai, gs leg
 853 Suchet Singh    k 7 Nov 1897 Karmana Darra
```

Pioneer
```
 671 Godar Bakhsh    k 7 Nov 1897 Karmana Darra
```

MALER-KOTLA IMPERIAL SERVICE SAPPERS & MINERS

Sapper
```
 179 Mazulla Khan    k 22 Nov 1897 Bagh, gs head
```

NABHA IMPERIAL SERVICE INFANTRY

Havildar
 513 Kishan Singh   k 9 Dec 1897 Waran Valley, gs left breast

Lance-Naik
 160 Hussain Khan   dang w 25 Oct 1897 Karappa, gs right shoulder

Sepoys
 821 Kishan Singh   sev w 9 Dec 1897 Waran Valley, gs leg
 956 Rur Singh   sev w 25 Oct 1897 Karappa, gs left arm

WAZIRISTAN 1901-02

From Maj-Gen C C Egerton, Commanding the Punjab Frontier District, dated Abbottabad 15 March 1902

I have the honour to submit, for the information of His Excellency the Commander-in-Chief in India, the following report on the raids undertaken against the Mahsud Waziris since the 24th November 1901.

2. During the hot weather the Mahsuds, who had been under blockade since November 1900, had been very active in raiding on and beyond the blockade cordon, even capturing some of our Militia and Border Police posts.

3. It was therefore arranged that the reliefs for the Dera Ismail Khan garrison and the blockading force should be simultaneously brought down to the Dera Ismail Khan border, and utilised for raiding purposes in conjunction with the blockade troops.

4. The first series of operations was directed against the Mahsuds of the Khaisara and Shahur, combined with demonstrations from Jandola into the Takhi Zam, and from Datta Khel against the north-western portion of Mahsud territory.

First series of operations.

5. The conduct of these operations was entrusted to Brigadier-General L. Dening, D.S.O., commanding the Derajat District. Their general object was to destroy all Mahsud defences, capture as many prisoners and cattle as possible, to carry off, or destroy, all grain and fodder found; and to return to their bases on the fourth day, after having inflicted all the damage possible.

The force was divided into four columns as under:

No. 1 Column.—From Datta Khel, under Lieutenant-Colonel V. C. Tonnochy, 3rd Sikhs.

No. 2 Column.—From Jandola, under Colonel H. N. McRae, C.B., A.-D.-C., 45th Sikhs.

No. 3 Column.—From Sarwakai, under Lieutenant-Colonel R. W. MacLeod, 29th Punjab Infantry.

No. 4 Column.—From Wana, under Lieutenant-Colonel W. E. Bunbury, 28th Punjab Infantry.

A Royal Engineer officer and demolition party was attached to each column.

6. The operations were carried into effect as follows:

No. 1 Column moved out from Datta Khel on November 23rd, and marched *viâ* the Shuidar Narai to Dodgul, where it bivouacked on the night of the 24th. On the 25th Dodgul was destroyed and the force proceeded down the Shuran Algad and bivouacked at a place called Bitt Malik Shahi (marked on the map as Mahsud) not far from the Razmak Kotal. On November 26th a reconnaissance was made towards the Shaktu. No opposition was met with. On November 27th Colonel Tonnochy made a dash for Makin, a considerable portion of which was destroyed. The force then retired to their bivouac at Bitt Malik Shahi. This was a very brilliant feat of arms, but at the same time a somewhat risky one, as had the column, as was probable, been heavily followed up, it would have been in a somewhat serious position. However, the result justified Colonel Tonnochy's judgment and enterprise, and had a marked effect upon the enemy. On November 28th, the column returned to Datta Khel, being followed up half-heartedly by the enemy for part of the way.

No. 2 Column left Jandola on the night of the 24th November and proceeded to Kot Shingi, which was partially destroyed. At Kot Shingi serious opposition was encountered, and as there had been several casualties, Colonel McRae decided to return to Jandola, which he reached on the afternoon of the 25th, being followed up by the enemy to within about four miles of Jandola and having suffered about twenty casualties. Next day the column reconnoitred up to the Shahur Tangi, and returned the same day, not having encountered any opposition.

No. 2 Column.

No. 3 Column left Sarwakai in the early morning of November 25th, and penetrated to Badshah Khan's village. They returned to Sarwakai on November 27th.

No. 3 Column.

No. 4 Column. No. 4 Column left Wana on the night of the 24th November, and proceeded *via* the Insar Narai into the Khaisara valley. During this and the three following days this column, aided by a small mixed column detached from the Wana garrison under Captain A. E. McBarnet, 5th Punjab Cavalry, on the 25th and 27th, completely gutted the Khaisara villages. The column returned to Wana on the 28th.

7. Simultaneously with the operations of the above columns the Southern Waziristan Militia, under Major R. Harman, D.S.O., operated in the Shaman Khel country, rendering excellent service.

8. Feeling it to be of great importance that the blow thus struck should be followed up as quickly as possible, General Dening, in consultation with the Commissioner on special duty, Mr. W. Merk, C.S.I., now submitted proposals for further operations, and at the same time asked for two additional battalions to enable him to carry them out. The proposals received sanction, and two additional regiments, *viz.*, the 32nd Pioneers and the 38th Dogras, together with two sections of a field hospital, were despatched to Tank. In the meantime, I had been directed to proceed to Tank and assume control of the operations, and four additional regiments were being sent me.

9. On the 4th December 1901, Brigadier-General Dening marched to Kot Shingi,
Second series of operations. which was destroyed, and bivouacked at Derajat Kalai. General Dening had subdivided his force into two columns under Colonel H. N. McRae, C. B., A.-D.-C., 45th Sikhs, and Lieutenant-Colonel W. duG. Gray, 1st Punjab Infantry.

10. The next day (5th) the force moved out, destroying several villages. The troops were then ordered to bivouac: Lieutenant-Colonel Gray's column, with the baggage, leading, and Colonel McRae's column covering the retirement. Lieutenant-Colonel Gray's column met with little or no opposition, and the march was continued to Guri Khel, where bivouac was formed. Meanwhile, the rear column under Colonel McRae became heavily engaged, and owing to the unauthorised withdrawal of a picquet, his left flank was so seriously threatened that he deemed it necessary to retake the position. By this time it was nearly dark, so Colonel McRae decided to remain where he was for the night, and continued his march next day across the Umar Raghza to Guri Khel, where he arrived about 11 A. M.

11. The force remained in bivouac at Guri Khel during the 6th. The enemy made frequent attacks on the picquets, but were invariably repulsed, on one occasion at the point of the bayonet by a company of the 29th Punjab Infantry under Captain H. A. Vallings.

12. The enemy were now seen in large numbers working round both flanks, and fearing for the safety of a convoy, which he had ordered to come out from Jandola with supplies, General Dening resolved to retire on Jandola.

13. On the 7th December the force retired to Murga Band, the enemy following up the picquets and rear-guard. On one occasion they attempted to rush a picquet of the 29th Punjab Infantry under Captain Vallings, but were repulsed with a loss of forty killed.

14. Their losses on this and the previous day must have been very heavy, as they made no further attempt to follow up the column, which returned to Jandola on the evening of the 8th. The retirement on this day was covered by the 38th Dogras, under Colonel F. G. Vivian, which I had sent out from Jandola for that purpose.

15. The previous operations towards the Shinkai had shown General Dening that large
Third series of operations. villages were situated in the Dwe and Tre branches of the nullah, while at the same time the Splitoi had not yet been visited. Proposals were therefore submitted for operations in that portion of the country. In the meantime the following movements had taken place:

On the 10th December a column under Lieutenant-Colonel A. F. Hogge, 23rd Pioneers, marched from Jandola to Sarwakai, which it reached on the 11th. On the 15th December a reconnaissance under Colonel Hogge was made to Turan China; no opposition was met with. On the 17th December a demonstration was made by Major F. G. Lucas, D.S.O., 5th Gurkhas, commanding at Wana, into the Khaisara.

16. On the 19th December a force left Jandola under command of Brigadier-General Dening, and proceeded to Umar Raghza. No opposition was encountered.

17. On the same date a column left Sarwakai under command of Lieutenant-Colonel Hogge, 23rd Pioneers, and proceeded up the Shahur. Their orders were to move into the Splitoi and, having hurried this valley, to cross the range forming its northern boundary and to effect a junction with General Dening's force on the evening of the 21st at Darakai, in the Tre Shinkai.

18. General Dening's operations in the meantime had been as follows :—

On the 20th December the force moved to Ahmadwan, and thence up to the Tre nullah for some three or four miles, the enemy offering but slight resistance. Heliographic communication was established during the day with Colonel Hogge's column from Sarwakai. The force bivouacked near Paridal. On 21st December a force of 550 rifles under Major Harman, D.S.O., Commandant, Southern Waziristan Militia, covered the left flank, while the main body moved down the Tre to meet the Sarwakai column. Slight opposition was encountered. After being joined by Colonel Hogge's column, the whole force bivouacked at Dwe Shinkai. On the 22nd December, leaving the two pioneer regiments to guard the bivouac, the remainder of the force moved up the Dwe Shinkai in three columns.

No 1 Column (Colonel McRae) reconnoitred towards the Wacha Khwar, and met with some opposition.

No. 2 Column (Colonel Gray) moved east, and No. 3 Column (Colonel Vivian) moved south-east.

On the 23rd General Dening detached a column under Lieutenant-Colonel Gray into the Wacha Khwar, while Major Drew, with the 29th, was detached to the Guri Khel villages, north of Ahmadwan. He himself with the rest of the force returned to Guri Khel. Some opposition was encountered. The whole force bivouacked at Guri Khel. In the meantime, on the 22nd, I had detached a column from Jandola, under the command of Lieutenant-Colonel H. Godfray, 9th Bombay Infantry ; it covered the retirement of General Dening's force. The whole force returned to Jandola on the 24th December. On this day a small column from Sarwakai, in conjunction with some Bhittanis, raided into the Danaoti nullah.

19. In the meantime, the extra regiments had arrived, and troops were now placed in position for another series of operations in the north-eastern and eastern portions of Mahsud territory.

Fourth series of operations.

20. The object of these operations was to punish the Shabi Khel and other Mahsud sections having settlements in the Shaktu, Sharanna and Shuza Algads.

21. Three columns advanced simultaneously from Datta Khel, Janikhel and Jandola, respectively:

No. 1 Column, Jandola, Brigadier-General L. Dening, D. S. O., consisted of 30 sabres 4 guns and 2,450 rifles.

No. 2 Column, Colonel H. N. McRae, C.B., A.-D.-C., 45th Sikhs, consisted of 4 guns and 1,400 rifles.

No. 3 Column, Datta Khel, Lieutenant-Colonel V. C. Tonnochy, 3rd Sikhs, consisted of 2 guns and 1,400 rifles.

Besides the above, some 300 of the Northern Waziristan Militia, under Captain A. F. Ferguson-Davie, D.S.O., and 300 of the Southern Waziristan Militia, under Major R. Harman, D. S. O., were employed to crown the Babargarh range and prevent the Mahsuds from escaping into the Bhittani country.

On the 1st January 1902, No. 1 Column moved from Jandola up the Takhi Zam to Kot Shingi, where it bivouacked.

No. 2 Column to Kirkanwam at the mouth of the Shaktu.

No. 3 Column from Datta Khel *via* Manirogha to Wachfakiran in the Khaisara.

The Northern Waziristan Militia moved to Kirkanwam, and the Southern Waziristan Militia to the Torkhar Narai in the Bhittani country.

No opposition was encountered.

2nd January 1902.—No. 1 Column detaching a party of 600 rifles under Major Drew, 29th Punjab Infantry, to search the hills to the east of Zeriwam, moved on to Shilmanzai Kach, whence it crossed a *kotal*, over which a route connects the Zam with Shuza. The rear-guard was slightly engaged. The force bivouacked on the *kotal*. No. 2 Column marched up the Shaktu to Mandwam Kach, where it bivouacked encountering slight opposition. No. 3 Column marched to Waladin, where some resistance was encountered. *January 3rd.*—No. 1 Column marched to the junction of the Shuza and Weshtanai Algads, and bivouacked there. No. 2 Column moved on to the Sodgarh range and down into the Sheranna, and destroyed the chief settlements of the Jalal Khels. No. 3 Column marched down the Shaktu and bivouacked on the Khar Kach, sending a force along the Ziarat range. *January 4th.*—No. 1 Column moved up the Shuza, pushing out columns to north and west. No. 2 Column, sending two guns and 500 infantry with the baggage, proceeded over the Sodgarh range. No. 3 Column, leaving their baggage in bivouac with a guard, proceeded to Barari Narai. *January 5th.*—No. 1 Column moved down the Shuza to the junction of the Wariamana. No. 2 Column proceed to Kikarai where it bivouacked, effecting a junction with No. 3 Column. No. 3 Column moved out over the Barai Narai on to the watershed of the Takhi Zam. The enemy opposed them all day and followed up the retirement till after dark. On return to bivouac No. 3 Column joined force with No. 2. *January 6th.*—No. 1 Column marched to Murghaband. Nos. 2 and 3 Columns moved up the Shaktu. *7th January.*—No. 1 Column moved to Jandola; Nos. 2 and 3 Columns marched to Dosalli. *8th January.*—The two columns returned to Datta Khel.

22. The troops, or rather the greater portion of them, had now been marching and fighting since the 24th November and much needed a rest. I therefore withdrew the bulk of the Jandola Column into standing camp at Zam, the 38th Dogras and the 2nd Gurkhas to Miranshah and the Murree Mountain Battery, the 3rd Gurkhas and the 27th Punjab Infantry to Baran on the Bannu border. These places were selected with a view to further operations, should such be necessary. The Militia returned to their usual stations.

23. Great damage had been inflicted on the Mahsud settlements in the Shaktu; they had lost heavily both in men and live-stock, and the knowledge that our troops could penetrate anywhere and everywhere into their territory, had convinced them of their inability to cope with us. A deputation of Saiads from Kaniguram was sent in to ask for a cessation of hostilities until they could hold a *jirga*, and discuss matters amongst themselves. The Commissioner on special duty agreed to a suspension of hostilities for some days, and also consented to receive their *jirga* on their complying with certain preliminary conditions. These have since been complied with and the blockade raised.

24. I beg to commend the services of the troops employed in the blockading force to the favourable notice of His Excellency the Commander-in-Chief. They have had hard marching and hard fighting on occasions. They have bivouacked in the open for nights on end, and throughout their conduct has been exemplary. I trust that His Excellency may see fit to commend their services to Government.

GUJARAT MOUNTAIN BATTERY

<u>Gunner-Naik</u>
408 Faiz Bakhsh   sl w 5 Dec 1901 Umar Raghza

<u>Driver</u>
486 Sundar Singh   sev w 5 Dec 1901 Umar Raghza

MURREE MOUNTAIN BATTERY

<u>Gunner</u>
16 Bishen Singh   sl w 3 Jan 1902 Sheranna

23rd (PUNJAB) REGIMENT OF BENGAL INFANTRY (PIONEERS)

<u>Naik</u>
3035 Bhagwan Singh   sev w 5 Dec 1901 Umar Raghza

<u>Sepoys</u>
2838 Anokh Singh   sev w 25 Nov 1901 Khaisara
2121 Bagga Singh   sl w 5 Dec 1901 Umar Raghza
3520 Budh Singh   sev w 20 Dec 1901 Splitoi
4077 Bur Singh   sl w 26 Nov 1901 Khaisara
3711 Gujjar Singh   sl w 26 Nov 1901 Khaisara
3778 Gunda Singh   k 26 Nov 1901 Khaisara
3675 Jwala Singh   sl w 26 Nov 1901 Khaisara
4075 Khem Singh   sev w 26 Nov 1901 Khaisara, since dow
3272 Labh Singh   sev w 5 Dec 1901 Umar Raghza
3485 Maggar Singh   sev w 25 Nov 1901 Khaisara
3330 Pahu Singh   k 26 Nov 1901 Khaisara
4003 Ram Singh   sev w 26 Nov 1901 Khaisara
3824 Sundar Singh   sl w 26 Nov 1901 Khaisara
2665 Wazir Singh   sl w 26 Nov 1901 Khaisara

27th (PUNJAB) REGIMENT OF BENGAL INFANTRY

<u>Sepoy</u>
3513 Dyal Singh   sev w 2 Jan 1902 Shaktu

28th (PUNJAB) REGIMENT OF BENGAL INFANTRY

Sepoys
3657 Achhar   k 26 Nov 1901 Khaisara
3418 Ali Ahmed   sev w 22 Dec 1901 Dwe Shinkai, since dow
3480 Chaudri   sl w 26 Nov 1901 Khaisara
3492 Kesar Singh   sev w 26 Nov 1901 Khaisara
3766 Khawaz Khan   sl w 26 Nov 1901 Khaisara
3996 Khiali Khan   sl w 28 Dec 1901 Khaisara
3948 Lehnoo   sev w 6 Jan 1902 Shuza
4101 Majhi Khan   sev w 22 Dec 1901 Dwe Shinkai
4192 Mir Akhmed   sl w 26 Nov 1901 Khaisara
3998 Naurang   k 5 Dec 1901 Umar Raghza
4143 Niaz Gul   k 28 Nov 1901 Khaisara
3604 Noorulla Khan   sev w 2 Dec 1901 Khaisara
4029 Rahim Shah   sl w 22 Dec 1901 Dwe Shinkai
4146 Rahimuddin   k 5 Dec 1901 Umar Raghza
4082 Shamal Khan   sev w 22 Dec 1901 Dwe Shinkai

29th (PUNJAB) REGIMENT OF BENGAL INFANTRY

Subadar
Harditt Singh   sev w 6 Dec 1901 Umar Raghza, since dow

Havildar
2975 Fazl Dad   k 7 Dec 1901 Takhi Zam

Naik
3098 Man Singh   sev w 5 Jan 1902 Shuza

Lance-Naik
3017 Kale Khan   sl w 7 Dec 1901 Takhi Zam

Sepoys
3169 Alla Ditta   sev w 21 Dec 1901 Splitoi
3596 Atta-ullah   sl w 7 Dec 1901 Takhi Zam
3683 Chajja Singh   sev w 22 Dec 1901 Dwe Shinkai
3538 Firman Ali   sl w 7 Dec 1901 Takhi Zam
3220 Firoze Khan   sev w 21 Dec 1901 Splitoi
3766 Gurditt Singh   sev w 22 Dec 1901 Dwe Shinkai
3727 Mirza Khan   k 7 Dec 1901 Takhi Zam
3301 Sirdar Khan   k 7 Dec 1901 Takhi Zam
3213 Wazira   sev w 22 Dec 1901 Dwe Shinkai

32nd (PUNJAB) REGIMENT OF BENGAL INFANTRY (PIONEERS)

Havildar
2244 Ram Singh   sev w 21 Dec 1901 Splitoi

Sepoy
3703 Dulip Singh   sev w 10 Jan 1902 Sarwekai

35th (SIKH) REGIMENT OF BENGAL INFANTRY

Captain
Cassels, Gilbert Robert   sev w 24 Dec 1901 Umar Raghza

38th (DOGRA) REGIMENT OF BENGAL INFANTRY

Sepoys
 524 Chaukas   sev w 23 Dec 1901 Umar Raghza
1558 Dhaja Singh   sl w 23 Dec 1901 Umar Raghza
 305 Kirpa   sl w 23 Dec 1901 Umar Raghza
 683 Nathu   sev w 23 Dec 1901 Umar Raghza
 996 Puran   sl w 23 Dec 1901 Umar Raghza
 923 Sadhu   sl w 22 Dec 1901 Dwe Shinkai
1366 Sohanu   sl w 23 Dec 1901 Umar Raghza
1318 Tota   sl w 23 Dec 1901 Umar Raghza

45th (RATTRAY'S SIKH) REGIMENT OF BENGAL INFANTRY

Captain
McVean, Donald Archibald Dugald   sev w 5 Dec 1901 Umar Raghza; awarded DSO

Jemadars
Kishan Singh   k 5 Dec 1901 Umar Raghza
Mall Singh   sev w 5 Dec 1901 Umar Raghza

Lance-Naiks
```
3082 Jowala Singh    k  5 Dec 1901 Umar Raghza
2491 Kahan Singh     k  5 Dec 1901 Umar Raghza
5314 Mangal Singh    sl w 25 Nov 1901 Kot Shingi
3139 Prem Singh      sl w 25 Nov 1901 Kot Shingi
```

Sepoys
```
3423 Arjun Singh     sev w 25 Nov 1901 Kot Shingi
4112 Arjun Singh     sev w  3 Jan 1902 Shuza
3776 Attar Singh     k  5 Dec 1901 Umar Raghza
4336 Bagh Singh      sev w  5 Dec 1901 Umar Raghza
3902 Bhagwan Singh   k 25 Nov 1901 Kot Shingi
4278 Bishen Singh    sev w 25 Nov 1901 Kot Shingi
4067 Fauja Singh     k  5 Dec 1901 Umar Raghza
4493 Gulab Singh     sl w 25 Nov 1901 Kot Shingi
3349 Gurdit Singh    k  5 Dec 1901 Umar Raghza
4236 Hakim Singh     sl w 23 Dec 1901 Umar Raghza
3490 Harnam Singh    sev w 25 Nov 1901 Kot Shingi
3690 Kakud Singh     sev w 25 Nov 1901 Kot Shingi
2810 Lachman Singh   k  5 Dec 1901 Umar Raghza
3445 Mall Singh      sev w  5 Dec 1901 Umar Raghza
3675 Partab Singh    sl w 25 Nov 1901 Kot Shingi
4047 Phuman Singh    sl w  3 Jan 1901 Shuza
4352 Ram Singh       sev w  5 Dec 1901 Umar Raghza
3391 Thaman Singh    sev w  5 Dec 1901 Umar Raghza
```

1st Btn 2nd GURKHA (RIFLE) REGIMENT (SIRMOOR RIFLES)

Naik
```
2343 Dhojbir Thapa   sev w 5 Jan 1902 Barari Narai
```

Lance-Naik
```
2345 Mittarlal Thapa sev w 2 Jan 1902 Waladin
```

Riflemen
```
 955 Dargamani Thapa sev w 5 Jan 1902 Barari Narai
3207 Harkbir Pun     k 5 Jan 1902 Barari Narai
3315 Kalu Gurung     sev w 3 Jan 1902 Shakhtu
3090 Kansu Gurung    sl w 2 Jan 1902 Waladin
3016 Randoj Gurung   sev w 7 Jan 1902 Sham Plain
```

1st Btn 3rd GURKHA (RIFLE) REGIMENT

Riflemen
2775 Badrabir Gurung   sev w 3 Jan 1902 Sheranna
1807 Karnia Thapa   sev w 2 Jan 1902 Shakhtu
1807 Mukum Singh Gurung   k 3 Jan 1902 Sheranna [sic]
2166 Pitambar Ale   sl w 3 Jan 1902 Sheranna

1st REGIMENT OF PUNJAB CAVALRY, PUNJAB FRONTIER FORCE

Sowar
2833 Sohan Singh   sev w 4 Dec 1901, since dow

5th REGIMENT OF PUNJAB CAVALRY, PUNJAB FRONTIER FORCE

Lance-Daffadars
2654 Phula Singh   sev w 24 Nov 1901 Inzar Narai
2588 Pir Bad Shah   sev w 24 Nov 1901 Inzar Narai

Sowar
2689 Sheikh Ramzan   sev w 24 Nov 1901 Inzar Narai

3rd REGIMENT OF SIKH INFANTRY, PUNJAB FRONTIER FORCE

Sepoys
2836 Masti Khan   sl w 28 Nov 1901 Razmak
2937 Sardar Khan   sev w 27 Nov 1901 Makin, since dow

1st REGIMENT OF PUNJAB INFANTRY, PUNJAB FRONTIER FORCE

Surgeon-Lieutenant
Peile, Harry Diamond   sl w 24 Nov 1901 Kot Shingi

Subadar
Muhammad Gul   k 24 Nov 1901 Kot Shingi; widow awarded pension
                of IOM 3rd Class

Jemadar
Arjan Singh   sl w 24 Nov 1901 Kot Shingi

Havildar
4339 Inchar Khan   sev w 24 Nov 1901 Kot Shingi, since dow

Naik
 583 Sher Din   sl w 24 Nov 1901 Kot Shingi

Sepoys
  679 Bardam Singh   sev w 24 Nov 1901 Kot Shingi
 1159 Bila Singh   sev w 24 Nov 1901 Kot Shingi
  394 Boor Singh   sl w 23 Dec 1901 Wacha Khwar
  677 Dant Singh   sl w 23 Dec 1901 Wacha Khwar
 1247 Hamir Khan   sev w 3 Dec 1901 Kot Shingi
  694 Harnam Singh   sl w 24 Nov 1901 Kot Shingi
 1160 Jabbar Singh   sev w 23 Dec 1901 Wacha Khwar
 1174 Karandan Khan   sev w 24 Nov 1901 Kot Shingi
 1097 Narain Singh   sl w 23 Dec 1901 Wacha Khwar

2nd REGIMENT OF PUNJAB INFANTRY, PUNJAB FRONTIER FORCE

Captain
Forster, Philip Byron Bohun   sev w 25 Nov 1901 Shuran Algad

Subadar
Sharam Singh   sl w 28 Nov 1901 Razmak

Havildar
4095 Chandu Singh   sl w 28 Nov 1901 Razmak

Lance-Naik
4388 Maluk Singh   k 28 Nov 1901 Razmak

Sepoys
  247 Aizad Khan   sev w 28 Nov 1901 Razmak
  547 Biram Singh   sl w 28 Nov 1901 Razmak
  360 Bishen Singh   k 28 Nov 1901 Razmak
  482 Fakir Khan   sev w 28 Nov 1901 Razmak
  545 Hira Singh   sev w 28 Nov 1901 Razmak
  555 Hira Singh   sl w 28 Nov 1901 Razmak
  942 Jhanda Singh   sev w 28 Nov 1901 Razmak
  647 Mula Singh   sl w 28 Nov 1901 Razmak
 6435 Nadhan Singh   sl w 28 Nov 1901 Razmak
  512 Pal Singh   sev w 28 Nov 1901 Razmak
  659 Sham Singh   sev w 28 Nov 1901 Razmak
  817 Sham Singh   sl w 28 Nov 1901 Razmak

5th REGIMENT OF PUNJAB INFANTRY, PUNJAB FRONTIER FORCE

<u>Sepoys</u>
1929 Atta Muhammad   sev w 6 Jan 1902 Tutia Khel
2157 Farangi   sev w 6 Jan 1902 Tutia Khel

9th REGIMENT OF BOMBAY INFANTRY

<u>Sepoys</u>
1144 Kuri Khan   sl w 24 Nov 1901 Kot Shingi
 859 Mamle Khan   sl w 24 Nov 1901 Kot Shingi
 882 Mir Zaman   k 24 Nov 1901 Kot Shingi

PUNJAB COMMISSION

<u>Captain</u>
Down, Cecil Patton   sev w 6 Jan 1902 Tutia Khel, dow 7 Jan

ABBREVIATIONS

actg	acting
attchd	attached
Bgde	Brigade
Mmdr	Bombardier
Bty	Battery
Cav	Cavalry
cmdg	commanding
Cmdt	Commandant
Col-Sgt	Colour Sergeant
Corp	Corporal
Cpt	Captain
d	dead/died
dang	dangerously
dow	died of wounds
Drm	Drummer
Dvr	Driver
Fus	Fusiliers
GGO	Government of India General Order
Gnr	Gunner
gs	gunshot
Hldrs	Highlanders
Inf	Infantry
IOM	Indian Order of Merit
k	killed
Lce	Lance
Lcrs	Lancers
LG	London Gazette
Lt	Lieutenant
miss	missing
mort	mortally
Mtn	Mountain
NI	Native Infantry
offic	officiating
PFF	Punjab Frontier Force
Pte	Private
QM	Quarter Master
Regt	Regiment
sev	severely
Sgt	Sergeant
Sgt-Maj	Sergeant-Major
sl	slightly
S & M	Sappers & Miners
Tmptr	Trumpeter
2-i-c	second-in-command
w	wounded

www.ingramcontent.com/pod-product-compliance
Lightning Source LLC
Chambersburg PA
CBHW082013220426
43670CB00014B/2615